21,95

The Arc of Ascent

The Arc of Ascent

Ascent

The Purpose of Physical Reality II

by

John S. Hatcher

GEORGE RONALD

OXFORD

GEORGE RONALD, Publisher
46 High Street, Kidlington, Oxford OX5 2DN

A Cataloguing-in-Publication entry is available from the British Library

ISBN 0–85398–371–2

Printed and bound in Great Britain by
Biddles Ltd, Guildford and King's Lynn

If thou wishest the divine knowledge and recognition, purify thy heart from all beside God, be wholly attracted to the ideal beloved One; search for and choose Him and apply thyself to rational and authoritative arguments. For arguments are a guide to the path and by this the heart will be turned unto the Sun of Truth. And when the heart is turned unto the Sun, then the eye will be opened and will recognize the Sun through the Sun itself.[1]

'Abdu'l-Bahá

. . . [f]rom the beginning to the end of the arc of ascent, there are numerous spiritual degrees. The arc of descent is called beginning, and that of ascent is called progress. The arc of descent ends in materialities, and the arc of ascent ends in spiritualities. The point of the compass in describing a circle makes no retrograde motion, for this would be contrary to the natural movement and the divine order; otherwise the symmetry of the circle would be spoiled . . . No, through the Eternal Bounty the worth and true ability of man becomes apparent and visible by traversing the degrees of existence, and not by returning. When the shell is once opened, it will be apparent and evident whether it contains a pearl or worthless matter. When once the plant has grown it will bring forth either thorns or flowers; there is no need for it to grow up again.[2]

'Abdu'l-Bahá

Acknowledgements

I am indebted to the workers at the Research Department at the Bahá'í World Centre for graciously responding to my many queries, and I am also grateful to Dr Duane Troxel and the American Bahá'í Publishing Trust for providing me with software which greatly assisted my research. I would also like to express my appreciation to the Research Council at the University of South Florida for awarding me a grant for this project and to my dean and chairman for providing me release from my teaching duties to complete this book. Most of all, I wish to express my gratitude to my wife Lucia, my daughter Helen Grace, and my son James Varqá for understanding why the door to my room must be shut from breakfast until two p.m. Finally, I am grateful to my grandfather, Dr William Benjamin Hardman, without whose wisdom and foresight, this project would not have been possible.

Table of Contents

Acknowledgements   vi

Preface   xi

1. **The Subtle Art of Human Ascent: The**
   Wilful Linkage between Two Worlds   1

   The Two Components of Human Purpose   51
   Parallel Statements of these Two Duties   8
   The Enunciation of these Capacities in the
      Kitáb-i-Aqdas   12
   Parallel of Twin Duties to Twin Stations of
      the Prophets   18
   The Twin Duties and the Art of Salvation   22
   The Twin Duties and the Female and Male
      Principles of Complementarity   35

2. **The Social Imperative and the Emergence**
   of a Global Identity   45

   The Social Dimension of Individual Salvation   45
   The Social Self as Confirmed by the Sciences   51
   The Bahá'í Concept of the Social Self   55
   The Seven Valleys as a Paradigm for the Wilful
   Achieving Selflessness in a Contemporary
      Environment   78

3. A Wheel within a Wheel: The Bahá'í
    Paradigm of Human History   91

    The Bahá'í Concept of Universal Organization   91
    The Paradigm of Human Development   98
    Religion as the Process by which the
        Manifestations Educate Humankind   104
    The Cyclical Paradigm of Human History   114
    The Special Significance of the Present Age   119

4. New Wine and Old Skins: The Divine Art
    of Progressive Revelation   128

    The Relationship of the Wineskin to the Wine   129
    The Problem of Recognizing the Manifestation   138
    Continuity after the Passing of the Manifestation   151

5. Adam and Eve Get Divorced: How
    Christian Antinomianism Begets
    Western Materialism   160

    The Origins of Christian Antinomianism   162
    The Further Development of the Schism between
        the Twin Duties   177
    Children of Divorce: The Modern Heritage of
        the Schism   194

6. The Choice Wine at the Family Reunion   202

    Symbolic Terms Associated with a New
        Dispensation   203
    Unsealing the Choice Wine   209
    Preparing to Partake of the Vintage: Some
        Requisites for Just Governance   222

7. From the Lesser Peace to a Golden Age: Stages in the Evolution of a World Commonwealth   235

The Birth of a Global Identity   237
The Lesser Peace   251
The Stage of Establishment   269

8. The Kingdom Come: A Model of the Bahá'í Commonwealth   277

The Emergence of the Most Great Peace   277
The Structure of the Bahá'í Commonwealth   290
The 'Arc' as Metaphor for the Administrative
  Order   298
The Prospect for the Future   303

9. The Heart of the Commonwealth: The Local Community as Tribal Ethos   309

Relationship between the 'Super-State' and the
  Local Community   309
The Individual and the Tribal Perspective   321
Law Enforcement and the Community   331
An Abiding Image of a World Commonwealth   336

Appendixes   343

A. Some Distinctive Features of Operation   343
B. A Divine Economy   352

Bibliography   364

References   369

Preface

The first volume of this study *The Purpose of Physical Reality: The Kingdom of Names* examines the hypothesis that the justification for essentially spiritual beings taking their beginning in a physical environment is that physical reality as the initial stage in the endless journey of the human soul is a precisely devised classroom whereby autonomous transformation is initiated and assisted as preparation for birth into a spiritual existence. In such a context, our individual objective in this life is to acquire those tools and capacities that will best prepare us for the continuation of our lives in a non-physical reality, much as the gestation of the child in the womb prepares the infant for successful existence in the physical world.

However, one essential ingredient in this process of preparation may not be readily apparent in that study: the relationship between personal spiritual preparation and a social imperative. For where that first volume purposefully focuses on the question of theodicy (discovering God's justice in an ostensibly unjust world) from an individual or personal perspective, implicit in that discussion and explicit throughout the Bahá'í writings is the inextricable connection between learning spiritual lessons and involvement with others who are attempting the same thing. On the simplest level, this imperative is evident in the fact that spiritual virtues almost inevitably involve some sort of human relationship. Or put another way, until a virtue becomes practised and exercised, it is mostly theoretical because the majority of spiritual attributes, like justice, kindness and human goodness in all its forms, imply interaction with others.

But the social imperative is also evident in another aspect of the paradigm of human spiritual development. In the first volume we defined human purpose in the physical world as a twofold process whereby we discern spiritual verities as they are given concrete form in physical reality and then we manifest that understanding in some metaphorical action. We further surmised that such a process can enable us to achieve successively higher levels of insight followed subsequently by ever more eloquent expressions of that knowledge in action. And yet what may not be apparent is that this process is not an end in itself, but the means to an end.

A further study of the Bahá'í writings makes it clear that the underlying objective of this exercise is the expanded sense of self. For not only do each of these successive levels of understanding and action require ever more expansive social relationships, each level of comprehension also reveals, in an ever more complete way, that our individual reality has meaning only insofar as it relates to increasingly more inclusive expressions of ourselves:

> Every imperfect soul is self-centred and thinketh only of his own good. But as his thoughts expand a little he will begin to think of the welfare and comfort of his family. If his ideas still more widen, his concern will be the felicity of his fellow citizens; and if still they widen, he will be thinking of the glory of his land and of his race. But when ideas and views reach the utmost degree of expansion and attain the stage of perfection, then will he be interested in the exaltation of humankind. He will then be the well-wisher of all men and the seeker of the weal and prosperity of all lands. This is indicative of perfection.[1]

Consequently, the ultimate goal of spiritual ascent is,

when properly understood, the achievement of a kind of selflessness that results not from self-effacement or self-deprivation, or self-neglect, but from a fulfilment that occurs when we freely choose to become a functioning part of a greater expression of ourselves. Therefore, where the first volume discusses God's justice in conjunction with our personal relationship to physical reality, this continuation of that study emphasizes the relationship of that personal transformation to the entire plan of divine justice at work in the world. In particular, this discussion focuses on the Bahá'í belief that human history itself is a divinely guided process whereby spiritual principles are gradually and progressively expressed in social institutions. From this perspective, humankind is viewed as one coherent organism whose collective history parallels the stages of development characteristic of individual spiritual evolution.

Just as a cell in the human body can ill afford to be unconcerned with the health of the organism to which it is inextricably linked, so the aspirant to spiritual transformation cannot view personal health and development as being possible apart from the progress of human society as a whole. This study will attempt to demonstrate how the social order revealed in the Bahá'í scriptures provides the long-awaited workshop by which the collective social advancement of civilization will support and work in concert with the individual's attempt to fulfil inherent purpose.

for the tireless workers
in the Vineyard
who gladly labour
in quiet anonymity

The Subtle Art of Human Ascent

The Wilful Linkage between Two Worlds

> The spiritual world is like unto the phenomenal world. They are the exact counterpart of each other. Whatever objects appear in this world of existence are the outer pictures of the world of heaven.[1]
>
> *'Abdu'l-Bahá*

The Two Components of Human Purpose

In the short obligatory prayer revealed by Bahá'u'lláh, one finds what appears to be a succinct statement of human purpose in terms of this metaphorical process: 'I bear witness, O my God, that Thou hast created me to know Thee and to worship Thee.'[2]

The enunciation of this dictum in the obligatory prayer is a particularly valuable statement of human purpose because it is recited as a fundamental testimony of creed as well as a daily renewal of one's individual participation in the Eternal Covenant. Let us examine how this prayer exemplifies this two-part process.

To Know Thee

The first of these twin objectives of coming 'to know' God is, when properly understood, tantamount to the previously mentioned process of discerning spiritual lessons metaphorized in physical experience. That is, the Bahá'í writings assert that God is essentially unknowable:

> From time immemorial He hath been veiled in the ineffable sanctity of His exalted Self, and will everlastingly continue to be wrapt in the impenetrable mystery of His unknowable Essence. Every attempt to attain to an understanding of His inaccessible Reality hath ended in complete bewilderment, and every effort to approach His exalted Self and envisage His Essence hath resulted in hopelessness and failure.[3]

In another passage Bahá'u'lláh cites the inability of God's creation to know Him directly as one reason for the advent of the Prophets:

> And since there can be no tie of direct intercourse to bind the one true God with His creation, and no resemblance what-ever can exist between the transient and the Eternal, the contingent and the Absolute, He hath ordained that in every age and dispensation a pure and stainless Soul be made manifest in the kingdoms of earth and heaven.[4]

On one level, then, the response to the problem of how we can be mandated to love a Being that is essentially unknowable and unapproachable is fairly simple – we may never comprehend the 'Essence' of the Deity because God is infinite and essentially spiritual in nature; but we can understand the attributes of that Divine nature as they are dramatized for us through metaphorical expression, par-ticularly through the exemplary lives and teachings of the Manifestations. Therefore, when Christ states that to know Him is to know God (John 14:10) and that no one comes to God but through Him (John 14:6), He is stating this same principle. Bahá'u'lláh similarly observes that one of the crucial functions of the Manifestations is to provide humanity with a concretized analogue for the

Deity by translating the infinite and unknowable into perceptible form:

> These Tabernacles of Holiness, these primal Mirrors which reflect the light of unfading glory, are but expressions of Him Who is the Invisible of the Invisibles. By the revelation of these Gems of Divine virtue all the names and attributes of God, such as knowledge and power, sovereignty and dominion, mercy and wisdom, glory, bounty and grace, are made manifest.[5]

As we noted in *The Purpose of Physical Reality*, the infinite and essentially unknowable essence of God may also be perceived through the metaphorical expression of spiritual attributes in the myriad analogues of the natural world:

> Know thou that every created thing is a sign of the revelation of God. Each, according to its capacity, is, and will ever remain, a token of the Almighty. Inasmuch as He, the sovereign Lord of all, hath willed to reveal His sovereignty in the kingdom of names and attributes, each and every created thing hath, through the act of the Divine Will, been made a sign of His glory. So pervasive and general is this revelation that nothing whatsoever in the whole universe can be discovered that doth not reflect His splendour.[6]

But regardless of how we come to understand divine attributes, it is clear that the knowledge of God as expressed in the obligatory prayer implies neither physical proximity nor intimacy in any common sense of the word, but rather a familiarity with divine virtues, however they may become accessible to us.

Of course, this concept of the knowledge of God as perception of spiritual attributes may be erroneous or misconstrued if by it we infer either intellectual comprehension only or else some vague attachment or attraction to the personality of the Prophet. One result of the former assumption is that religious truth may become regarded as the exclusive property of some elite group of ecclesiastical authorities or scholars. An equally unfortunate result of the latter is that attachment to the Prophet may degenerate into adoration of a Manifestation's personality, even to the point of idolatry or deification, the very thing that occurred early in Christianity.* Consequently, to appreciate more accurately the connotative meaning of what this prayer might intend by the word *know*, let us consider briefly the Bahá'í concept of epistemology and education.

A teacher of mine would often begin by asking our class what we had done that day that any well-trained animal could not do as well or better. Beyond this wry and cynical humour was a profound statement of a theory of education – that the unexamined thought was not worth having, that education as rote programming of the mind was, in the final analysis, not education, but mere parroting someone else's learning – mere imposition of will, mere imitation, the virtual antithesis of true learning (and often a grievous impediment to justice). The Bahá'í teachings affirm that since each individual is held accountable for his or her personal spiritual development, acquiring the knowledge of God as a part of this process is likewise an individual responsibility and therefore available to all alike.

> . . . every man hath been, and will continue to be, able of himself to appreciate the Beauty of God, the Glorified. Had he not been endowed with such a capacity, how could he be called to account for his failure? . . . For the faith of no man can be conditioned by any one except himself.[7]

> He hath endowed every soul with the capacity to recognize the signs of God. How could He, otherwise, have fulfilled

---

* The view of Christ as God incarnate became official Christian doctrine as a result of the Council of Nicaea in 325. Until that synod, the question of Christology had been hotly debated.

His testimony unto men, if ye be of them that ponder His Cause in their hearts. He will never deal unjustly with any one, neither will He task a soul beyond its power.[8]

This concept of personal accountability does not imply that the acquisition of understanding occurs independently of external assistance or even that it is independent of traditional sorts of learning; it simply means that such understanding is not dependent on traditional learning, or what Bahá'u'lláh alludes to as 'learning current amongst men'.[9] The Bahá'í writings make clear that without guidance humanity cannot ascend, whether that external influence be in the form of restrictive ordinance or in the form of affirmative exhortation to achieve: 'Regard man as a mine rich in gems of inestimable value. Education can, alone, cause it to reveal its treasures, and enable mankind to benefit therefrom.'[10]

Yet it is equally clear that the type of learning alluded to as the common property of all alike is not the acquisition of a body of fact nor is it academic in nature, though it may be confirmed by scholarship or intellectual study. In this connection, Bahá'u'lláh states that we may receive guidance from others in striving for knowledge of spiritual matters, but we should not necessarily seek such insight or enlightenment from ecclesiastics or scholars nor through the aid of traditional learning:

Inasmuch as it hath been clearly shown that only those who are initiated into the divine mysteries can comprehend the melodies uttered by the Bird of Heaven, it is therefore incumbent upon every one to seek enlightenment from the illumined in heart and from the Treasuries of divine mysteries regarding the intricacies of God's Faith and the abstruse allusions in the utterances of the Day-springs of Holiness. Thus will these mysteries be unravelled, not by the aid of acquired learning, but solely through the assistance of God and the outpourings of His grace.[11]

Consequently, the more one attains such spiritual perception and knowledge, the better one is able to understand how the physical world, the so-called 'real' world, provides clues to the spiritual dominion that it reflects:

> Know thou that the Kingdom is the real world, and this nether place is only its shadow stretching out. A shadow hath no life of its own; its existence is only a fantasy, and nothing more; it is but images reflected in water, and seeming as pictures to the eye.[12]

In short, the first of the two duties that define human purpose in the short obligatory prayer implies neither memorization of doctrine nor blind adherence to dogma, but a capacity of discernment, of judgement, a type of poetic sensibility available to all alike, an ability to discover spiritual meanings that have been given phenomenal expression.

To Worship Thee

If the knowledge implied by this statement of purpose is subtle, the concept of worship implied in the second part of these twin obligations is more so. For while in its obvious or literal meaning the worship of God might be considered an admirable course of action for one aspiring to piety, one might infer that the ideal condition would be for the suppliant to remain in some sustained condition of meditation and prayer, the very conclusion that various ascetic orders in other religions have assumed to be the most efficacious path to piety. But Bahá'u'lláh makes it clear that this is not the proper assumption. Not only does Bahá'u'lláh exalt work to the station of worship and command that all have a profession, He explicitly condemns those who do not bring forth noble deeds: 'The basest of men are they that yield no fruit on earth.'[13]

Of course, one might argue that this 'fruit' need not be literal deeds, such as a vocation, but in proscribing asceticism and monasticism, Bahá'u'lláh makes it clear that this is precisely what He does mean:

> The pious deeds of the monks and priests among the followers of the Spirit . . . are remembered in His presence. In this Day, however, let them give up the life of seclusion and direct their steps towards the open world and busy themselves with that which will profit themselves and others. We have granted them leave to enter into wedlock that they may bring forth one who will make mention of God, the Lord of the seen and the unseen, the Lord of the Exalted Throne.[14]

Similarly, in the concluding passages of the *Hidden Words*, itself a synthesis of spiritual verities, Bahá'u'lláh states:

> The best of men are they that earn a livelihood by their calling and spend upon themselves and upon their kindred for the love of God, the Lord of all worlds.[15]

Such passages obviously do not imply that prayer and other forms of literal worship are not also intended by the second part of this credo. Indeed, for the Bahá'í, prayer is an obligatory and indispensable source of daily sustenance. But in the context of this statement of human purpose, prayer, or any other action expressive of this second duty, is not separate from or independent of knowledge; rather, it is a sign of understanding, a completion of the process, the translation of understanding into dramatic action.

This inference becomes clearer when we look briefly at several statements about the purpose and nature of worship in its literal sense. For example, 'Abdu'l-Bahá states that prayer 'need not be in words, but rather in thought and attitude'.[16] Likewise, the Báb states that the sincerity of prayer is what matters, not its duration – 'its prolongation hath not been and is not beloved by God'.[17]

Similarly, while Bahá'u'lláh makes prayer obligatory, He states that one should be obedient to His ordinances, not from fear of retribution, but 'for the love of My beauty'.[18] Indeed, the Báb explicitly cautions against praying from fear of punishment or for desire for rewards:

> Shouldst thou worship Him because of fear, this would be unseemly in the sanctified Court of His presence, and could not be regarded as an act by thee dedicated to the Oneness of His Being. Or if thy gaze should be on paradise, and thou shouldst worship Him while cherishing such a hope, thou wouldst make God's creation a partner with Him, notwithstanding the fact that paradise is desired by men.
>
> Fire and paradise both bow down and prostrate themselves before God. That which is worthy of His Essence is to worship Him for His sake, without fear of fire, or hope of paradise.
>
> Although when true worship is offered, the worshipper is delivered from the fire, and entereth the paradise of God's good-pleasure, yet such should not be the motive of his act.[19]

We conclude, then, that *worship* in this context implies a whole range of pious acts that have in common some physical act that demonstrates one's recognition of and allegiance to the divine essence given earthly expression through the Manifestations. Worship in its most literal sense may be among these actions, but even these have as their essential purpose the production of reformed character: 'Prayer and meditation are very important factors in deepening the spiritual life of the individual, but with them must go also action and example, as these are the tangible results of the former. Both are essential.'[20]

Parallel Statements of these Two Duties

Having established some of the less obvious implications of the statement of human purpose in the short obligatory prayer as 'knowing' and 'worshipping' God, we can explore some of the appearances of this enunciation of human purpose in other passages from the Bahá'í writings in order to attempt an even more complete understanding of this process by which human spiritualization and salvation take place.

Capacities Unique to Human Beings

In a particularly valuable parallel statement of these twin duties, Bahá'u'lláh observes that the capacity to accomplish these two tasks is unique to human beings:

> Having created the world and all that liveth and moveth therein, He, through the direct operation of His unconstrained and sovereign Will, chose to confer upon man the unique distinction and capacity to know Him and to love Him – a capacity that must needs be regarded as the generating impulse and the primary purpose underlying the whole of creation.[21]

In *The Purpose of Physical Reality* we noted that the source of this capacity in human beings is the existence of the soul[22] because those powers we commonly associate with human capacity (such as abstract thought, reason, self-awareness, will) are but faculties of this essentially spiritual reality:

> Know, verily, that the soul is a sign of God, a heavenly gem whose reality the most learned of men hath failed to grasp, and whose mystery no mind, however acute, can ever hope to unravel. It is the first among all created things to declare the excellence of its Creator, the first to recognize His glory, to cleave to His truth, and to bow down in adoration before Him.[23]

As we also noted in *The Purpose of Physical Reality*, the soul, which takes its association with the physical body at conception but continues its existence after the body's demise, distinguishes the human reality from the rest of creation:

> If there were no man, the perfections of the spirit would not appear, and the light of the mind would not be resplendent in this world. This world would be like a body without a soul.
>   This world is also in the condition of a fruit tree, and man is like the fruit; without fruit the tree would be useless.[24]

Or stated more simply, physical creation has as its animating purpose the providing of a classroom environment wherein the distinguishing capacities of the human reality can become manifest and trained.

These observations thus focus on these twin duties. That is, the capacity to 'know Thee' and 'worship Thee' is unique to human beings because only human beings possess the faculties to perform these subtle tasks. And human beings possess this faculty because human beings have a soul. And because human beings have a soul and these capacities, the human reality is the fruit of creation; because the purpose of creation is to bring forth beings capable of appreciating and benefiting from knowing their creator and then wilfully acting out that understanding in an 'ever-advancing civilization'.[25] And as we will discuss throughout this study, that civilization is an expression in social relationships of the spiritual laws and realities of the unseen world, the spiritual world.

For now, the most important thing we can observe is that these two capacities are not only unique to human beings and therefore define the distinguishing characteristics of what it means to be human, they also represent the essential purpose of creation itself – the process by which human beings collectively exercise these capacities in such a way as to bring forth an ever more complete expression of the spiritual world in human society.

Of course, it is well worth noting that in this parallel statement of these twin capacities, the 'worship' of God has been expressed as the 'love' of God. This distinction indicates that what is meant by worship is not a mindless subservience, but a proper appreciation of the essential benignity of God and His dealings with His human creation. In effect, we cannot be mandated to love, but if we truly understand the Creator, love will most likely follow. Therefore, when Bahá'u'lláh states in the Kitáb-i-Aqdas, 'Observe My commandments, for the love of My beauty',[26] He implies that our goal is to become sufficiently informed about the ordinances of the Manifestation that we appreciate the divine logic and wisdom implicit in divinely-ordained assistance. Thus, to love the 'beauty' of God in this context implies obeying commandments because we have achieved insight about the essential justice and grace underlying God's methods in educating humanity.

Worship as Action

As we have already noted, worship in the context of the Bahá'í writings implies any sort of action that expresses metaphorically the spiritual verities we have come to understand. But in yet another parallel statement of these twin capacities, Bahá'u'lláh implies that the objective of this process is the transformation of character:

> From among all created things He hath singled out for His special favour the pure, the gem-like reality of man, and invested it with a unique capacity of knowing Him and of reflecting the greatness of His glory. This twofold distinction conferred upon him hath cleansed away from his heart the rust of every vain desire, and made him worthy of the vesture with which his Creator hath deigned to clothe him.

It hath served to rescue his soul from the wretchedness of ignorance.[27]

In this passage, the second part of the process, the worship or love of God, is expressed in terms of personal transformation resulting from obedience to guidance. In effect, the love evokes worship, the worship is expressed in daily action, and the habituating of these actions enables one to assume the virtue or attribute that these actions dramatize. In this way one puts on the 'vesture' of holiness.

The Enunciation of these Capacities in the Kitáb-i-Aqdas

Though the parallel to the obligatory prayer may not be immediately apparent, the most powerful and weighty enunciation of these same two actions appears as the virtual preamble to the Kitáb-i-Aqdas, Bahá'u'lláh's Most Holy Book, His book of laws and ordinances, the work which establishes the foundation for the Bahá'í administrative order. In the opening passage of this work, Bahá'u'lláh states that two duties are incumbent on every individual:

> The first duty prescribed by God for His servants is the recognition of Him Who is the Dayspring of His Revelation and the Fountain of His laws, Who representeth the Godhead in both the Kingdom of His Cause and the world of creation. Whoso achieveth this duty hath attained unto all good; and whoso is deprived thereof, hath gone astray, though he be the author of every righteous deed. It behoveth every one who reacheth this most sublime station, this summit of transcendent glory, to observe every ordinance of Him Who is the Desire of the world.[28]

As we have already noted, recognition of the station and purpose of the Prophet is, in the physical reality, tantamount to the knowledge of God. Bahá'u'lláh states that in their station of 'essential unity,'[29] the Prophets possess the authority and attributes of the Deity:

> Were any of the all-embracing Manifestations of God to declare: 'I am God!' He verily speaketh the truth, and no doubt attacheth thereto. For it hath been repeatedly demonstrated that through their Revelation, their attributes and names, the Revelation of God, His name and His attributes, are made manifest in the world.[30]

'Abdu'l-Bahá confirms the crucial nature of this access to the divine Reality when He explains that without this continual assistance, humankind would be totally deprived of any progress in this world:

> The enlightenment of the world of thought comes from these centres of light and sources of mysteries. Without the bounty of the splendour and the instructions of these Holy Beings the world of souls and thoughts would be opaque darkness. Without the irrefutable teachings of those sources of mysteries the human world would become the pasture of animal appetites and qualities, the existence of everything would be unreal, and there would be no true life. That is why it is said in the Gospel: 'In the beginning was the Word,' meaning that it became the cause of all life.[31]

If we accept this premise that the Manifestation represents the means by which we gain knowledge of God, then it is no less apparent that acceding to the guidance of the Prophets, whose laws, ordinances and exhortations are explicitly for our benefit, is the most efficacious means by which we can act out our understanding. In short, to recognize the Manifestation is equivalent to attaining a knowledge of God, and obeying the ordinances of the Manifestations is equivalent to worshipping God; because those ordinances are specifically designed to train us, to transform us, to 'save' us by showing us how to express our understanding in a regimen of metaphorical actions.

The Integral Nature of this Process

There are numerous other passages in the Bahá'í sacred texts that likewise demonstrate the importance of this simple but powerful pattern of response as being at the heart of human purpose. Bahá'u'lláh states that 'The beginning of all things is the knowledge of God, and the end of all things is strict observance of whatsoever hath been sent down from the empyrean of the Divine Will.'[32] Similarly, Shoghi Effendi states that the 'very purpose' of the Bahá'í community as a whole is 'regulated by the twin directing principles of the worship of God and of service to one's fellow-men'.[33]

But regardless of the precise context or description of these twin duties or twin aspects of human purpose, the pattern is inevitably the same – knowledge coupled with action. Nevertheless, obvious as these passages might appear to be in their meaning, a closer scrutiny of this paradigm reveals that these two actions are in reality two inextricably related parts of one integral process. The inextricable relationship between these two actions is hinted at by Bahá'u'lláh in this same opening passage of the Kitáb-i-Aqdas: 'These twin duties are inseparable. Neither is acceptable without the other.'[34]

There is a noticeable similarity between the exhortation implied in these twin aspects of human purpose and the often-cited formula enunciated by 'Abdu'l-Bahá as a means for achieving success in all human endeavours. 'Abdu'l-Bahá observes that any human enterprise consists of knowledge, volition and action: 'The attainment of any object is conditioned upon knowledge, volition and action. Unless these three conditions are forthcoming, there is no execution or accomplishment.'[35]

What 'Abdu'l-Bahá seems to suggest here is not three separate actions, but three aspects of one single response, all of which are causally related. One must know before one can decide to do. Or stated in terms of our paradigm of human purpose, one will not likely decide to respond to the guidance of the Manifestation until one recognizes His station and authority, though one might do some worthy action.

The word *acceptable* in this context implies that unless both parts of the paradigm are followed, the process is incomplete. For example, 'Abdu'l-Bahá observes that good deeds of every sort are beneficial, but unless one has an understanding of the relationship between action and human purpose, deeds by themselves offer an inadequate solution to the human condition:

> Know that such actions, such efforts and such words are praiseworthy and approved, and are the glory of humanity. But these actions alone are not sufficient; they are a body of the greatest loveliness, but without spirit.[36]

He then goes on to explain how the knowledge of God induces action:

> . . . if to the knowledge of God is joined the love of God, and attraction, ecstasy and goodwill, a righteous action is then perfect and complete. Otherwise, though a good action is praiseworthy, yet if it is not sustained by the knowledge of God, the love of God, and a sincere intention, it is imperfect.[37]

The knowledge of God as indicated by recognition of the Manifestation must necessarily precede the expression of that knowledge in deeds; in that sense, knowledge has primacy in order. Yet the recognition by itself means little if it does not result in altered behaviour, a transformed human being. The acceptance of the Manifestation as one's 'Saviour' is not a completed act until that recognition is demonstrated through action, through obedience to the guidance the Prophet brings. Or stated another way, how can one be said to have recognized the station and nature of the Manifestation if one does not also realize the necessity of obedience to His guidance.

Attributes of this Process

In addition to being inseparable, these two actions, or 'twin duties', possess other noteworthy attributes which we must consider if we are to see how this paradigm plays itself out throughout the Bahá'í portrayal of the organization of physical reality. For example, these two actions are distinct but inseparable because they are complementary and reciprocal parts of one action. Each action enhances our ability to perform the other.

Because knowledge induces action, there is also a causal relationship. But that sequence of causality does not cease with the metaphorical action. As we also noted in *The Purpose of Physical Reality*,[38] action increases our understanding of an attribute and thereby provides the basis for a more profound or more expansive expression of that increased knowledge. Indeed, probably the most subtle and noteworthy attribute in the relationship between these twin aspects of human purpose is the fact that at no point is this process finished or completed. It is for this reason that in *The Purpose of Physical Reality* we defined salvation as being in forward motion since there is no final point of attainment wherein all knowledge is translated into all possible actions. In fact, there is no final point for the application of this process to a single virtue or attribute. The process of applying these twin responses is thus inexhaustible.

The attributes of the relationship between these twin responses are thus impressive: inseparable, complementary, reciprocal, progressive, inexhaustible. But these observations hardly provide a complete picture of how important this dual paradigm is in relation to the Bahá'í teachings about cosmology and theology and theodicy. For example, since some passages in the Bahá'í writings seem to indicate that the physical world is but a shadowy reflection of the divine world, we might think it hardly worthy of our attention, and many passages caution against becoming too attached to the physical world: 'Abandon not the everlasting beauty for a beauty that must die, and set not your affections on this mortal world of dust.'[39]

Yet a more careful consideration of the Bahá'í writings reveals that the physical world, in addition to being a means by which we can gain insights about the unseen world, has an inherent value of its own. That is, the Bahá'í writings indicate that these twin duties parallel the twin aspects of creation (the spiritual and the physical). Therefore, the relationship between the physical and the spiritual is distinct from a neo-Platonic doctrine whereby the physical world functions solely to give us clues about the world of ideas and abstract forms. For unlike the commonly-accepted neo-Platonic perspective of the goal in this life being to abstain from the things of this world, escape from this illusory 'cave',* and ascend mystically to the eternal realm, the Bahá'í writings portray the physical world as a thoroughly spiritualized expression of the unseen spiritual world, a classroom not to be disdained, but to be respected, cherished, utilized and esteemed:

---

* In Book VII of Plato's *Republic*, Socrates makes an elaborate conceit commonly known as the 'allegory of the cave', in which he compares the physical world to an inferior expression of the ineffable world of forms and ideas which the physical world reflects. However, one may see in this Socratic doctrine an appreciation for physical reality inasmuch as it provides the images of that spiritual world, and thus the means for our ascent.

> The spiritual world is like unto the phenomenal world. They are the exact counterpart of each other. Whatever objects appear in this world of existence are the outer pictures of the world of heaven.[40]

In this sense, phenomenal reality, because it is an eternal reality that co-exists with the spiritual reality, is the outward or visible aspect of spiritual reality, not merely a guidepost or a symbol, but the spiritual world given concrete expression.

The implications of this relationship between the spiritual and physical world are profound and manifold. For example, what we are doing when we respond to the twin duties enunciated by Bahá'u'lláh is acting out this same process – we are giving poetic expression to our spiritual realities. Thus, if we liken the relationship between the spiritual world and the physical world to the relationship between the human soul and the human body, we can observe that this linkage is, from the beginning, an inherent property of creation itself.

Parallel of Twin Duties to Twin Stations of the Prophets

This linkage or interplay between the two realities is clearly demonstrated in the Bahá'í concept of how human society advances through the process of progressive revelation; for it is the Manifestations who in their character and teachings explicate this crucial linkage between these two aspects of reality, between these two worlds. In the broadest sense, it is their mission to explain and demonstrate how phenomenal reality functions as an outward expression of the spiritual world. In this vein, it is axiomatic in discussions of Bahá'í theology to note how the Prophets of God provide two categories of information – the one, a reiteration of eternal spiritual verities;

the other, an enunciation of the laws, ordinances and social methodology whereby that spiritual insight can be expressed through dramatic, metaphorical action.

A part of this same distinction is the observation that where the first sort of instruction alludes to a reality that is eternal and constant, the second alludes to a creation that is in a constant state of change and evolution. Consequently, the spiritual verities enunciated by the Prophets are in accord, whereas their laws, ordinances and social teachings often vary, sometimes significantly, because they are guiding a constantly changing organism, the human body politic, through myriad changes of 'an ever-advancing civilization'. In short, while eternal attributes of the spiritual world are constant, the implementation of them in the phenomenal world is always relative and capable of infinite progression towards the eternal ideal without ever becoming that ideal.

Obviously the distinction between these two categories of information and the realities they represent parallel the twin duties of human purpose. The insights about the spiritual verities relate to the recognition of those attributes as they are manifested through the appearance of the Prophets; and the Prophet's guidance about how to act out those verities in the phenomenal world convey the most effective means of 'worshipping' God at any given point in the historical progress of the human family. Thus, as we noted in the first volume of this study, there is a parallel between the 'twofold' language which the Manifestations employ and these two categories of information. The language conveying spiritual verities will most often be allusive, poetic and abstruse because the reality it is attempting to reveal is unseen, ephemeral and veiled. However, the language delineating the law, though sometimes embellished with imagery, will often be direct, straightforward, exact, 'devoid of allusions', 'unconcealed and unveiled; that it may be a guiding lamp and a beaconing light whereby wayfarers may attain the heights of holiness, and seekers may advance into the realm of eternal reunion'.[41]*

But perhaps the most important parallel between these twin duties of human purpose and the appearance of the Manifestations concerns the dual stations which Bahá'u'lláh states are applicable to each Prophet.

The Station of Essential Unity

Related to the first of these duties (the knowledge of God as signalled by the recognition of the Prophet) is the station of 'essential unity' appropriate to each of the Manifestations. In explaining this station, Bahá'u'lláh observes that all the Manifestations are like mirrors reflecting the same essential divine force:

> Thus, viewed from the standpoint of their oneness and sublime detachment, the attributes of Godhead, Divinity, Supreme Singleness, and Inmost Essence, have been and are applicable to those Essences of being [the Manifestations], inasmuch as they all abide on the throne of divine Revelation, and are established upon the seat of divine Concealment. Through their appearance the Revelation of God is made manifest, and by their countenance the Beauty of God is revealed. Thus it is that the accents of God Himself have been heard uttered by these Manifestations of the divine Being.[42]

In this context, the essential truth of each revelation is the same, even though the language of the Messengers may be veiled in a poetic garment distinctly calculated to teach

---

* As we will note in more detail later, much of the Kitáb-i-Aqdas defies this expectation because the laws are imbedded in or surrounded by metaphorical analogies and poetic homilies that explicate the context in which the law must operate.

humanity in a particular social or historical milieu. Thus, Bahá'u'lláh observes, 'Wherefore, should any one of these Manifestations of Holiness proclaim saying: "I am the return of all the Prophets," He verily speaketh the truth. In like manner, in every subsequent Revelation, the return of the former Revelation is a fact, the truth of which is firmly established.'[43]

The Station of Distinction

In relation to the second duty of 'worshipping' God, or acting out recognition of spiritual principles as conveyed by the Prophets in daily action, is the second station of the Manifestations, what Bahá'u'lláh terms the 'station of distinction'. In this station the Manifestations reveal specific guidance calculated to direct the daily affairs of humanity for a specific duration of time and to befit the exigencies of a particular period in the history of human advancement:

> The other is the station of distinction, and pertaineth to the world of creation and to the limitations thereof. In this respect, each Manifestation of God hath a distinct individuality, a definitely prescribed mission, a predestined Revelation, and specially designated limitations. Each one of them is known by a different name, is characterized by a special attribute, fulfils a definite Mission, and is entrusted with a particular Revelation.[44]

Because the Manifestation thus serves to elucidate the spiritual reality and, through creative laws and guidance, demonstrates to humankind how to employ wilful actions to fashion a critical linkage between these realities in terms of human behaviour and social structures, He effectively joins and knits together these twin realities. It is perhaps this very process that is being alluded to when Bahá'u'lláh in the long obligatory prayer refers to the Manifestation as the one 'through Whom the letters B and E (Be) have been joined and knit together'.[45] That is, it is the Manifestation who brings creation into being by linking together for human understanding the eternal, changeless world of the spirit with the contingent reality by creating a social edifice capable of translating that unseen reality into a visible but divine artifice wherein we ourselves collaborate as artisans, or to use one of 'Abdu'l-Bahá's metaphors, as labourers in the vineyard of God.[46]

The Twin Duties and the Art of Salvation

There are other important parallels between this process and the appearance of the Manifestations, particularly as regards the attempt to establish an institution to promulgate and protect the revelation of a Prophet. But before we examine these further implications of this paradigm of human purpose, we would do well to gain a more ample understanding of why this process is such an effective means of educating human beings that God has chosen to employ it consistently with every succeeding dispensation. Or stated in terms of our abiding theme, let us examine more carefully how this process brings about salvation.

Because the Bahá'í perception of history views God as a divine artificer fashioning a civilization that is increasingly capable of reflecting divine attributes, it is extremely useful to examine the twin duties of human purpose in terms of the artistic process, since both practices fashion raw materials into expressions of abstract thought. In such a context, the Manifestation is artisan and foreman, author, teacher and organizer of other artisans.

Of course, theories of art abound and few cogent expressions of art as a process could be considered universally accepted. However, an examination of two particular theories of poetry may serve well to explicate the twin duties of human ascent in terms of a process whereby each of us is empowered to become a co-creator fashioning God's poem from the earthly materials of our own lives.

The Causality of Art

In the poem 'Peter Quince at the Clavier', the speaker, Peter Quince, sits at the keyboard of a clavier, inspired in his playing by the 'blue-shadowed silk' of a woman whose beauty has moved him to play:

> Just as my fingers on these keys
> Make music, so the selfsame sounds
> On my spirit make a music, too.
>
> Music is feeling, then, not sound;
> And thus it is that what I feel
> Here in this room, desiring you,
>
> Thinking of your blue-shadowed silk,
> Is music. It is like the strain
> Waked in the elders by Susanna.
>
> Of a green evening, clear and warm,
> She bathed in her still garden, while
> The red-eyed elders watching, felt
>
> The bases of their beings throb
> In witching chords, and their thin blood
> Pulse pizzicati of Hosanna.[47]

On the most obvious level, the speaker is, we can assume, comparing the passion he feels for the woman to the lust the elders felt upon seeing Susanna. But in truth, the poem is tightly focused not on the evocative power of feminine pulchritude, but on the process whereby that momentary vision of beauty or feeling of passion becomes translated into some corporeal form or sensually perceptible medium.

In Wallace Stevens's poem, the medium is music. Thus,

like the elders, Peter Quince, inspired by the beauty
emanating from the young woman, translates his emotion
into a concrete or sensually perceptible form, into music.
Subsequently, the very music he has created affects him
again: 'so the selfsame sounds/ On my spirit make a
music, too'. The resulting paradigm of causality runs
something like this: 1) beauty as a divine attribute is
metaphorized in the form of the beautiful woman; 2) the
emanation of this attribute attracts Peter Quince so powerfully that he is inspired to translate his emotion into artistic
form; 3) he composes the music in his mind and transmits
those strains onto the keyboard through the instrumentality of his fingers; 4) the clavier translates the speaker's
passion into melodic line; 5) when he hears the selfsame
music, his own spirit is reinvigorated and his passion
renewed.

The speaker concludes, as he ponders this cyclical
relationship, that art gives a permanence to the ephemeral,
renders the forms and abstractions of the unseen world
into something understandable in the physical world:

> Beauty is momentary in the mind –
> The fitful tracing of a portal;
> But in flesh it is immortal.
> The body dies, the body's beauty lives.

To a certain extent, Stevens in this poem seems to be
exploring the same qualities of art conveyed in Keats'
proverbial dictum about life and art at the end of 'Ode on a
Grecian Urn'. After marvelling at how an ancient relic can
so preserve in time the fleeting vision that was in the mind
of the Greek artisan, the speaker in Keats' poem concludes
that though civilizations and ages may pass, the ideas and
truths of those ages endure because art has the capacity to
give concrete form to spiritual verities by freezing a
moment's vision into lasting image:

When old age shall this generation waste,
  Thou shalt remain, in midst of other woe
Than ours, a friend to man, to whom thou say'st,
  'Beauty is truth, truth beauty.' – that is all
    Ye know on earth, and all ye need to know.[48]

In the same way that the artisan gives permanence and form to his vision of the Grecian village by fashioning the urn, so Keats as artisan constructs in poetic form the music produced when the beauty of that artifact plays upon the instrument of his own creative faculties.

But Stevens is also making a further statement about the nature of this process. Peter Quince is a character in Shakespeare's *Midsummer-Night's Dream*, the director of the bumbling interlude about Pyramus and Thisbe. Consequently, we infer that Stevens here is alluding to the inadequacy of the artist, and perhaps of the art as well, to render accurately the unseen reality into perceptible form. The poem seems to imply that all art must invariably be imprecise and allusive. Artifice may hint at abstraction, allude to it, evoke it, even recall it, but never hope to reproduce or duplicate it. Art may serve us well, as well as anything could, but it is necessarily the 'fitful tracing of a portal', a window in the physical world through which we may gain a fleeting glimpse of the eternal reality.

The Artist as Visionary

Another useful statement of the artistic process as parallel to the twin duties of human purpose is exemplified in Coleridge's theory of primary and secondary imagination, especially as that theory is implied in the familiar poem 'Kubla Khan'. In this dreamlike piece, the poet begins with a mystical vision of a surreal edifice, a 'stately pleasure-dome' wrought by the mighty emperor Kubla Khan. The edifice is described as containing crystalline 'caves of ice' formed where Alph, the sacred river, is forced up like a fountain from between the rocks:

> And from this chasm, with ceaseless turmoil seething,
> As if this earth in fast thick pants were breathing,
> A mighty fountain momentarily was forced:
> Amid whose swift half-intermittent burst
> Huge fragments vaulted like rebounding hail,
> Or chaffy grain beneath the thresher's flail:
> And 'mid these dancing rocks at once and ever
> It flung up momentarily the sacred river.[49]

While the poem invites various readings,* the narrator/persona's response to the vision seems to make clear that at the heart of the poem is a symbolic statement of the artistic process. The narrator, reflecting on the great Khan's feat, wonders if he, too, could translate his own recollected visions into artistic form. In particular he recalls a vision he once had of a beautiful woman:

> A damsel with a dulcimer
> In a vision once I saw:
> It was an Abyssinian maid,
> And on her dulcimer she played,
> Singing of Mount Abora.
> Could I revive within me
> Her symphony and song,
> To such a deep delight 'twould win me,
> That with music loud and long
> I would build that dome in air,
> That sunny dome! those caves of ice![50]

Just as Peter Quince's translation of desire and longing into music plays on the instrument of his own imagin-

---

* Among the most popular is Coleridge's own assertion that the work is the poet's spontaneous transcription of an opium-induced dream. See *English Romantic Poetry and Prose*, p. 391.

ation, this narrator likewise wishes to render his recollected vision so vibrant that it would inspire him anew ("twould win me').

In both cases, then, one gauge of the artist's success is the continuity of causality – the capacity of the artifice, like an electrical transformer, to reinvigorate the imaginative or inspirational power of the original vision. But while Stevens implies that the artist must ultimately fall short of exactitude or completeness, Coleridge implies another, somewhat more unfortunate, result of this noble effort – the alienation of the artist from society:

> And all who heard should see them there,
> And all should cry, Beware! Beware!
> His flashing eyes, his floating hair!
> Weave a circle round him thrice,
> And close your eyes with holy dread,
> For he on honey-dew hath fed,
> And drunk the milk of Paradise.[51]

Like visionaries or seers in the classical tradition (Cassandra, Tiresias, etc.) and, of course, like the Prophets in religious history, the poet as visionary is perceived as strange, alien, dangerous. Consequently, instead of appreciating the service he has rendered, the generality of people wish to protect themselves from the artist's influence. They are frightened by the truth the artist reveals and revert to superstition in order to veil themselves from the disturbing information it imparts. Implicit in this rejection, of course, is the persecution of the visionary.

That Coleridge means for this vision to imply a spiritual insight or sacred intimation is made clear by the appellations he ascribes to the initial symbols in the poem as they relate to his essay on art in *Biographia Literaria*. In discussing the artistic process, Coleridge describes two parts whereby inspiration is rendered into concrete form. The first part, the 'primary imagination', is a passive

capacity of the poet to be attuned to or in touch with
spiritual insights, the verities latent in the fabric of the
universe itself. To a certain extent, the receptivity to inspiration, this intuition, is a fundamentally human capacity
available to everyone, not an esoteric sensibility specialized
for the poet. Thus, in 'Kubla Khan' the constant avail-
ability of this eternal truth might well be represented
by the sacred river as the creative word or ubiquitous
source of human insight (the 'Alpha and Omega'). When
the sacred river is 'flung up momentarily', insight is
briefly gained. Otherwise, the river proceeds to sink 'in
tumult to a lifeless ocean' where one hears 'ancestral voices
prophesying war!'

It is in the second part of the process that the specialized
faculties of the artist become employed. By subtle combination of determination and genius, the artist manages to
forge the momentary burst of insight into metaphorical
referent:

> The power [of the 'imagination'], first put in action of the
> will and understanding, and retained under their irremissive,
> though gentle and unnoticed, control . . . reveals itself in the
> balance or reconciliation of opposite or discordant qualities:
> of sameness, with difference, of general, with the concrete;
> the idea, with the image; the individual with the representa-
> tive . . .[52]

The fact that the 'sunny pleasure dome' is constructed of
ice seems to imply that the artist must necessarily possess
daring, imagination and deft skills in order to fabricate an
edifice from that momentary vision, that burst of water
flung up from the sacred river.

Thus, the ironic ending to Coleridge's poem is important. Though little appreciated for his efforts, the poet
renders a vital service to humanity by giving voice to
those insights that are at the heart of the human experience
and by providing access to and understanding of the world

of ideas – the spiritual or divine reality. It may well be this practical application of poetry which prompted Bahá'u-'lláh to ascribe to the arts the epithets 'wings to man's life' and 'a ladder for his ascent'.[53] This is also the essence of Shelley's meaning when he describes the capacity of poetry to enlighten not only the poet, but all who use the art to exercise these faculties:

> But poetry acts in another and diviner manner. It awakens and enlarges the mind itself by rendering it the receptacle of a thousand unapprehended combinations of thought. Poetry lifts the veil from the hidden beauty of the world . . .[54]

Spiritual Ascent as Artistic Process

The fundamental parallel between these two portrayals of the artistic process and the twin duties that, according to Bahá'í scripture, delineate human purpose are not difficult to spot. In both processes, abstraction is made concrete by the wilful use of metaphor. In the same way that the artist must flesh out the unseen intimations of immortality through words, clay, colour, song, so the aspirant to spiritual transcendence must articulate spiritual verities through wilful daily action. But there are more subtle implications in this analogy that help demonstrate further the divine wisdom whereby human creation as an essentially spiritual organism is initially trained and educated in the ostensibly awkward, constraining and often contrary medium of physical reality.

First of all, from meditating on the artistic process as we have discussed it, we come to see more clearly why there are two parts to the process of human development and how each part is essential for the other. Without insight, the artist has nothing important to say to us. Conversely, without the wilful discipline to develop the tools and craft of his medium, the artist, however full of divine fire, can hardly render even a 'fitful tracing of a portal' to reveal or unveil the ephemeral reality. This interdependence of the two parts of the process parallels the inseparability Bahá'u'lláh attributes to the recognition of the Manifestation and the obedience to His guidance.

Secondly, we can discern in the two aspects of these processes two parallel sets of requisite skills or human capacities. For example, the first part of these twin duties – recognition of truth – implies receptivity, clarity of perception, purity of motive. For some of the poets of the English Romantic Movement, the Aeolian harp became a symbol of this sensibility or capacity:

> In Coleridge's poem 'The Eolian Harp' the speaker calls his 'indolent and passive brain' a 'subject Lute' whereon play 'Full many a thought uncall'd and undertain'd/ And many idle flitting phantasies'. In his essay 'In Defence of Poetry' Shelley uses the same metaphor: 'Man is an instrument over which a series of external and internal impressions are driven, like the alternations of an ever-changing wind over an Æolian lyre, which move it by their motion to ever-changing melody.' The transcendentalist Emerson used the metaphor of a lightning rod to portray essentially the same quality of passivity on the poet's part.[55]

Spiritually this capacity relates to the admonition repeated in the scripture of virtually every religion about not allowing impediments to veil one's receptivity to the truth. For example, Christ explains that He uses the artistic device of the parable because the people He teaches are so attached to the literal aspects of religion (laws, rituals and other trappings) that they are no longer open to the essential truth underlying their belief:

> This is why I speak to them in parables, because seeing they do not see, and hearing they do not hear, nor do they understand. With them indeed is fulfilled the prophecy of

Isaiah which says: 'You shall indeed hear but never understand, and you shall indeed see but never perceive.'[56]*

The Bahá'í scriptures are likewise replete with references
to this quality of perception. Bahá'u'lláh states:

> We cherish the hope that through the loving-kindness of the
> All-Wise, the All-Knowing, obscuring dust may be dispelled
> and the power of perception enhanced, that the people may
> discover the purpose for which they have been called into
> being.[57]

As we noted in the first volume, Bahá'u'lláh's *Hidden
Words* equates the virtue of this independence of thought
with internal justice, stating that

> The best beloved of all things in My sight is Justice; turn
> not away therefrom if thou desirest Me, and neglect it not
> that I may confide in thee. By its aid thou shalt see with thine
> own eyes and not through the eyes of others, and shalt know
> of thine own knowledge and not through the knowledge of
> thy neighbour. Ponder this in thy heart; how it behooveth
> thee to be.[58]

The second part of the artistic process likewise parallels
what we have alluded to in the twin duties as the
translation of perception into action. In this capacity, the
artist is active and struggles with the materials of his
medium to represent through sound, stone, paint or
language what he has glimpsed or heard from the unseen
world of spiritual forms. Therefore, this second sort of
artistic faculty is not passive, but an active source of
enlightenment for humanity, a lamp, a 'candle of the
Lord', which throws 'its beams into the external world'.[59]
     A third parallel between these two processes, and

---

* This and all subsequent citations from the Bible are from the Revised
Standard Version.

perhaps the most significant one, is the fact that this capacity, though latent in everyone, can be exercised only through struggle, through wilful, dutiful and rigorous discipline. 'It truly disturbs me', Bahá'í artist and writer Roger Bansemer remarked, 'when people see my work and tell me how *talented* I am. Such comments seem to imply that because I have *talent*, what I do is easy or effortless. They are unaware of the countless days, months and years I have spent studying my craft, developing and honing the skills I have, the untold lonely hours of persistence and drudgery.'[60] In the same way that the artist must wrestle daily with the subtleties of art to give form to the formless, so the believer as aspirant to personal transformation must constantly struggle to discover how best to dramatize the tenets of faith in daily action, to fashion from mundane affairs forms of worship.

A fourth similarity between these two processes lies in the reciprocal and progressive relationship between the two parts. Once the ephemeral is given representative form, the mind need not re-experience that mystic vision in order to recall the insight. The artifice, or the action, having fashioned a portal through which the eternal may be glimpsed, serves to give the meditative faculty a foothold for further consideration of that same verity. Whether literally or figuratively, the aspirant to growth can revisit the artifice to regain or recollect the insight which has been clothed in the garment of metaphor.

Some Essential Implications in this Process

We could continue endlessly to note other parallels between these processes, but the essential relationship is perhaps sufficiently apparent for us to conclude that both the artistic process and the Bahá'í paradigm of human advancement are essentially the same mechanism. However, we should note a few other dynamic principles that govern both processes.

For both the artist and the aspirant to spiritual transformation, there must be some first principle; otherwise, the art and the spiritual quest become merely existential grace at best or, at worst, vain imaginings that must needs degenerate into solipsism, fanaticism or superstition. In short, we must presume that once the doors of perception are opened, there is an external spiritual reality to perceive.

For the agnostic, the secular humanist or the post modern theorist, such an issue may seem unnecessary. For them, the human condition may be adequately defined in terms of each individual's noble attempt to impose order on disorder, meaning on chaos. For them it may seem fruitless or even detrimental to presume that beyond particular human perceptions is a reliable cognitive force or even an objective metaphysical reality. However, such is not the case for the Romantic artist and theorist who affirms the Platonic notion of physical reality as a metaphorical expression of divine reality, nor for the believer in a spiritual reality for which the physical experience is a foundational preparation. For one who comes to affirm the objective existence of a spiritual reality, such perceptions are not naive inner reflections, but the awakening and hearkening of the soul to the 'real' world. For these souls, 'Nature is animated, alive, filled with God or the Spirit of the World; it is mysteriously present, it gives a discipline of fear and ministry of pleasure. Nature is also a language, a system of symbols.'[61]

Besides the necessity of an external spiritual reality, a second essential prerequisite for the success of such beliefs is the concept of renewal. We have noted how the very process of clothing abstraction in the garment of sensually perceived form invests the form with the capacity to advance understanding, just as Peter Quince's own music affects his spirit. At some point, however, the law of entropy dictates that one must in time return again to the source of inspiration. For while the process of creating form from inspiration may yield further insight, it is insufficient to maintain an endless causal process of transformation without the need for further sustenance.

This leads us to yet a third principle governing this process. If spiritual reality is itself organic and dynamic, then at some point as more and more of the essential ingredients of that reality become translated into human social analogues, social reality will take on the properties of that spiritual reality until it operates as a spiritual dynamism. In time, the artifice will be consonant with, even in a sense synonymous with the spiritual reality it metaphorizes. For while the natural world inherently reflects the laws and realities of the spiritual world, the human social reality is only potentially spiritual until, through a process of divinely assisted effort, spiritual principles become wilfully translated into social relationships. Since the physical can only allude to the abstract and infinite, the human social reality can never become the spiritual reality, although its essential dynamic can become spiritually based and its progress towards that reality ever more refined.

Finally, when (through the interplay of divine will and guidance with human understanding, volition and action) this process fashions human society into an essentially spiritual organism, we can rightly designate that society as God's artifice, God's poem, the heavenly kingdom translated into social metaphor, the unseen given concrete form. Humanity as a whole may become the 'jobbers' and artisans in this process, like the villagers who helped piece together the wondrous mosques in Islamic culture or the mediaeval cathedrals in Western Christendom. But the blueprint, the vision, the inherent capacity of society to manifest the divine world, all these are revealed to humankind through God's master craftsmen, the Manifestations.

The Twin Duties and the Female and Male Principles of Complementarity

Having established how the twin duties incumbent on humanity parallel the twin stations of the Prophet and the dynamic process in art whereby abstract reality becomes wilfully translated into concrete or artistic form, we are prepared to study how the Manifestation functions as artist and art instructor. But for our immediate purposes, we can best conclude this introduction to the Bahá'í paradigm of spiritual ascent by noting how the interplay between understanding and action in this dynamic process of knowing and worshipping God is most obviously borne out in the subtle interplay in this life between the soul and the body. For where in some religious traditions the body is perceived to be antithetical to the purposes of the so-called higher self (the spiritual or rational faculties), the Bahá'í writings depict a complementarity between these twin aspects of self.

Enigmas in the Adamic Myth

From the Bahá'í perspective, the physical self need not be the enemy of the spiritual self. Properly ordered and directed, the body becomes the minion of the soul, its functionary and representative, the outward expression of the soul's advancement and a primary instrument through which the 'worship' of God is accomplished. Therefore, the laws revealed in the Kitáb-i-Aqdas are not perceived as

restrictive or puritanical, but as delineating the most
efficacious means of harnessing the capacities of the physical
self (even the passions and emotions) towards constructive
ends: 'We approve of liberty in certain circumstances,
and refuse to sanction it in others. We, verily, are the
All-Knowing.'[62] While Bahá'u'lláh's statement might be
inferred to connote some authoritarian or arbitrary tenor,
he goes on to observe that the objective for each one
should be to study the laws in order to perceive the divine
rationale, justice and benignity underlying each law:

> Were men to observe that which We have sent down unto
> them from the Heaven of Revelation, they would, of a
> certainty, attain unto perfect liberty. Happy is the man that
> hath apprehended the Purpose of God in whatever He hath
> revealed from the Heaven of His Will that pervadeth all
> created things.[63]

Curiously, one of the more effective means of understanding this subtle interplay between soul and body as
paralleling the twin duties in the process of spiritual ascent
is to be found in what is one of the most influential and
certainly the most misunderstood mythological treat-
ments of this theme, the Adamic myth.* From a Bahá'í
perspective, the story of Adam is in part an allusion to an
historical figure, a Manifestation who appeared approximately six thousand years ago and ministered to a particular
people. Of course, most people in the West are familiar
with the story as told in Genesis.† In general, the story has
been studied as a creation myth or else it has been used

---

* See *The Purpose of Physical Reality* pp. 22–7 and 37–45 for a further
discussion of the Adamic myth in relation to Bahá'í theodicy.
† The version of the story in the Qur'án is quite different, as we noted in
our discussion in *The Purpose of Physical Reality*.

historically in much of the Judaeo-Christian tradition to justify a view of women as subordinate to men, to portray women as the source of temptations of the flesh and therefore as the cause of human failure, and to substantiate the Christian doctrine of primal sin. But following 'Abdu'l-Bahá's suggestion about how this myth functions as a poetic device, we can see in the story an entirely different meaning which demonstrates dramatically the complementary relationship between the twin duties of human purpose as they relate to the dual aspects (or twin stations) of human nature.

According to the narration of the story of Adam in the second chapter of Genesis, God decides to give Adam a 'helper'[64] and produces the beasts of the field, which Adam proceeds to name. Yet the sequence of events seems out of sync with the first chapter wherein God creates man only after he has created the birds and beasts. Therefore, we might assume that what is now being narrated is the making of man in the image of God: 'Let us make man in our image, after our likeness.'[65] While the physical man has already evolved, as have the beasts and birds, they are 'given' to man in the sense that humanity becomes endowed with the capacity to utilize them, to domesticate the beasts that they might indeed be fit 'helpers'.

Yet we are told that 'for the man there was not found a helper fit for him' until God caused a 'deep sleep to fall upon the man' and from one of Adam's ribs fashioned woman.[66] If we are to take this myth as being literal in any sense, we are clearly lost, for in no way does woman evolve from man. Clearly some metaphorical or allegorical meaning is implied. Furthermore, since from a Bahá'í perspective, men and women are inherently equal, even some sense of subordination seems erroneous. In addition, why is it that Eve, not Adam, is tempted by the serpent?

Some Allegorical Solutions

To a certain extent, the logical problems of the story result from the perception of the work as a literal narration of creation rather than as an attempt to render abstruse matter into symbolic or allegorical terms, to view the story as a mythological tale similar to other creation myths from various other cultures. This does not mean that the story is less true or misleading. Myth, after all, is not a lie any more than all other forms of art are lies. As we have noted, all attempts to translate spiritual matter into concrete form ultimately fall short of exactitude or precise accuracy. But the capacity of myth to convey that ineffable reality depends on a willing and witting audience, on individuals aware of how myth operates and what it requires of us.

But to gain access to the reality underlying such mythological art, one must be willing to invest sufficient energy to uncover the veiled or metaphorical meaning, the same kind of effort that any work of art requires of us. Therefore, in assisting us to understand this myth, 'Abdu'l-Bahá notes in *Some Answered Questions* that the story, like all allegory, has a variety of possible meanings.[67] He notes, for example, that it was often the case in ancient poetic traditions for a female figure to represent the soul or the spiritual aspect of a human being. Thus, the character of Adam might represent an evolving humankind, and the appearance of Eve might symbolize humanity's becoming aware of its spiritual or intellectual faculties and capacities.

Following this suggestion, we can easily resolve several of the ostensible enigmatic problems of the story. For example, if Eve represents the soul, then humanity's loneliness or incompleteness as depicted in the story derives from the incompleteness of human development.

And yet, if collective human evolution parallels the evolutionary development of an individual human being, as the Bahá'í writings affirm, then the spiritual or intellectual self is not something that is added, any more than the soul is added to an individual's physical being. Instead, an inherent or latent or potential capacity is made apparent or kinetic.

Thus, if there is a parallel between individual human development and the collective evolution of the species, and if the soul of the individual is extant from conception, then we must conclude that the soul of humankind was an integral part of human creation from the beginning. Consequently, the myth does not state that God added something to human reality; He transformed something already extant into a companion – a rib into Eve. In other words, God through His Manifestations endowed humankind with the capacity to recognize and utilize the inherent powers of the soul, and these powers, as we have noted, focus on the ability to recognize spiritual attributes and then, through the power of will, to act out that insight in obedience to spiritual principles.

As the story proceeds, Eve is tempted to eat of the tree in the 'midst of the garden'[68] by the serpent who tells her that 'when you eat of it your eyes will be opened, and you will be like God, knowing good and evil'.[69] Since the Bahá'í writings assert that the concept of Satan, which the serpent symbolizes, represents the ego, the desire to exalt oneself above others,* then why does the ego assault Eve and not Adam?

Following our allegorical interpretation, we can con-

---

* This lower nature in man is symbolized as Satan – the evil ego within us, not an evil personality outside (see 'Abdu'l-Bahá, *Promulgation of Universal Peace*, p. 287).

clude that where the physical or appetitive self might fall prey to temptations of the flesh, it is precisely the spiritual or intellectual self that would fall prey to self-aggrandizement or hubris. Therefore, Eve is tempted to transcend the limitations of human knowledge and power, and in her desire for such distinction, she begins to question God's justice and to perceive the laws of God as capricious or restrictive.

While on a literal level the story implies that Adam falls because he accedes to his wife's iniquity, a figurative or poetic reading implies that the physical or appetitive self will inevitably follow the wilful desires of the soul, since volition is a property of the soul. This interpretation also clarifies what is meant when Adam defends his sin by stating that his failure was the fault of the helpmate God had given him: 'The woman whom thou gavest to be with me, she gave me fruit of the tree, and I ate.'[70] Eve, who as the spiritual or intellectual self is charged with responsibility for providing guidance and will power, readily acknowledges complete culpability and replies, 'The serpent beguiled me, and I ate.'[71]

The implicit antipathy in Adam's response also highlights another subtle point: these two complementary aspects of self have become one organism ('they shall become one flesh'[72]). In part, we infer, the susceptibility of each results from their becoming divided instead working in concert to fulfil their ordained or inherent purpose.

Finally, this allegorical interpretation also clarifies the distinction in God's judgement of the two aspects of self. God first curses the serpent (the ego), and puts 'enmity between you and the woman',[73] meaning enmity between the ego and the soul. Such an inference seems well vindicated by the observation in virtually all religious literature about pride, or ego or the love of self being the greatest deterrent to the spiritual progress of the soul.

God then judges the spiritual self in the following manner: 'I will greatly multiply your pain in childbearing; in pain you shall bring forth children, yet your desire shall be for your husband, and he shall rule over you.'[74] If, as we have suggested, the offspring of the soul are the perceptions of spiritual attributes expressed in some form of changed behaviour, then this judgement implies that the human being is destined to achieve spiritual insight only with difficulty and to act out that insight only through struggle. Whereas in a state of innocence these insights might have been intuited, the soul must now strive to achieve insight by piercing the metaphorical veils which, in this life, conceal spiritual realities, and then wilfully struggling to incorporate that understanding into metaphorical deeds.

The second part of Eve's judgement also becomes clear in this context. God is not enunciating the proper relationship between husband and wife, but rather describing how the spiritual self will be susceptible to being dominated by desires of the flesh. Thus, one of the greatest forces deterring the soul from its proper condition will be the temptations of the body or the flesh, the temptation to allow the appetitive self to gain primacy over the spiritual and rational self. Far from suggesting that this relationship is proper, God is cautioning Eve as the responsible party in this relationship that she will be susceptible to the 'desire' to let her husband (her physical or appetitive nature) overrule her good judgement.

The enigma of a literal interpretation is likewise removed when we apply this allegorical interpretation to God's judgement of Adam, the physical self:

. . . cursed is the ground because of you; in toil you shall eat of it all the days of your life; thorns and thistles it shall bring forth to you; and you shall eat the plants of the field.
In the sweat of your face you shall eat bread till you return

to the ground, for out of it you were taken; you are dust . . .[75]

Because the body became subject to the selfish desires of the ego, the body must labour to sustain itself, enduring thorns and thistles – the inevitable pain, disease and suffering that is the lot of the physical life. Then, after struggling to sustain itself, the body will become dust again. So it is that while the physical self must inevitably decline and pass into dust from which it came, the soul will return to the spiritual kingdom from which it emanated. *

A Partial Matrix

Obviously this brief exegesis of the story of Adam and Eve is hardly a complete or sufficient explication of how it functions to imply an ancient perception of God's justice. But perhaps this explanation does help us begin to appreciate that this theme of the interplay between the dual aspects of our existence as they relate to the twin duties of human purpose is hardly new or something confined to the Bahá'í writings. In fact, as we proceed with our discussion of the social implications of Bahá'í concepts of theodicy, we will note further how this two-part process functions at the heart of divine methodology by which essentially spiritual beings are trained in an environment ostensibly antithetical to spiritual purposes.

As a useful conclusion to this initial treatment of the mechanism of human advancement as enunciated in the

---

* In this connection, Bahá'u'lláh commands in the Kitáb-i-Aqdas that on the deceased should be placed a burial ring bearing the inscription, 'I came forth from God, and return unto Him, detached from all save Him, holding fast to His Name, the Merciful, the Compassionate' (Bahá'u'lláh, *The Kitáb-i-Aqdas*, no. 129).

short obligatory prayer, we might find it useful to assemble some of the parallels we have thus far delineated. As we examine them, we can observe that inevitably the parallels to the first 'duty' relate to the spiritual reality, whereas those activities relating to the second 'duty' involve expressing spiritual insight in physical action. Or stated another way, the process itself gives dramatic evidence of the critical linkage between the two worlds or realities. Therefore, the end result of this process or exercise is to demonstrate for the individual that the two realities are really but aspects of one organic creation. Consequently, the artistic process is a means by which we use each aspect of creation to gain access to the other, even though, as 'Abdu'l-Bahá notes, 'the world of existence is a single world, although its stations are various and distinct'.[76]

Some Parallels to the Twofold Duty of Human Purpose

Parallels	First Duty (Spiritual Reality)	Second Duty (Physical Reality)
obligatory prayer	to know Thee	to worship Thee
exhortation in the Kitáb-i-Aqdas	recognition of Manifestation	obedience to His laws
personal application	perception of spiritual attributes	translation of insight into daily action
artistic methodology	inspiration or insight	translation of ideas into perceptible form
Coleridge's theory	primary imagination	secondary imagination
dual nature of Manifestations	station of essential unity	station of distinction
dual nature of their teachings	reiteration of spiritual verities	revelation of laws, ordinances and institutions
Divine Plan as God's poem	essentially spiritual nature of physical reality	evolution of social forms as expression of spiritual verities
Adamic myth	Eve as human capacity for spiritual or intellectual insight	Adam as capacity and obligation to act out spiritual understanding on daily basis

2

The Social Imperative

And the Emergence of a Global Identity

... when ideas and views reach the utmost degree of
expansion and attain the stage of perfection, then will he be
interested in the exaltation of humankind.[1]

'Abdu'l-Bahá

We now can understand more amply how the acts of
knowing and worshipping God enunciated in the short
obligatory prayer as constituting human purpose actually
allude to a subtle process by which we can achieve spiritual
ascent. We likewise see some of the larger implications of
this process, particularly as they allude to the twin duties
incumbent on every soul as discussed by Bahá'u'lláh in the
opening passages of the Kitáb-i-Aqdas (i.e. the recognition
of the Manifestation and obedience to His commandments). Furthermore, as we noted in the first volume of
this study and at the outset of the previous chapter, while
these twin duties may delineate human purpose in terms of
the essential properties of human spiritualization, the goal
of this process is not some final point of achievement, but
rather the condition of being in forward motion.

The Social Dimension of Individual Salvation

Salvation, according to the Bahá'í teachings, is thus not
achieved merely through recognition of the station of the

Prophet or through a single act of commitment to the guidance he gives. Salvation involves a constant monitoring of one's condition, a persistent evaluation of one's performance coupled with an ever more expansive expression of one's emerging understanding in daily action.

Such a process does not imply that one must defer indefinitely a sense of well-being or a confirmation of one's spiritual security. The existential rewards of this forward motion are immediate, just as one need not await some final point of physical conditioning to feel the benefits of daily exercise. And yet, while spiritualization as a process and salvation as a state of being are sustained by this forward motion, this progress is but a symptom or a property of the really substantive change that is occurring and not the change itself; a means to spiritual growth, not a definition of that growth. For while the struggle for self-improvement that this process seems to imply is certainly desirable, a further study of the Bahá'í writings indicates that implicit and explicit in all human development is a growing awareness of the collective or social self. Stated simply, individual spiritual growth cannot take place in a vacuum; it requires interaction with others.

Why Virtue Implies Interaction

The implications of this observation are profound and complex. On the simplest level, this verity implies that however pious one might aspire to be and however much spiritual ascent requires independent thought and will power, this process cannot be conducted outside a social context. One explanation for this observation is that the virtues which we attempt to express in daily action almost invariably derive meaning from our relationships with other people.

For example, consider the solitary life of an ascetic. Can someone who lives isolated from others be considered good or kind when such a one has never had the opportunity to put that virtue into meaningful action? Can the ascetic claim to be a just person merely because of having studied philosophical or theological treatises on justice, or even from having meditated and prayed about it? Clearly, attributes like justice, kindness, love, trustworthiness and the myriad other admirable virtues that we associate with individual spiritual progress are almost entirely theoretical until learned and practised in a social milieu. For example, can one truly be said to understand patience until one has raised children?

Revelation Focuses on Collective Ascent

There is, however, another more weighty significance to the social aspect of individual progress. The Bahá'í writings repeatedly assert that the overall objective of divine guidance at work in creation is not the random salvation of a select few individuals, not solely the establishment of an effective workshop for individual aspirants to human spiritualization, but the systematic advancement of human civilization as a whole: 'All men have been created to carry forward an ever-advancing civilization.'[2]

Of course, it quickly becomes apparent that individual purpose as expressed in the twin duties and the collective purpose of advancing civilization are not mutually exclusive or even conflicting. In fact, the two statements of purpose are in concert, are synonymous. One's attempt to give overt expression to one's spiritual condition must necessarily involve participating in the collective goals of human society, a society which is itself attempting to employ the same dual process to bring about the collective advancement of humankind.

In this sense, the Manifestations minister to both the individual and the collective self by instituting processes that will enable each to assist the other: the individual is exhorted to assist others, and society is devised to create a spiritual environment wherein one's individual spiritual development can be instigated and nurtured. Thus, Manifestations invariably inaugurate some form of social order whereby the individual effort at spiritual transformation is an integral part of a social programme. This aspect of the revelation of Bahá'u'lláh takes its foundation in His revelation of the Kitáb-i-Aqdas.

The Ever-Expanding Sense of Self

Even if we affirm this social dimension of individual spiritual progress, we still have not enunciated with clarity why individual salvation and spiritual transformation are necessarily dependent on social change. Perhaps we see why the exercise of virtue usually implies relationships with others, but is not the individual's success independent of how the rest of society does? Are we not responsible primarily for our own individual progress quite apart from how everyone else is doing? After all, Bahá'u'lláh said that 'the faith of no man can be conditioned by any one except himself'.[3]

At the close of our discussion in The Purpose of Physical Reality, we noted that the physical stage of our lives functions primarily as preparation for our birth into the spiritual realm. We noted that because of this relationship of the physical experience to the life beyond, the proper function of our physical lives is to establish the foundation of our spiritual development in preparation for the growth that will occur after we are no longer in need of relating spiritual verities and realities to metaphorical physical action. In short, once we are experiencing that ineffable reality first hand, we will no longer need such indirect procedures for gaining understanding and insight.

Once we have established that foundation in this life, we are enabled to become detached from the physical world and, like a child whose period of gestation is finished, we are ready for that transition or birth into the world beyond. In this sense, we observed in *The Purpose of Physical Reality* that one of the clearest indices of our progress is the 'detachment' we have about this life: we utilize the physical analogues, yet realize that their primary value is as tools for our development.[4]

However, there is another kind of detachment also crucially related to our progress and purpose in this life, a detachment from self that derives from a social imperative. For example, we first understand a virtue from the narrow perspective of self-interest or else in relation to one or two others, to our siblings, to our parents or family. But as we acquire a more expansive experience and define ourselves in terms of more inclusive groups, our understanding of this virtue also expands and we become capable of relating it to these ever more encompassing social environments: to our neighbourhood, to our community, to our city or country, and ultimately to humankind as a whole. Yet implicit in this expansive understanding and application of virtue is an expanding identity, an ever more inclusive sense of ourselves and a attendant detachment from selfishness.

Such a detachment or loss of self obviously does not imply self neglect or merely sympathy and empathy with the plight of our fellow human beings. Such detachment implies a palpable sense of our own individual condition and well-being as integral to and inseparable from the larger and more inclusive expression of ourselves as social beings, whether that expression of us be an extended family, a tribe, a nation or humankind as a planetary body politic. Indeed, 'Abdu'l-Bahá describes this increasingly expansive self as one of the clearest evidences of the progress of the human soul:

> Every imperfect soul is self-centred and thinketh only of his own good. But as his thoughts expand a little he will begin to think of the welfare and comfort of his family. If his ideas still more widen, his concern will be the felicity of his fellow citizens; and if still they widen, he will be thinking of the glory of his land and of his race. But when ideas and views reach the utmost degree of expansion and attain the stage of perfection, then will he be interested in the exaltation of humankind. He will then be the well-wisher of all men and the seeker of the weal and prosperity of all lands. This is indicative of perfection.[5]

While not precisely equating the condition of spiritualization or salvation with attaining this expanded sense of self, Bahá'u'lláh in the *Hidden Words* makes it unmistakably clear that achieving this awareness is one of the essential purposes of our creation:

> O CHILDREN OF MEN!
> Know ye not why We created you all from the same dust? That no one should exalt himself over the other. Ponder at all times in your hearts how ye were created. Since We have created you all from one same substance it is incumbent on you to be even as one soul, to walk with the same feet, eat with the same mouth and dwell in the same land, that from your inmost being, by your deeds and actions, the signs of oneness and the essence of detachment may be made manifest.[6]

Likewise, Bahá'u'lláh observes in another passage that the diversity among humankind which seems to function as a deterrent to inclusivity and a unified sense of self is, in reality, not an impediment but a device by which we can be trained to appreciate the essential unity underlying our apparent differences:

'If God had pleased He had surely made all men one people.' His purpose, however, is to enable the pure in spirit and the detached in heart to ascend, by virtue of their own innate powers, unto the shores of the Most Great Ocean, that thereby they who seek the Beauty of the All-Glorious may be distinguished and separated from the wayward and perverse.[7]

Thus, while our individual goal may be the progressive habituation of virtue by means of employing the twin duties of knowing and worshipping, the means by which we exercise this process is necessarily social in nature, and the true gauge of whether such progress has indeed occurred is the extent to which we become detached from being exclusively concerned with our individual progress and become increasingly aware of and involved in the progress or spiritualization of the social institutions which are, in reality, merely more inclusive expressions of our own identity. Indeed, it is this verity that underlies the most persistent theme of the Bahá'í religion: the oneness of humankind.

The Social Self as Confirmed by the Sciences

This idea of our individual salvation and spiritual progress as inextricably bound up in our social identity is hardly new nor is it the exclusive property of Bahá'í belief. When we employ the term *homo sapiens*, we necessarily refer to a biological organism with relatively few instinctive patterns of behaviour and, therefore, with little or no inherent autonomy.

The Individual as a Social Being

If the social sciences have anything to tell us about ourselves that is beyond much controversy, it is that as a species we have a fundamental need to relate our personal situation to some more inclusive enterprise. Therefore, when the sociologists or social psychologists employ terms such as *human* or *person*, they imply an organism that is by nature a social creature. Indeed, they imply that the human reality is inevitably dependent on a social relationship:

> The recognition that human behaviour is learned is basic to the study and understanding of behaviour. It is a discovery comparable in importance to the germ theory of disease in medicine. It orients the student's research into new and more fertile fields. No longer do we see society as composed of individuals each unique in his individually inherited behaviour. Rather, we see society as a complex of forces which shape the behaviour of the individual members, but which in turn is modified by its members.[8]

To a certain extent, the validity of this assertion is dramatically demonstrated by the rare but well-known examples of children fostered without human social intercourse, children who have survived in the wild nurtured by animals and who have lived without any human contact.[9] When these feral children have been introduced into a human social environment, none has been able to acquire 'human' capacities or characteristics. None has become socialized. One and all, they have soon deteriorated and died.

While such isolated occurrences may imply relatively few reliable generalizations about human nature, they do help confirm the obvious and inexorable axiom that being human means that we have an inherent need to relate individual identity and reality to a larger expression of self. Of course, the perception of ourselves as integral with or dependent upon some social relationship in no way implies the neglect or abnegation of self, nor the loss of independence and individuality. According to the seminal work of noted French cultural anthropologist Emile

Durkheim, we have within us an inherent duality: we are individuals and we are also members of a group.

There are two beings in him [the human being]: an individual being which has its foundation in the organism and the circle of whose activities is therefore strictly limited, and a social being which represents the highest reality in the intellectual and moral order that we can know by observation – I mean society . . . In so far as he belongs to society, the individual transcends himself, both when he thinks and when he acts.[10]

The Power of the Social Self

To a considerable extent, it is from this larger expression of self that we derive our greatest sense of achievement. Certainly it is in the name of this relationship that the majority of the most noble and heroic acts find their expression. Indeed, the common will or the collective opinion is perhaps the most impressive force that humankind as a species can martial in moulding human behaviour. Consequently, when that force is used to reinforce and sustain us, we as individuals are capable of super-human acts of sacrifice and courage. Conversely, when that same force of the collective self is turned against us, we are liable to become weakened and diminished to the point of extinction. What is more, when we become inured to such social influence, we are capable of becoming infinitely worse than beasts of the field:

How lofty is the station which man, if he but choose to fulfil his high destiny, can attain! To what depths of degradation he can sink, depths which the meanest of creatures have never reached![11]

Another important generalization about the crucial nature of this social sense of self is that the greater the integralness of the social organism with which our individual identity becomes associated, the more power it is capable of wielding in our lives. No doubt it is for this reason that in so many tribal communities the most grievous punishment one can suffer is not physical torture or even death, but separation from the group, whether such isolation be imposed as punishment or comes about through happenstance.

I. M. Finley notes that in the ancient Achaean civilization of 1200 BC separation from society was deemed the harshest fate one could endure:

> It was not out of mere sentiment for the fatherland that banishment was deemed the bitterest of fates. The exile was stripped of all ties that meant life itself; it made no difference in this regard whether one had been compelled to flee or had gone from home in the search for land by free choice.[12]

This same sentiment obtained with the Anglo-Saxon tribes almost two thousand years later. In one Anglo-Saxon lyric we find the following plaint:

> He who has felt such solitude
> knows how cruel a comrade is sorrow
> for one bereft of the company of friends.
> No wound gold for him, no fruit of the fields,
>
> only a freezing corpse and dark thoughts –
> images of warriors strutting in the hall,
> the doling of treasures at the feast,
> how his gold-friend indulged him in youth.[13]

This same strategic relationship pertains equally well to tribal societies of whatever historical or geographical setting. Indeed, the power of this need to belong and of the benefits derived from being appreciated by the social self can explain in large part the amazing acts of self-sacrifice we observe in times of war, even when the causes or objectives of the war are ambiguous.

The Bahá'í Concept of the Social Self

The Bahá'í writings confirm the essential truth of this social dimension to the human reality, both as it regards physical well-being and as it implies a spiritual obligation.

Essential Interdependence

'Abdu'l-Bahá observes that unlike some other creatures in nature, 'man cannot live singly and alone. He is in need of continuous cooperation and mutual help. For example, a man living alone in the wilderness will eventually starve. He can never . . . provide himself with all the necessities of existence.'[14] 'Abdu'l-Bahá goes on to explain, however, that this very interdependence of humanity is not a weakness, not a flaw or failing. The integrality of the human family is an essential reality of human existence designed to instigate and sustain individual and collective spiritual enlightenment:

> . . . each member of the body politic should live in the utmost comfort and welfare because each individual member of humanity is a member of the body politic and if one member of the members be in distress or be afflicted with some disease all the other members must necessarily suffer. For example, a member of the human organism is the eye. If the eye should be affected that affliction would affect the whole nervous system. Hence, if a member of the body politic becomes afflicted, in reality, from the standpoint of sympathetic connection, all will share that affliction since this (one afflicted) is a member of the group of members, a part of the whole. Is it possible for one member or part to be in distress and the other members to be at ease? It is impossible! Hence God has desired that in the body politic of humanity each one shall enjoy perfect welfare and comfort.[15]

In short, the Bahá'í concept of spiritual health envisions a mutuality of interests between the individual and society

wherein the health of the individual organism is inseparable from and in concert with the health of the body politic
as a whole.

Of course, as we have already noted, the Bahá'í scriptures affirm that the most meaningful aspect of this social
relationship cannot be imposed, but derives instead from
the willingness of the individual to foster the well-being of
society, not solely because he or she feels morally impelled
but, more importantly, because the individual has attained
a sense of self that transcends individual interests. Or
stated more accurately, the individual has come to realize
that self-interest is inseparable from collective interest.
Therefore, the achievement of a more inclusive sense of
self is not an incidental or ancillary benefit derived from
the individual practice of virtue. Properly understood, the
wilful relinquishing of selfish concerns to foster the well-
being of the body politic is itself the precise goal of
individual enlightenment and development.

A Further Examination of 'Detachment'

As we have noted, 'detachment' in such a context implies
not so much the forgoing of vain desires or the control of
the appetitive self, but rather a conjoining or alignment of
individual motives and objectives with those of the larger
self. But however logical and beneficial such a process may
ultimately be, we might understandably wonder how such
a process takes place and what part we have to play in
bringing about this transformation from self-interest to an
appreciation of ourselves as integral parts of the divine
creation.

As we noted in *The Purpose of Physical Reality*, the sort
of detachment that derives from the wise use of the
physical classroom is partially assisted by the natural

properties of life itself. That is, while our job is to extract spiritual lessons communicated to us through the phenomenal world without becoming infatuated with the medium through which these lessons are conveyed, the ageing process itself will see to it that we will in the course of our lives gradually relinquish our dependence on things physical and the sense of ourselves as purely physical beings.

In effect, we noted in *The Purpose of Physical Reality* that the physical classroom, while inherently benign and purposeful, is also perilous if we allow ourselves to become obsessed with the vehicle through which spiritual analogues are conveyed to us. Therefore, while we should not disdain or reject involvement in the physical world, we need to utilize this teaching device with a sense of detachment:

> As a quality, the term *detachment* denotes the capacity to use physical metaphors without becoming overly attracted to, infatuated with, or involved in the literal teaching device. As a process, the term implies a gradual relinquishing of our reliance on the physical vehicle to accomplish spiritual development. Our use of physical metaphors is purposely short-lived.[16]

The latter portion of this description, the gradual relinquishing of our need to understand the spiritual world through the physical world, relates, of course, to the process of ageing whereby we are incrementally bereft of our ability to use well the physical or metaphorical self. This imposed detachment can be easily demonstrated by a graph on which we plot the eventual ascent of our intellectual or spiritual self (it is to be hoped) simultaneously with the inevitable decline in our physical and sensual powers:

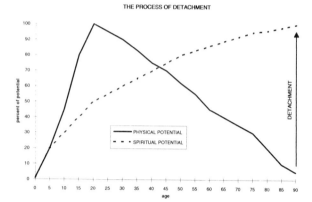

THE PROCESS OF DETACHMENT

Needless to say, the graph reflects only a general sort of observation, not the inevitable pattern of every life. The fundamental value of the chart is in demonstrating the inexorably widening gulf between what we have alluded to as the Evian or spiritual/intellectual self, and the Adamic or physical/sensual self. Or stated in terms of our discussion in *The Purpose of Physical Reality*, the chart shows the inevitable decline of the metaphorical self simultaneous with the steady ascent of the spiritual true or essential self (the soul), until the ultimate dissociation of the two selves at the time of one's departure from the physical world. Visually, the graph seems to portray the physical or metaphorical self being gradually stripped away as one might peel the rind from a choice fruit. Of course, if the fruit is not so choice or is not ripe, the rind comes off with difficulty.*

This sense of detachment implies a careful monitoring of our involvement with the Adamic or metaphorical self, and an ever greater realization of our essentially spiritual nature. Thus, the wise aspirant to spiritual transcendence will gradually desire detachment much as the persona in

---

* Aficionados of Dante might be tempted to see in this a less felicitous image of flaying.

Delmore Schwartz's poem 'The Heavy Bear' wishes he could become separated from the clumsy beast (his body) that inevitably seems to sabotage his 'spirit's motive':

> That inescapable animal walks with me,
> Has followed me since the black womb held,
> Moves where I move, distorting my gesture,
> A caricature, a swollen shadow,
> A stupid clown of the spirit's motive . . .[17]

Yeats' persona in his poem 'Sailing to Byzantium' expresses much the same consternation about the difficulty of achieving spiritual or intellectual objectives while 'fastened to a dying animal', observing that 'An aged man is but a paltry thing,/ A tattered coat upon a stick . . .' However, the speaker goes on to observe that spiritual transcendence is possible if the 'Soul clap its hands and sing, and louder sing/ For every tatter in its mortal dress . . .'[18]

But in the context of our present analysis of theodicy, *detachment* takes on the additional connotation of a selflessness derived from this definition of the individual as an inherently social organism. This form of detachment implies not a withdrawal from the physical world, but a more extensive participation in it. Therefore, we might think of this quality or attitude as indicative of the existential joy one might find in such common experiences as singing in a chorus, playing an instrument in an orchestra, or participating in any sort of team sport. In such circumstances, detachment does not imply the loss of individuality or the denial of self but an affirmation and fulfilment of self, an expansion of the self through the achievement of a more inclusive identity.

The example of a cell in the human body serves well as a further explication of this concept. On the one hand, the cell is autonomous, complete. It comes into being, it is nourished, thrives, and becomes integral to the thriving of the body. Like the human being, the cell is a thoroughly 'social' organism – its subsistence and meaning is inseparable from its relationship with the aggregate of other cells which comprise the entire organism of the body. The cell may participate in an intricate sequence of subordination – it may serve a finger, which serves a hand, which serves an arm, which assists the entire body.

If it had the capacity to do so, the cell might determine what part of the body it would serve – a leg, the liver, the heart, the brain. Had it the further capacity to understand its existence, the cell might take understandable pride in its worth and service, feel loyalty to the body it served and camaraderie with the other cells in their mutual effort to maintain the health of the body. The truly wise cell would also come to understand that in helping the body as a whole, it was likewise fostering its own well-being by creating a healthy environment. In fact, the cell would realize that without a healthy body to serve, it would cease to exist.

It is precisely in these distinctions that we find the unique challenge facing us as social creatures. For while we may speak of socialization as an involuntary process by which we are shaped, and while we may further attribute many of our achievements and failures to the external influence of social forces at work in our lives, the Bahá'í notion of how this kind of detachment is achieved (together with other sorts of social benefits) implies a distinctly wilful act of applying the twin processes we have already discussed.

The Seven Valleys as a Paradigm for the Wilful Attainment of Detachment

Throughout the Bahá'í writings one finds confirmation that this quality of detachment is at the heart of all efforts to transform human society. Because we must first approach this issue from a personal perspective before we can come to appreciate the implications it has for the body politic as a whole, we would benefit greatly from examining a work by Bahá'u'lláh which, among its other accomplishments, serves well as a paradigm of how detachment as an affirmation or fulfilment of self is best achieved. By studying the implications of this work in light of such an individual goal, we can better grasp how this goal of an expanded sense of self, when combined with the process of knowing and worshipping, is at the heart of coming to grips with the notion of history as a divinely guided process whereby humanity collectively achieves this same sort of detachment through acquiring a global identity.

The Literary and Historical Context

Because the world is so dominated by Western materialism, the modern cult hero has come to embody anti-social individualism. He is alone, emotionless, passionless, invulnerable, unapproachable, self-sufficient. In terms of our discussion so far, he is not at all human or humane. To such a figure, a concept of human purpose as defined by attributes like selflessness, detachment, and an expanded identity would seem alien or anathema, a threat to the fundamental basis for his existence. Unlike the tribal heroic ideal of past cultures, this hero does not uphold his society, he wars against it. Instead of exemplifying the highest ideals of his society, he becomes its inveterate enemy, the anti-hero.

In light of the massive deterioration of any social norms worthy of much admiration or self-sacrifice, such heroic ideals are an understandable index to the decay that has beset society worldwide. It is for this reason that Bahá'u'lláh's

Tablet *The Seven Valleys* is particularly valuable in this regard, because in this work Bahá'u'lláh responds to queries from a mystic, a Ṣúfí, someone who might have similar objections to our paradigm of individual fulfilment as involving a social imperative. That is, in most religious traditions the mystic is a solitary figure, perhaps fasting, rapt in prayer, or following some other form of independent spiritual exercise. He may not perceive religious institutions and society in general as detrimental, but usually he wants no part of that life and pursues instead a course of spiritual illumination and transformation through solitude and isolation.*

Bahá'u'lláh's general response to the mystic is to demonstrate that any attempt at personal transformation must inevitably involve action and involvement with others. But because Bahá'u'lláh is responding to questions posed by a Ṣúfí, He employs the language and style of the mystic writers, often alluding to the Ṣúfí traditions, particularly those of Rúmí.†

The structure of the work is likewise directly related to this tradition; like many mystic writers, Bahá'u'lláh discusses spiritual transformation in terms of stages of progressive enlightenment.

Bahá'u'lláh might thus seem to be vindicating the essence of the mystical quest – the individual striving for proximity to God and godliness through successive grades of transformation. Yet what is not so apparent is the manner in which Bahá'u'lláh employs the language, imagery and concepts of the mystic tradition to instruct

---

* Obviously this is a gross simplification: some mystics live in communities and there are mystical elements in many religions that do not necessitate any sort of personal isolation or alienation.

† Jalálu'd-Dín Rúmí (1207–73), called Mawláná ('our Master'), acknowledged to be the greatest Persian Ṣúfí poet and founder of the 'whirling' dervish order.

subtly this learned correspondent by exhorting him to a process and a truth beyond, and in some ways contradictory to, the traditional Ṣūfī notion of the religious life.

THE MYSTICAL PATH

The general goal of the mystic, regardless of religious or cultural orientation and largely without regard to historical period, is the attainment of, or experience of, proximity to God or to some universal source of spiritual energy. Though clearly such nearness has allegorical implications, the occurrence is usually described and experienced as a sensually perceived phenomenon, not simply as insight, enlightenment or other more general sorts of heightened spiritual awareness.

This goal of union or reunion with God or with some divine force or essence might be described in terms of Nirvana to the Hindu, of being in the presence of the 'Good' to the neo-Platonist, of having a vision of Christ to the Christian, of attaining the presence of the 'Friend' to the Ṣūfī. One hesitates to give specific parameters to such an experience because it is entirely subjective and therefore variously portrayed. But at the heart of the mystical experience is the sensation of being utterly detached from mortal concerns or selfish desires and of experiencing a union (perhaps 'reunion' would be more appropriate) with the spiritual forces of the universe.* In this sense, the emotional objective is not at all alien to what one might feel as a result of achieving an expanded sense of self. But for the mystic, these emotions derive largely from sensual perception, not from social action.

---

* The descriptions of this experience by mystics is not unlike, and perhaps not unrelated to, the present-day descriptions of encounters with the afterlife by 'NDErs' (those who have had a 'near death experience'). Perhaps the best of these descriptions in terms of enunciating the experience as a coalescing of detachment and reunion is Melvin Morse, *Closer to the Light.*

How the mystic achieves this condition is likewise variable. In some tribal religions hallucinogens are used. In some ascetic orders the mystic may employ various forms of deprivation to achieve detachment and reunion – extended periods of prayer, fasting, isolation or meditation. Some orders of Ṣūfīs arrive at a state of ecstasy by means of whirling dances (hence the term 'whirling dervish'). Fairly common to all the varieties of mysticism is that the process occurs in successive stages of intensity until some final and more or less complete state of ecstasy is attained. In this state of ecstasy the mystic often has a sense of immense insight, universal knowledge, ineffable tranquillity and detachment from the physical world and the physical self.

Interestingly, it is fairly common that in describing this process many mystics portray a predictable sequence of stages of successive intensity. For example, the mediaeval English mystic Richard Rolle of Hampole (1300–49) described his own experience in terms of three successive levels of perception characterized by three sensual indices: *Calor* (heat), *Canor* (song), *Dulcor* (sweetness).* In this state, heat or warmth was not metaphorical, but a literal sensation that Rolle experienced after periods of intense contemplation in his isolated cell. Likewise, the song he describes as a heavenly music was literally heard. The final stage of ecstasy, the sense of sweetness or inexpressible joy, is typical of the sort of experience that mystics from whatever background try in vain to describe, an ineffable sense of detachment from self coupled with a sensation of

---

* While mystical subjects dominate most of his work, the autobiographical discussions of this paradigm are found in his best-known writing, the *Incendium Amoris* and *Emendatio Vitae*. See Hope Emily Allen, *Writings Ascribed to Richard Rolle, Hermit of Hampole*, New York, 1927 or George G. Perry, *English Prose Treatises of Richard Rolle of Hampole*, Early English Text Society, OS 20, London, 1866.

oneness or union, a blissful and fulfilling merging of the individual self with spiritual forces of the universe.

In the broadest of terms, Ṣúfism as an approach to this process is divided into two classifications – those who affirm the necessity of working within the institution, of abiding by the law of the Qur'án and the fundamental requisites of Islamic law, and those who, though regarding themselves as Muslims in a general sense, believe themselves beyond the need of law or ecclesiastical authority. A *darvísh* or *faqír* as a Ṣúfí may belong to any of the numerous orders of Islamic mystics, but he can usually be classified as ascribing to one of these two orientations towards religious authority:

> A member of the former [those who live by Qur'ánic law] is known as a traveller (*sálik*) on the pathway (*taríqat*) to heaven. The latter are *ázád*, free, or *majdhub*, rapt, abstracted, attracted.[19]

Of course, in the broadest sense all religious life is related to mystical experience. Shoghi Effendi observes, 'The Bahá'í Faith, like all other Divine religions, is thus fundamentally mystic in character. Its chief goal is the development of the individual and society, through the acquisition of spiritual virtues and powers.'[20] Indeed, Bahá'u'lláh's description of His first intimation of His own revelation when He was in the Síyáh-Chál is portrayed as a mystical experience, and when we describe the initial exuberance of a new believer in a religion as being 'on fire' with faith, we are describing an emotional tenor and a spiritual ecstasy that calls to mind the mystical process.

There are, however, important distinctions between a single mystical experience or the mystical aspect of religious belief and the religious practice of mysticism. For example, the mystic typically perceives the ecstatic experience as an end in itself. Therefore, instead of attempting to translate this ineffable experience into some concrete form, some practical course of action, the mystic's objective most often becomes trying to achieve this transcendent condition more intensely or with greater frequency.

THE PROBLEM WITH MYSTICISM IN RELATION TO INSTITUTIONALIZED RELIGION

Mysticism is thus inherently susceptible to emotionalism, to the rejection of religious orthodoxy, and often to any profound sense of social imperatives or obligations. The religious experience becomes, in effect, a purely personal and private matter, or else something to be shared solely with those few who are initiated into its practices.

It may be understandable, then, that mysticism is frequently proscribed by ecclesiastical authority. Indeed, in this same vein, in the Kitáb-i-Aqdas Bahá'u'lláh Himself proscribes asceticism and monasticism, a subject He treats in a later Tablet, *The Glad-Tidings*, with the affirmation that the services of these holy ones are needed in the world.*

Because the mystical experience is subjective and empirical, the mystic may also reject any concept of the necessity for intermediaries between himself and God or for any law imposed by social or religious authority. Such a rejection may be confined to the intercession that official ecclesiastical doctrine or sanctioned procedures impose, but it may also imply a rejection of the entire notion of Prophets or Manifestations as essential vehicles for human spiritual development. It is in this connection that one of the most noted Bahá'í scholars, Mírzá Abu'l-Faḍl, denounces mysticism as a movement and 'Sufi'ism' in particular. In discussing the writings of Bahá'u'lláh,

---

* See p. 70 for text.

specifically the Kitáb-i-Aqdas, he reiterates the abolition of asceticism and the commandment that all have a profession, and then observes:

> He [Bahá'u'lláh] has clearly demonstrated to intelligent men, that corruptions of Divine Religions, and the appearances of ruinous, discordant beliefs, divisions, sects and heresies, have been invented worships resulting from Sufi'ism and asceticism . . . Indeed, if we consider the manner of the rise of monkhood in Christianity and Sufi'ism in Islam, we readily understand that their origin was the Platonic philosophy.[21]

Bahá'u'lláh's Use of the Mystical Treatise

However, in spite of the inherent problems with mysticism as a way of life, Bahá'u'lláh in His response to questions put to Him by a Ṣúfí employed the literary device of a mystical treatise to enunciate with poetic power a paradigm of spiritual ascent in His work *The Seven Valleys.* More specifically, Bahá'u'lláh compares spiritual ascent to a journey through seven successive valleys. By resorting to the language and concepts familiar to the mystic, He teaches a view distinct from some of the tenets of mysticism, but being a revered friend to many Ṣúfís, He lovingly avoids any hint of disdain or condescension.

THE PLANE OF LIMITATIONS

The first three valleys or stages in this journey (Search, Love and Knowledge), though framed in the analogy of an evolving human love relationship, very clearly establish a paradigm of the stages through which any seeker must pass who searches for, discovers and accepts the new Manifestation of God. Yet, inasmuch as all three of these are essentially intellectually oriented, they seem to apply primarily to the first part of the two-part process we have already described, the knowledge or recognition of the spiritual verities. In effect, the process is incomplete.

So it is that Bahá'u'lláh describes the first three valleys as existing on the plane of limitation and the last four valleys (which are depicted in terms of various forms of union with divine reality rather than mere intellectual comprehension of that relationship) as being experienced beyond the plane of limitation.

In the first valley, the Valley of Search, Bahá'u'lláh elucidates the qualities of the true seeker by ascribing to him (or prescribing for him) the metaphorical steed of patience wherewith he can traverse this valley. He adds to this quality of patience the attributes of determination and independence – 'they turn away from imitation, which is following the traces of their forefathers . . .'[22]

The sense of this seems to be that even though as yet unaware of the identity of the Manifestation, the true seeker reaches a point of understanding wherein he perceives that all creation is empowered and made meaningful through the advent of the Prophet of God and His Revelation. For where the Ṣúfí most often employs the term 'Friend' to designate various sorts of spiritual guides or spiritually endowed teachers (possibly including the Prophets of God), Bahá'u'lláh in this work seems to use the term specifically to designate the Manifestation.

The second stage, the Valley of Love or the 'city' of love, is enigmatic in its mixture of positive and negative images. On the one hand, it is depicted as a necessary step towards spiritual progress. The wayfarer has caught scent of the fragrance of the Beloved and is in a state of complete attraction and awe. But the experience, though rife with passionate intensity, is also chaotic and marked by perplexity and consternation.

The most immediate sense of the condition recalls similar descriptions in the Petrarchan sonnets of the late fourteenth century.* In these poems the speaker attempts to describe his confusion at being simultaneously overwhelmed by longing and yet unable to attain the object of his desire. He thus employs oxymoronic imagery to convey this bewildering and confounding emotional state. Consequently, many Petrarchan sonnets emphasize the irony that the same beloved who is the source of the lover's delight is simultaneously the source of his despair: 'I feed me in sorrow, and laugh in all my pain./ Likewise displeaseth me both death and life/ And my delight is causer of this strife.'[23]

Bahá'u'lláh describes the wayfarer, who is burning with the fire of this sort of love and passion, in precisely these terms. He is a lover consumed by attraction so that his longing for union 'burneth to ashes the harvest of reason'. He 'seeth neither ignorance nor knowledge, neither doubt nor certitude; he knoweth not the morn of guidance from the night of error'.[24]

What becomes clear in Bahá'u'lláh's description of this phenomenon is that love as existential passion and ecstatic confluence of oxymoronic experience (pain and joy, nearness and longing) is valuable when it leads to higher understanding of the source of this condition, but negative when it is perceived as the end itself. For this reason, much of this second valley is portrayed as perilous and undesirable. Indeed, Bahá'u'lláh makes it abundantly clear that emotionally powerful as this initial attraction is when one first discovers the identity of the Manifestation, this stage in spiritual development is intended to be a temporary condition. Otherwise, the believer neurotically attempts to sustain the intense pitch of this emotionality, or else,

---

* According to many scholars, the primary source of the courtly love tradition that is the heart of the Petrarchan lyric is mystic strains of Arabic love poetry.

once the emotions have abated, attempts to discover other relationships capable of reinducing these same powerful emotions rather than proceeding beyond this initial enthralment to the stages of understanding, growth, development and maturity of response.

The third stage of spiritual ascent, the Valley of Knowledge, Bahá'u'lláh conveys, largely by means of a parable, the theme of which concerns how one acquires the ability to discern the end in the beginning. A virtual definition of theodicy or justice in man's relationship with God, this parable further alludes to the process as a developing love relationship.

The story describes a lover who despairs after years of separation from his beloved. Then one night, as he ventures out into the marketplace, he is pursued by a watchman whom he presumes to be some malefactor. He breaks into a run, his heart filled with terror, and tries every way he can to escape this villain. He thinks the pursuer is a murderer: 'Surely this watchman is 'Izrá'íl, my angel of death.' At last, the lover traverses a garden wall with 'untold pain', leaps down into the garden, and discovers 'his beloved with a lamp in her hand, searching for a ring she had lost'.[25]

Bahá'u'lláh summarizes the theme of the analogy by stating that had the lover possessed true knowledge, he would have understood in the beginning that what seemed to be a chastening was actually guidance and preparation. By analogy, one who acquires divine knowledge is able in time to understand theodicy, how over time God's justice is played out in our individual lives and in the entirety of human history: the believer 'beholdeth justice in injustice, and in justice, grace'.[26]

Once such insight or foresight is attained, belief is no longer experienced as blind attraction, not a leap of faith, but as confidence in the justice and benignity of the divine methods by which God educates essentially spiritual beings in the phenomenal stage of their existence.

BEYOND THE PLANE OF LIMITATIONS

Bahá'u'lláh states that the Valley of Knowledge is 'the last plane of limitation',[27] by which He would seem to imply that beyond intellectual comprehension of divine justice (perceiving the long-range divine wisdom latent in seeming injustice and disorder) is a more empirically based understanding wherein one experiences subjectively the essential harmony, unity and divine logic that permeates creation. Therefore, the last four valleys or stages in this paradigm of spiritual ascent are portrayed as predominantly intense, ineffable and exalted beyond intellect or language. And yet, by the end it becomes clear that the completion of this process requires action back in the physical domain.

The stage of unity, for example, implies a condition of empirical experience of divine justice and the organic unity of creation. Or, more pertinent to our purposes here, the Valley of Unity implies that one transcends the particular manifestations of divine attributes in physical forms and has instead a subjective awareness of the divine reality, an experience tantamount to the more advanced stages of experience that the mystic seeks.

Because this stage is an experience of divine unity rather than an intellectual understanding of it, such a condition cannot be explained with exactitude; it can only be shared 'heart to heart' and 'breast to breast'.[28] The Valley of Unity is thus transitional between the two sets of three valleys, the first three pertaining to the acquisition of fundamental belief or faith, and the last three relating to the ineffable delights of certitude, confirmation and detachment which result from direct experience of spiritual realities: 'The tongue faileth in describing these three

Valleys, and speech falleth short.'[29] Yet because this transitional valley is itself beyond 'the last plane of limitation', the sojourner in this valley does not perceive himself as distinct from or relative to creation, but integral with it. Instead of an intellectual perception of the relatedness or integrality of creation, one has an empirical or subjective encounter with the essential unity of creation wherein 'the first is the last itself, and the last is but the first'.[30]

In such a state, one appreciates the limitations of 'acquired learning' as opposed to 'the divine bestowal',[31] and grasps the significance of the hadíth (Islamic tradition) which notes how intellectuality often compounds error instead of leading the seeker to true knowledge: 'Knowledge is a single point, but the ignorant have multiplied it.'[32]

The remaining three valleys or stages are relatively brief and treat more or less the same theme – the emotions that accompany the full realization of the self as an eternal spiritual expression of divine Will. Furthermore, since these succeeding stages must be experienced to be understood, Bahá'u'lláh concentrates often on the imagistic equivalents of these abstract conditions, what T. S. Eliot calls the 'objective correlatives'* for emotions associated with such a condition rather than on any logical exposition of it. In effect, these poetic equivalents of thought serve as indices to the experiences.

The fifth valley, the Valley of Contentment, is more or less the emotional aspect of experiencing this unity of the

---

* According to the definition of the term in *A Handbook to Literature* (p. 342), the term was used by Eliot 'to describe a pattern of objects, actions, or events, or a situation that can serve effectively to awaken in the reader an emotional response without being a direct statement of that subjective emotion'.

fourth valley. Having perceived and then experienced the overall purposefulness, justice and integrity of creation, the wayfarer feels totally at peace with the Will of God. The sixth valley, the Valley of Wonderment, seems to be an intensification of this emotion – the wayfarer is caught in a 'whirlwind of wonderment'.[33]

But there is something more at work here. Having experienced the full implications of God's justice, the soul can now fix its enlightened gaze back on the particular ingredients of physical creation to see in the mortal world of forms the lofty wisdom it metaphorizes and conceals. In short, the wayfarer at this level becomes possessed of the ability to unravel what he previously considered to be the mysteries of the physical world:

> Indeed, O Brother, if we ponder each created thing, we shall witness a myriad perfect wisdoms and learn a myriad new and wondrous truths.[34]

The emotion resulting from this unveiled wisdom is a sense of empowerment and vigour. Where the soul was content with the Will of God, the soul is now excited, astonished, delighted at being able to see the particular examples of the unified enterprise at work.

To an extent, the emotional aspect of this valley is akin to the intensity of experience appropriate to the Valley of Love, except that here the wayfarer knows precisely the basis for the affection. Furthermore, where the lover was content to bask in the ecstasy of emotion, the wayfarer at this stage becomes aware that it is now his task to return to the world of forms and express this insight in action.

As with the other levels of experience, Bahá'u'lláh does not confine His portraiture of this penultimate plane to mere generalities, even though the treatment is succinct. Rather, He presents this emotionally-charged perspective

in three ways. First, He gives a general description of the
emotional content – the wayfarer is amazed, delighted,
tossed about in the tumult of joy and awe because 'at every
moment his wonder groweth' as he increasingly becomes
'struck dumb with the beauty of the All-Glorious . . .'[35]

Interestingly, Bahá'u'lláh describes this as an exhausting
experience, since, we infer, there is no end to the wonders
one perceives in such a state of enlightened joy:

> . . . in this Valley the traveller is flung into confusion, albeit,
> in the eye of him who hath attained, such marvels are
> esteemed and well beloved. At every moment he beholdeth a
> wondrous world, a new creation, and goeth from astonish-
> ment to astonishment, and is lost in awe at the works of the
> Lord of Oneness.[36]

Bahá'u'lláh then discusses one of the kinds of marvels that
the soul at this stage can discern – the world of dreams. To
the casual reader, this discussion of dreams may seem to be
digressive, but it is not. Bahá'u'lláh notes two curious
mysteries about dreams – marvels which, He implies, the
soul intoxicated with the wine of astonishment can discern.

He observes how in the dream state the soul without
movement of the body wanders in a 'far-off city'.[37]
Bahá'u'lláh then observes that sometimes the very things
we dream may later come to pass. His conclusion is that
God has placed dreams in men 'to the end that philosophers may not deny the mysteries of the life beyond nor
belittle that which hath been promised them'.[38]*

Thirdly, Bahá'u'lláh observes how 'all these planes and
states are folded up and hidden away'[39] within the creation
of man. Therefore, similar to the way in which the

---

* 'Abdu'l-Bahá discusses this same proof or observation at great length in a
number of places. See, for example, *Promulgation of Universal Peace*,
pp. 416, 464, and *Some Answered Questions*, pp. 227–8.

realities of God (first, last, seen and hidden) are experienced metaphorically by every human being, so the realities of the spiritual world are proven by this common phenomenon of dreams.

Attainment Implies Selflessness Coupled with Action

It is with Bahá'u'lláh's description of the final stage of spiritual ascent that we come to understand most clearly how Bahá'u'lláh is using this literary form of the mystical treatise to portray the means by which one can achieve a sense of selflessness that is affirmative and fulfilling.

The title of this final seventh valley, 'True Poverty and Absolute Nothingness', hardly seems positive at all. Instead of representing the fulfilment and completion of spiritual development, such a condition sounds defeating, as if one is being asked to deny or sacrifice his or her individuality, special gifts and talents. In one sense, the solution to such an inference is obvious – lasting wealth and true fulfilment of self can only result from the acquisition of spiritual attributes and detachment from the things of this world. As we have noted, self-realization involves not perceiving oneself as exalted above, in competition with, or even as distinct from the rest of creation. Neither does it imply the neglecting of individual capacities and talents. Instead, the most lofty condition, as well as the most satisfying, is coming to appreciate how individual action can be vitally linked to a coherent divine plan and universal structure: 'Ecstasy alone can encompass this theme, not utterance nor argument; and whosoever hath dwelt at this stage of the journey, or caught a breath from this garden land, knoweth whereof We speak.'[40]

We must be careful not to infer from this an allusion to a sort of 'oversoul' wherein all individual souls ultimately become merged into a transcendental world soul or where individual consciousness is obliterated or reincarnated.* And yet, we do infer that while we may we retain our individual consciousness and personality, our greatest joy is in the perception of ourselves and of our actions as integral to our more expansive identity.

This concluding discussion also seems to allude to the previously mentioned two-part paradigm for spiritual advancement that we have analyzed in relation to the artistic process. For example Bahá'u'lláh alludes to the three stages of Ṣúfí life:

> In all these journeys the traveller must stray not the breadth of a hair from the 'Law', for this is indeed the secret of the 'Path' and the fruit of the Tree of 'Truth'; and in all these stages he must cling to the robe of obedience to the commandments, and hold fast to the cord of shunning all forbidden things, that he may be nourished from the cup of the Law and informed of the mysteries of Truth.[41]

To explain the relevance of heeding the law to the concluding passages of a mystical treatise, Bahá'u'lláh alludes to His own presence, as He does several times in the *Hidden Words*, stating that this is a precious springtime, and that 'though the grace of the All-Bounteous One is never stilled and never ceasing, yet to each time and era a portion is allotted and a bounty set apart, this in a given measure'.[42] In effect, Bahá'u'lláh seems to be alluding to the potentialities of this turning point in human history, and also to the preciousness of the time during which

---

* These concepts and terms, usually coupled with a belief in reincarnation, are employed by various philosophical and theological orientations. American readers would perhaps be most familiar with these terms as discussed by nineteenth-century thinkers such as Ralph Waldo Emerson and the so-called transcendentalists or by the Theosophical movement introduced into America by Helena Petrovna Blavatsky. The terms and ideas have also been used more recently by so-called New Age thought. The source for all of these movements is Eastern religion and philosophy.

He is physically present on earth. More generally, He admonishes the hearer to take advantage of one's earthly opportunities to recognize the Prophet and carry out His guidance:

> . . . make thou an effort, that haply in this dustheap of the mortal world thou mayest catch a fragrance from the everlasting garden, and live forever in the shadow of the peoples of this city.[43]

The third part of this final division He states succinctly in several paragraphs. He begins with the observation that in this ultimate stage of spiritual attainment the wayfarer transcends the necessity of understanding the divine world in terms of the physical world because the wayfarer has come to understand how the worlds of God are inextricable parts of one organic reality. However, Bahá'u'lláh then admonishes us to return to the existential response – obedience, the law, the daily exercise of translating spiritual insight into the physical experience.

This is a powerful turn, especially following on the heels of His observations about the persistent heedlessness of humanity historically to recognize and follow the 'True Friend', the very one sent to provide guidance. Not only is this exhortation startling in the context of responding to a mystic whose very life is ascetically oriented; it also serves to reiterate powerfully that the goal of this life is not escape from it but to achieve the spiritualization or sanctification of materiality by means of wilful application of divine principles to human social structures.

It is, therefore, entirely appropriate that after the loftiness of spiritual insight and ascent, the believer is exhorted, like the Philosopher King in Plato's *Republic*, to re-enter the world of shadows, to apply this heady insight to uplifting the human condition, to make the terrestrial realm into a social metaphor of the spiritual kingdom. Or

stated in terms of this final valley, 'True Poverty and
Absolute Nothingness' implies not the neglect of things
physical, but a more intense devotion to them; not the
abnegation of self, but the exploration, utilization and
ultimate fulfilment of self.

Thus, the paradigm of selflessness as delineated by
Bahá'u'lláh in *The Seven Valleys* demonstrates poetically
the achievement of detachment as an emotionally charged
vision of the essentially spiritual nature of physical reality.
In addition, it recalls the axiomatic verities we noted
regarding the inexorable relationship between insight and
action because the sojourner returns from the mystic
journey and the ephemeral vision to the essential obligation to express that vision in the most practical of terms.

So it is that Bahá'u'lláh in this mystic treatise makes it
abundantly clear that even the most ecstatic encounter
with the mysteries of the spiritual world have the fundamental and essential purpose of enabling us to experience a
union (or reunion) with the rest of creation in order that
we might express that vision in social structures. Therefore, though ostensibly intended for the individual, this
paradigm is equally applicable to the collective progress of
humankind.

Achieving Selflessness in a Contemporary Environment

We have thus established that the twin duties of human
purpose have as their primary goal an achieved state of
selflessness wherein the individual is enabled to appreciate
how the human body politic and creation as a whole are
integral aspects of one organic and divinely guided process.
Yet this perception, however ecstatic, is only potentially
valuable until it becomes translated into action. And since
we are integral parts of a social reality, our own individual

ascent and well-being cannot be properly nurtured until the social organism of which we are a part is likewise aware of its essential nature and proper destiny. In effect, individual ascent is inseparable from collective ascent.

Of course, even when society becomes aware of this essential reality, we as individuals are, while in the physical plane of existence, never able to achieve some final or permanent or sufficient vision of the divine reality. Since we are always being tempted to reject this larger perspective and resort to self-interest, we must constantly struggle to maintain both parts of this process and to keep them in balance. That is, we are constantly in need of reinvigorating our vision of the transcendental reality and then of finding inventive and creative ways of expressing that vision in action so that through entropy our ascent does not grind to a halt. Like the artist, we are constantly in need of discovering more varied and expansive ways to express our love of the divine beauty, a process which, as we have noted, enhances and clarifies the love we are expressing:

> These journeys have no visible ending in the world of time, but the severed wayfarer − if invisible confirmation descend upon him and the Guardian of the Cause assist him − may cross the seven stages in seven steps, nay rather in seven breaths, nay rather in a single breath, if God will and desire it.[44]

But if the Bahá'í writings justify and explain the purpose of physical reality by delineating the essential goal and means to that goal, we are still faced with a weighty and immediate dilemma. How do we initiate this process when the very same social environment through which we are exhorted to achieve these purposes is so profoundly antithetical to such noble aspirations?

Social Identity in a Period of Transition

The Bahá'í writings acknowledge the complexity and consternation of attempting such lofty aspirations in the context of contemporary society. In addition, however, to enunciating the trials that must inevitably beset humankind in this age of transition to a global identity, the Bahá'í writings also spell out in specific terms what course these trials will take, how this turmoil will in time lead to the very means by which the collective ascent portrayed in *The Seven Valleys* can take place.

In times past, coal miners took caged canaries with them into the dark reaches of their nether world, not to have the comfort of beauteous song, but to detect the presence of deadly but odourless methane gas. The bird's delicate system would quickly succumb to the poisonous fumes, and the limp canary would serve as the miners' call to alarm. With the aid of modern science, we can now easily confirm what anyone not totally bereft of sensibilities has for some time perceived empirically – that our present global society is littered with the carcasses of dead canaries. Our whole environment is deteriorating at such a rapid and lethal pace that we now experience a humane quality of life (those of us fortunate enough to experience it at all) only in snatches or in nostalgic recollection of what we may now perceive as a more innocent and naive era.

Caught up as we now are in the fundamental exigencies of sustaining some degree of physical viability, we barely have time to contemplate the more subtle ills that this condition perpetrates upon us – the disappearance of leisure, the disintegration of the family, the decline of any generally endorsed moral imperatives that might nourish our souls, deter the malevolent or coordinate our individual efforts to become human. Our educational systems have, by and large, degenerated into warehouses for our most cherished hopes. There remain few if any sanctuaries from the ubiquitous and pernicious fear of violence and abuse. To the underdeveloped areas of the world where mere subsistence is questionable, even these issues would be deemed a luxury in light of even more primitive matters of survival.

It is ironic, then, that at the very time when social disintegration seems intent on savaging whatever vestiges of civilization we thought we had, there has simultaneously emerged over the past several years a vision of a 'new world order', of the world community as a collective enterprise, of the human race as one integral organism, and of our struggle to combat the social and environmental ills (that we as a species have largely perpetrated on ourselves) as a common and collective undertaking.

No doubt part of this rapidly emerging sense of ourselves derives from the sometimes desperate hope that such a vision may impel us towards unified action against the rampant forces destroying our human possibilities as individuals. A significant source of this vision, however, derives from a relatively newly-emerged reality – a truly planetary society where no people, no nation, no portion of this increasingly small world community is, or can afford to be, autonomous or in any way insulated from our common plight. Whether we like it or not, we have become one integral community, and whether we like it or not, we are all on some level of consciousness frighteningly aware of the imminence of vast and dramatic change and how precisely between identities we all are – the one, archaic and no longer applicable to our world; the other, a sense of self that is yet to be born.

It is true that writers, thinkers, artists, philosophers have for virtually the entire course of the past century noted this period as an age of transition. But we now no longer require prophecies about the destiny of our age. We experience it on a daily basis. Old value systems no longer can pretend to define or sustain us, and yet no new perspective seems sufficiently developed or implemented to yield much future hope.

Bahá'í poet Robert Hayden rendered a powerful image of what on some level we all now experience with an almost unremitting constancy in what he termed 'our deathbed childbed age'.[45] In his poem 'Richard Hunt's "Arachne"' he describes the terrible consternation of Arachne as she is transformed from a woman into a spider:

> Human face becoming locked insect face
> mouth of agony shaping a cry it cannot utter
> eyes bulging brimming with the horrors
> of her becoming
>
> Dazed crazed
> by godly vivisection husking her
> gutting her
> cutting hubris its fat and bones away
>
> In goggling terror fleeing powerless to flee
> Arachne not yet arachnid and no longer woman
> In the moment's centrifuge of dying
> becoming[46]

The sense of this wrenching change, of struggling to survive precisely between identities in the 'moment's centrifuge of dying/becoming' has been the theme of perhaps the majority of modern and post-modern art, but often these images convey an ambivalence. There is on the one hand understandable lamentation and insecurity, sometimes the stark terror associated with the loss of individual identity and fundamental human values, something that Matthew Arnold observed at the very beginning of the Modern Age in his poem 'Dover Beach' published in 1867:

Ah, love, let us be true
To one another! for the world, which seems
To lie before us like a land of dreams,
So various, so beautiful, so new,
Hath really neither joy, nor love, nor light,
Nor certitude, nor peace, nor help for pain;
And we are here as on a darkling plain
Swept with confused alarms of struggle and flight,
Where ignorant armies clash by night.[47]

Instead of being challenged to discover a more inclusive identity, the speaker in this piece is defeated by the confusion and chaos in the macrocosm. His only solution is to turn inward, to become insular and attempt some degree of integrity in the microcosmic world over which he still has a modicum of control.

On the other hand, during these same years there were others who sensed in the decline of archaic and outmoded value systems the dawning of human potential, a release from what they perceived to be outworn, superficial, narrow and often oppressive perspectives. Walt Whitman saw in the rapid changes occurring in American society a reason to experiment with and exult in individual human potential apart from institutions and institutionalized thought. In his poem 'Song of Myself' begun in 1855 he states:

I celebrate myself, and sing myself,
And what I assume you shall assume,
For every atom belonging to me as good belongs to you.

I loaf and invite my soul,
I lean and loaf at my ease observing a spear of summer
    grass.

My tongue, every atom of my blood, form'd from this soil,
    this air,
Born here of parents born here from parents the same, and
    their parents the same,

I, now thirty-seven years old in perfect health begin,
Hoping to cease not till death.

Creeds and schools in abeyance,
Retiring back a while sufficed at what they are, but never
  forgotten,
I harbour for good or bad, I permit to speak at every hazard,
Nature without check with original energy.[48]

Even among religionists, we find this dichotomy. Some
have seen in the vast and rapid transformation of our
planetary society the fulfilment of any number of prophetic
visions of everything from world peace to the end of time,
from a golden age of a unified global community to something akin to Yeats' famous image of the Second Coming
as a dire decline in the cyclical spiral of human history:

Surely some revelation is at hand:
Surely the Second Coming is at hand.
The Second Coming! Hardly are those words out
When a vast image out of *Spiritus Mundi*
Troubles my sight: somewhere in sands of the desert
A shape with lion body and the head of a man,
A gaze blank and pitiless as the sun,
Is moving its slow thighs, while all about it
Reel shadows of the indignant desert birds.
The darkness drops again; but now I know
That twenty centuries of stony sleep
Were vexed to nightmare by a rocking cradle,
And what rough beast, its hour come round at last,
Slouches towards Bethlehem to be born?[49]

The Dual Nature of the Bahá'í Perspective about this Period

As we will later discuss, the Bahá'í writings assert that the
social laws, exhortations and institutions revealed by
Bahá'u'lláh offer practical methods for responding to the
exigencies of a world that, though suddenly become a

single community, is largely devoid of any coherent or integrated sense of how to function as a unified social organism. But in spite of the largely optimistic vision that the Bahá'í perspective offers, we also discover in the Bahá'í writings a forthright analysis of the difficulties and challenges that must needs characterize this transitional period until the emergence of a functioning global society.

Consequently, some passages in the Bahá'í scriptures exult in the expectation of this age as the fulfilment of human history, as the 'consummation of all the Dispensations within the Adamic Cycle, inaugurating an era of at least a thousand years' duration, and a cycle destined to last no less than five thousand centuries, signalizing the end of the Prophetic Era and the beginning of the Era of Fulfilment'.[50] And yet, because the majority of humanity is oblivious to or does not share such an optimistic vision of the future, and because the Bahá'í teachings assert that severe trials must precede the emergence of a global civilization, other passages lament the sad state of moral decline and speak with foreboding about the pangs that must accompany the birth of our new collective identity. These passages portray a contemporary society charged with a feeling of imminent disaster.

Shoghi Effendi portrays dramatically the dual nature of the Bahá'í perspective in the opening passages of his work *The Promised Day is Come*:

A tempest, unprecedented in its violence, unpredictable in its course, catastrophic in its immediate effects, unimaginably glorious in its ultimate consequences, is at present sweeping the face of the earth. Its driving power is remorselessly gaining in range and momentum. Its cleansing force, however much undetected, is increasing with every passing day. Humanity, gripped in the clutches of its devastating power, is smitten by the evidences of its resistless fury. It can neither perceive its origin, nor probe its significance, nor discern its outcome. Bewildered, agonized and helpless, it watches this great and mighty wind of God invading the remotest and fairest regions of the earth, rocking its foundations, deranging its equilibrium, sundering its nations, disrupting the homes of its peoples, wasting its cities, driving into exile its kings, pulling down its bulwarks, uprooting its institutions, dimming its light, and harrowing up the souls of its inhabitants.[51]

Clearly implicit in this portrayal is an underlying vision of a propitious outcome to the transition. And yet, as his work goes on to explain, the hope latent in this analysis of the twofold process of disintegration and reformation is hardly a desperate plea that we make a virtue of necessity. From the Bahá'í view, the social evolution of planetary society proceeds in a predictable and orderly fashion, similar to the way in which the geophysical earth and its inhabitants have likewise come into being and have progressed through predictable and orderly stages of growth before reaching fruition:

All created things have their degree or stage of maturity. The period of maturity in the life of a tree is the time of its fruit-bearing . . . The animal attains a stage of full growth and completeness, and in the human kingdom man reaches his maturity when the light of his intelligence attains its greatest power and development . . . Similarly there are periods and stages in the collective life of humanity. At one time it was passing through its stage of childhood, at another its period of youth, but now it has entered its long-predicted phase of maturity, the evidences of which are everywhere apparent . . . That which was applicable to human needs during the early history of the race can neither meet nor satisfy the demands of this day, this period of newness and consummation. Humanity has emerged from its former state of limitation and preliminary training. Man must now become imbued with new virtues and powers, new moral standards, new capacities. New bounties, perfect bestowals, are awaiting and already descending upon him. The gifts and blessings of the period of youth, although timely and sufficient during the adolescence of mankind, are now incapable of meeting the requirements of its maturity.[52]

In other words, human history, though not precisely linear in its progress, does in time manifest the inherent process by which we emerge from crude beginnings in the dust into one fully integral social organism. Therefore, in discussing the 'oneness' of humanity, the authoritative Bahá'í writings portray the unification of human society on our planet not solely as the desire of human hearts nor the obstinate imposition of order on disorder, but rather as the end result of a process inherent in creation itself:

> Let there be no mistake. The principle of the Oneness of Mankind – the pivot round which all the teachings of Bahá'u'lláh revolve – is no mere outburst of ignorant emotionalism or an expression of vague and pious hope. Its appeal is not to be merely identified with a reawakening of the spirit of brotherhood and good-will among men, nor does it aim solely at the fostering of harmonious cooperation among individual peoples and nations . . . It implies an organic change in the structure of present-day society, a change such as the world has not yet experienced.[53]

More specifically, Shoghi Effendi states that the collective ascent of human society can be viewed in terms of an ever-expanding social identity as expressed in successively more encompassing social institutions:

> It represents the consummation of human evolution – an evolution that has had its earliest beginnings in the birth of family life, its subsequent development in the achievement of tribal solidarity, leading in turn to the constitution of the city-state, and expanding later into the institution of independent and sovereign nations.[54]

This expanding sense of collective identity as expressed in

evolutionary social structures is thus portrayed as an inherent human capacity and even as a fore-ordained process initiated and sustained by divine intervention:

> The principle of the Oneness of Mankind, as proclaimed by Bahá'u'lláh, carries with it no more and no less than a solemn assertion that attainment to this final stage in this stupendous evolution is not only necessary but inevitable, that its realization is fast approaching, and that nothing short of a power that is born of God can succeed in establishing it.[55]

The Importance of Human Volition in this Process

The ostensible paradox of the last part of this statement is important, implying as it does that while the process is self–sustaining and inherent, it also involves human volition, even though it is dependent for its ultimate 'realization' on a 'power that is born of God'.

But this assertion is no less enigmatic than are the opening passages of Bahá'u'lláh's own analysis of the course of human history in the *Kitáb-i-Íqán* where He observes how, because of wilful human perversity, God's explicit guidance and assistance has been consistently abused and neglected. In particular He notes the irony that the very people who have 'yearningly awaited the advent of the Manifestations of God' are almost inevitably the ones who turn away from 'His face' and persecute the very source of human guidance and salvation.[56] This observation is in substance and tone essentially the same assertion made by Muḥammad when He states:

> So oft then as an apostle cometh to you with that which your souls desire not, swell ye with pride, and treat some as impostors, and slay others?[57]*

---

* This and all subsequent citations from the Qur'án are from *The Koran*, trans. H. M. Rodwell.

Muḥammad's elucidation of human perversity is almost verbatim what Christ had stated six hundred years earlier:

> O Jerusalem, Jerusalem, killing the prophets and stoning those who are sent to you! How often would I have gathered your children together as a hen gathers her brood under her wings, and you would not![58]

Logically and theologically, such observations might seem to raise significant doubts about the felicitous outcome of human history instead of inducing us to accept a vision of impending change as heralding a quantum leap forward in the emergence of a just global society. Yet the Bahá'í writings presage and affirm that such a society will emerge and that the initial foundation of a global community and a world government may well emerge 'ere the close of this century'.[59]*

In view of the discrepancy between present world conditions and the optimistic vision of what the Bahá'í writings assert will emerge in less than a decade, we might well wonder what is the basis for such confidence. More particularly, we might want to know why, if it has been the eternal plan of God that human society proceed by degrees to foster an 'ever-advancing civilization', such steady progress does not seem to have occurred. Likewise, if such a reformation and transformation of human society is about to occur, what force or process will make the difference? For if the Manifestations themselves lament how divine intention has been waylaid by human perversity, what will suddenly reverse this process so that this same force of human volition which presently seems intent on bringing a closure to human possibilities will instead be marshalled to bring about the fruition of human social evolution? Because however comforting it might be to

---

* More will be said in later chapters about the sequence of future events as predicted in the Bahá'í writings.

recite passages from the Bahá'í scriptures asserting that the outcome of present consternation will be the fulfilment of the eternal plan of God, such assurance can by itself hardly assuage the stultifying and paralyzing effects of contemporary societal deterioration.

Therefore, before we pursue in detail a delineation of the Bahá'í paradigm regarding the process that will ultimately coalesce on a societal level the twin processes of human ascent with the goal of a global identity, we must first examine the fundamental Bahá'í tenets regarding history as a divine process. By this means we can attempt to ascertain why the divine plan of an omnipotent deity seems so often to have been deterred or perverted by feeble and fallible human beings. Only after such a discussion can we hope to appreciate why those same forces will not continue to inhibit the advent of planetary consciousness and the establishment of the global commonwealth the foundations of which the Bahá'í writings affirm have already been firmly established.

3

A Wheel within a Wheel

The Bahá'í Paradigm of Human History

So you will find the smallest atoms in the universal system are similar to the greatest beings of the universe. It is clear that they come into existence from one laboratory of might under one natural system and one universal law; therefore, they may be compared to one another.[1]

'Abdu'l-Bahá

According to Bahá'í belief, the organic structure of the smallest systems is parallel to that of the largest systems. Therefore, we might presume that the conclusions we have inferred about how individual purpose is achieved are likewise applicable to humanity as a whole. In effect, the twin duties enunciated in the first chapter and the goal of an expanding collective identity discussed in the second should be as applicable to the advancement of the human body politic as they are to the individual. By examining the Bahá'í paradigm of history, we can discern how the artistic process and the goal of an ever more inclusive sense of identity are apparent in the ascent of human society.

The Bahá'í Concept of Universal Organization

In the first volume of this study, we alluded to the Bahá'í concept of human history as a divinely-guided process of human education.[2] But since any inferences we make about human history depend on these assumptions, we would do well to review some of the more fundamental Bahá'í beliefs that support such an assertion.

The Creator and the Creation

The foundational belief of Bahá'í cosmology is the concept of God as Creator, the assertion that the Creator as a cognitive Being has wilfully produced a physical reality which functions as a metaphorical expression of spiritual reality. In this sense, all phenomenal reality, whether objects or relationships among those objects, have as their inherent purpose the statement in concrete or artistic form the essential principles at work in the unseen or meta-physical reality. Consequently, to the extent that it is the inherent capacity of physical reality to manifest divine attributes, the physical world is not in the process of becoming spiritual; it already is. Therefore, as the outward or visible aspect of the unseen world, physical reality is an inseparable and integral part of spiritual reality.

A corollary of this belief concerns the eternality of physical reality. Since it is the inherent attribute of the Creator to create and since He is eternal, then His creation is likewise eternal. Planets, solar systems, entire galaxies may come into composition and in time decompose, but the organism that is the universe itself continues in perpetuity. Therefore, while it may be useful from our terrestrial perspective to distinguish between these realities, as we have seen, the Bahá'í writings assert the unity of creation: '. . . know ye that the world of existence is a single world, although its stations are various and distinct.'[3]

A series of related axioms from the Bahá'í writings further explicate how the physical world gives sensual form to the unseen reality. First, 'Abdu'l-Bahá asserts that physical reality is an eternal, essential and calculated expression: since the Creator 'has neither beginning nor end – it is certain that this world of existence, this endless universe, has neither beginning nor end', even though parts of the universe 'may come into existence, or may be disintegrated'.[4] Second, all creation has as its animating purpose the rendering of spiritual attributes in sensually perceptible forms: 'Know thou that every created thing is a sign of the revelation of God.' Without this capacity, Bahá'u'lláh explains, 'the entire universe would become desolate and void'.[5]

Physical Creation Focused on the Human Reality

As we also noted in the first volume, the Bahá'í writings affirm that physical reality is a classroom designed specifically for human enlightenment: 'Out of the wastes of nothingness, with the clay of My command I made thee to appear, and have ordained for thy training every atom in existence and the essence of all created things.'[6] From such a perspective, the Creator's desire to fashion a phenomenal expression of spiritual reality is not an arbitrary or capricious act, but a teaching device by which human souls are made aware of spiritual attributes, then trained to use them.

The physical world from this perspective might well be described as a spawning ground for human souls as well as a classroom for the initial training of the soul in its preparation for birth into the spiritual world, something discussed at length in the first volume. Therefore, the relationship of the human reality to the physical reality is parallel to the relationship in a human being between the soul and the body:

By the appearance of the spirit in the physical form, this world is enlightened. As the spirit of man is the cause of the life of the body, so the world is in the condition of the body, and man is in the condition of the spirit. If there were no man, the perfections of the spirit would not appear, and the light of the mind would not be resplendent in this world. This world would be like a body without a soul.[7]

Yet, while the spawning and initial education of the human soul is at the heart of the purpose of physical reality, there is no implication in this that the human reality is separate from or independent of the rest of creation. As the fruit of this enterprise, the spiritual evolution of human society necessarily focuses on the education and progress of humankind. But humanity as an organic and integral part of that creation cannot correctly perceive itself as independent of creation any more than could an orange perceive itself to be independent of the orange tree which produced it.

Human Reality Focused on the Nature of the Soul

To a great extent the nature of the human soul is beyond comprehension: it is a 'sign of God, a heavenly gem whose reality the most learned of men hath failed to grasp, and whose mystery no mind, however acute, can ever hope to unravel'.[8] As we noted in the first chapter, the most distinguishing capacities of this spiritual essence is the power to perceive spiritual attributes and then to express that perception in terms of a wilful course of social action.

There are, however, other noteworthy aspects of the soul's existence we should mention here, most of which we elucidated in the first volume of this study.[9] For one thing, even though the human soul has a point of beginning when it associates with the body at conception, the soul is essentially spiritual and therefore unimpaired by the body's infirmity or demise: 'once it has come into existence, it is eternal.'[10]* As we have already noted, such a view does not imply that the physical experience of the soul is irrelevant. According to Bahá'í belief, the physical environment provides the soul with a period of gestation wherein it becomes introduced to spiritual concepts, albeit clothed in physical garment.

Thus, while the soul may benefit from its association with the body as preparation for the continuation of life beyond physical existence, the death of the body in no way affects the powers or the reality of the soul. After the death of the body, 'the disintegration of the members, dispersing of the particles, and the destruction of the composition, [the soul] persists and continues to act and to have power'.[11]† But what is that power and what sort of action will be possible in a non-physical environment?

According to the Bahá'í teachings, the powers of the soul are all those essential faculties that distinguish human-kind: the power of intellect, of reason, imagination, will, memory and the sense of identity or self. All of those faculties which we most commonly associate with human existence continue after the body's disintegration since they are, one and all, derived from the power of the soul:

> Now regarding the question whether the faculties of the mind and the human soul are one and the same. These faculties are but the inherent properties of the soul, such as the power of imagination, of thought, of understanding; powers that are the essential requisites of the reality of man, even as the solar ray is the inherent property of the sun. The

---

* The Bahá'í teachings specifically reject any notion of pre-existence; one's identity and essential reality begin at conception. But since the laws of physical and spiritual realities are parallel, we can presume that the spiritual essence that is the soul may exist in much the same way that the molecules that become our body have existed eternally.

† Whereas the dynamic force sustaining the body can cease to exist, the dynamic force sustaining the soul cannot.

temple of man is like unto a mirror, his soul is as the sun, and
his mental faculties even as the rays that emanate from that
source of light. The ray may cease to fall upon the mirror, but
it can in no wise be dissociated from the sun.[12]

The Perpetuity of Human Life and Planetary Systems

If we assert that the universe as a phenomenal expression
of the spiritual reality is perpetual and that its essential
purpose is to nurture souls in preparation for their birth into
the spiritual realm, then we must also assume that there have
always been human souls being generated in this manner.
Therefore, since our own planet has a beginning, we must
presume that there have been other planets on which this
same process has occurred or is presently occurring:

> . . . it is certain that this world of existence, this endless
> universe, has neither beginning nor end. Yes, it may be that
> one of the parts of the universe, one of the globes, for
> example, may come into existence, or may be disintegrated,
> but the other endless globes are still existing; the universe
> would not be disordered nor destroyed.[13]

In this sense, the universe as a whole, as a physical
metaphor for divine reality, is not in the process of
becoming or achieving purpose. It has always existed in a
state of completeness or perfection even though the parts
of this universal organism are in various stages of evolving
or disintegrating. Planets, solar systems, entire galaxies
may come into being, evolve through vast changes, and
eventually go out of being, but the infinite universe itself is
always in a condition of perpetuity and wholeness, yield-
ing its intended results – producing beings capable of
understanding the divine reality and acting out that understanding in terms of 'an ever-advancing civilization'.

So it is that the whole physical paradigm has as its
primary function the social imperative of demonstrating

to human souls the coherence and integrity of the entire design. The purpose of physical reality is not solely to churn out a few rare individuals capable of responding to the twin duties, but rather to set in motion a dynamic social process. Or stated more simply, human history is not the recounting of a few isolated success stories, but the delineation of the progress of planetary society as a whole. In the same way that we observed in the previous chapter how the gauge of individual progress is the extent to which one achieves an expanding sense of self, so the gauge of the progress of the planet as a spiritually dynamic enterprise is the extent to which human society as a whole achieves this same objective as expressed in ever more inclusive social paradigms.

In such a context, contemporary debates about whether or not the universe is expanding or contracting become relatively unimportant insofar as the viability of creation is concerned. No doubt vast portions of the universe are expanding while other parts are contracting and may in time fall back on themselves, then explode again to produce galaxies and other systems, like the contracting and expansion of a vast heart pulsing in the timeless reaches of infinite space.

The Earth as a Cell in the Universal Body

From this perspective, the debate between so-called cre-ationists and so-called evolutionists may be seen equally as pointless. We might describe this process as evolutionary, but it is a systematic part of a divine process, not a random process of mutation or a deterministic mechanism of natural selection. The planet comes into being, achieves its inherent purpose of expressing divine reality in terms of human civilization, perhaps in time coalesces with other such organisms within the galaxy, much as cells in the human body work in concert to form organs that serve in turn to give life to the body as a whole. In due course both the cell and the planet will pass out of existence and decompose, but the universal body lives on.

The Paradigm of Human Development

According to this cosmological perspective, it is the inherent destiny of our planet to pass through various stages of change until, having achieved geophysical maturity, it becomes capable of bringing forth human evolution. And yet, equally apparent in such a view is the distinct nature of humankind apart from other creatures on the planet.

The Fundamental Properties of Human Evolution

If the inception of humankind as a whole parallels the creation of individual human life, and if the individual human being begins with the association of the soul with the body at the point of conception, then we might infer that the human species begins at whatever point human-kind collectively is endowed with a soul.

According to the Bahá'í scriptures, this capacity is from the beginning, however latent it may be in the earlier stages of evolutionary change. Therefore, though affirm-ing that the human species has passed through a myriad stages of evolutionary physical change, the Bahá'í writings assert that the human being was from inception a distinct species:

> . . . as man in the womb of the mother passes from form to form, from shape to shape, changes and develops, and is still the human species from the beginning of the embryonic period – in the same way man, from the beginning of his existence in the matrix of the world, is also a distinct species –

that is, man – and has gradually evolved from one form to another. Therefore, this change of appearance, this evolution of members, this development and growth, even though we admit the reality of growth and progress, does not prevent the species from being original.[14]

A corollary of this belief is the assertion that the chronological precedence of other life forms does not imply that human life derived or mutated from that life:

> . . . the fact that the animal having preceded man is not a proof of the evolution, change and alteration of the species, nor that man was raised from the animal world to the human world. For while the individual appearance of these different beings is certain, it is possible that man came into existence after the animal. So when we examine the vegetable kingdom, we see that the fruits of the different trees do not arrive at maturity at one time; on the contrary, some come first and others afterward. This priority does not prove that the later fruit of one tree was produced from the earlier fruit of another tree.[15]

To accept these assertions is to view as erroneous any inference dictating that at some point we acquired the essential requisites for humanness. For in the same way that there is no point at which an embryo becomes human, so the species as a whole is always human, though in the earliest stages not capable of exercising its inherent capacities:

> So also the formation of man in the matrix of the world was in the beginning like the embryo; then gradually he made progress in perfectness, and grew and developed until he reached the state of maturity, when the mind and spirit became visible in the greatest power. In the beginning of his formation the mind and spirit also existed, but they were hidden; later they were manifested. In the womb of the world mind and spirit also existed in the embryo, but they were concealed; afterward they appeared. So it is that in the seed

the tree exists, but it is hidden and concealed; when it develops and grows, the complete tree appears.[16]

The Need for External Assistance

We noted in our definition of the human being as a social organism that individual aspirations to meaningful ascent must be initiated and assisted at every turn, that we are by definition reliant on external help in virtually every part of meaningful human development. Or stated another way, though our purpose as individuals is to achieve a kind of autonomy wherein we actively strive for ascent, we necessarily require training and nurture before such independent ascent can be attempted. Even then we require a social context for the expression of our enlightenment as well as continued assistance as we ascend.

This same principle is no less applicable to the ascent of humankind as a whole. Stated in terms of the laws of physics, since human society on a given planet is ostensibly a closed system, without some infusion of external resources capable of uplifting the human condition, human progress would not be possible. Furthermore, the law of entropy dictates that external assistance must be ongoing and not a single infusion of grace. Therefore, essential to the Bahá'í paradigm of human social evolution is the concept of the systematic assistance and guidance imparted to human society from 'outside' the system in the form of divine emissaries, what the Bahá'í writings refer to as *Manifestations*.

According to Bahá'í belief, these beings are not inspired humans, but are pre-existent beings, emissaries from the spiritual world who inherently possess a capacity beyond human limitations. They are thus capable of infusing into this ostensibly closed system a sufficient amount of light and heat to advance the human social condition. Indeed, the very cyclical nature of the Bahá'í paradigm of human history revolves around the periodic advent of these divinely-guided teachers. In effect, to study appropriately the process of human ascent, one must necessarily study the history of religion.

The Nature of the Manifestations

If there is no individual or collective advancement without the intervention or assistance of these messengers, we obviously need to understand something about their methods if we are to appreciate how this process of human advancement takes place.

As we noted in the first volume, perhaps foremost among the distinguishing attributes of the Manifestations is that they are a distinct creation: 'a Manifestation is not merely an enlightened human being; the Manifestation has a power, a capacity, a spiritual essence superior to the station and nature of human beings.'[17]

They are to outward seeming normal human beings who are subject to most of the same trials and difficulties of humankind, but the souls of the Manifestations are 'pre-existent'.[18] Consequently, where we must gradually acquire an understanding of the relationship between the physical world and the spiritual world it foreshadows, the Manifestation enters this reality possessing an innate knowledge and already fully aware of this relationship. The Manifestation is not merely a spiritually advanced or specially endowed human being, but a distinct creation whose specialized task is to function as an intermediary between the spiritual world and the phenomenal world and, as God's viceroy, to forge the critical link between these two realities.

A second distinguishing attribute of the Manifestation is

that He is spiritually exemplary. That is, where human beings have the capacity through wilful struggle to acquire divine attributes, the Manifestations already possess these attributes and reflect them perfectly in their lives. As we noted in the first volume, each Manifestation thereby functions to give concrete or metaphorical form to godliness itself.

Yet, superior beings though they be, the most critical distinguishing characteristic of the Manifestations is their role in relinquishing their own will to the Will of God in order to become a channel through which the Deity can convey guidance to human society. In this capacity, they one and all acknowledge that the instruction they provide is not of their own devising. Through a process of revelation, they are empowered to convey what God commands them, even as Christ explained: 'For I have not spoken on my own authority; the Father who sent me has himself given me commandment what to say and what to speak.'[19]

Common to the lives of these Manifestations, therefore, is the fact that until the point in their earthly lives when God begins to utilize them to instruct humanity, they are more or less concealed. As a result, we know relatively little about the lives of these Teachers until that point occurs, an event which is usually signalized or symbolized by some dramatic experience: Moses hears the voice emerge from the burning bush; Buddha becomes 'enlightened' sitting under the banyan tree; Christ experiences the descent of the holy spirit in the form of a dove as He is being baptized; Muḥammad sees a vision of the Angel Gabriel while meditating in a cave; the Báb has a vision of the martyred Imám Ḥusayn; and Bahá'u'lláh sees the veiled maiden while He is imprisoned in the Síyáh-Chál.

Quite possibly these transforming events are intended as

dramatic explanations for the benefit of their followers more than anything else – as if to explain why at some point these individuals who are ostensibly but other human beings are suddenly endued with a power or insight or station they did not have before. And yet, one senses in Bahá'u'lláh's description of this event that the Manifestations themselves are humbled and astonished by the power of this process of revelation, even though they demonstrate prior to this point an awareness that they are about their Father's business:

> . . . I felt as if something flowed from the crown of My head over My breast, even as a mighty torrent that precipitateth itself upon the earth from the summit of a lofty mountain. Every limb of My body would, as a result, be set afire.[20]

Another common attribute among the Manifestations is that they do not aspire to earthly ascendancy, material possession or public approbation. For even though their guidance relates to both spiritual and mundane affairs, they portray themselves as conveyers of information, not so much as earthly executors of social programmes. Therefore, when the masses attempt to crown Christ king, he flees,[21] and when Bahá'u'lláh is offered an opportunity to avoid the political machinations of the Persian theocracy, He rejects it.* In effect, the Manifestations surrender control of their lives to the Will of God, and their physical well-being to the caprice of authorities so that no one may question the purity of their motives or the source of the religious teachings they bring.

Other distinguishing attributes of these Educators relate

---

* Bahá'u'lláh avoided execution in the Síyáh-Chál largely because of the intervention on His behalf by the secretary of the Russian Legation and the Russian Minister. After His release, the Russian government 'offered Bahá'u'lláh a refuge in its own territories, but He chose to go to 'Iráq'. Balyuzi, *Bahá'u'lláh: The King of Glory*, p. 102.

to the process by which they gradually lead human society towards fulfilment. For while they all have equal capacity and status, the systematic method by which they gradually uplift the human condition demonstrates that they are fully coordinated in their efforts and therefore tailor their instruction to the exigencies of the age in which they appear.

Religion as the Process by which the Manifestations Educate Humanity

Stated with utmost simplicity, the Bahá'í view of human history on this planet focuses on the cyclical and gradual education induced by the Manifestations. Therefore, human history is inevitably religious history, and religious history is a single, coherent and coordinated process which necessarily occurs in definable stages of enlightenment:

> The religion of God is one religion, but it must ever be renewed. Moses, for example, was sent forth to man and He established a Law, and the Children of Israel, through that Mosaic Law, were delivered out of their ignorance and came into the light; they were lifted up from their abjectness and attained to a glory that fadeth not. Still, as the long years wore on, that radiance passed by, that splendour set, that bright day turned to night; and once that night grew triply dark, the star of the Messiah dawned, so that again a glory lit the world.
>
> Our meaning is this: the religion of God is one, and it is the educator of humankind, but still, it needs must be made new.[22]

As we discussed in the first volume and earlier in this same volume, such a process of instruction is subtle and in-direct, because true education cannot result from coercion, indoctrination or imposition of will. History as a divinely-ordained programme by which humanity is uplifted and trained is thus like wise parental guidance or a carefully-devised educational programme wherein the instruction is geared to the ever-changing capacities of the student. But what is particularly important to our present observations about how the artistic process relates to this education and to the goal of an ever more inclusive sense of self is the parallelism between the twofold identity of these Manifestations and the dual aspects of the instruction they provide.

The Two Stations of the Prophets

As we mentioned in the first chapter, the Manifestations reveal two distinct categories of guidance. The first is a reiteration of the timeless, changeless attributes and relationships of the spiritual world. Though expressed in terms appropriate to the capacity of human society at a given time, these eternal verities are the Manifestations' attempt to define the hidden or veiled or concealed reality for which the phenomenal world is the metaphorical body. The second aspect of revelation relates to the specific laws, ordinances, institutions and daily regimen with which the Manifestation trains society to advance its condition and thereby more fully understand and implement the updated and incrementally more complete revelation of human purpose.

We noted in the first chapter parallels between the twin duties of human purpose, the dual parts of the artistic process, and the dual aspects of divine revelation as they parallel the 'twofold station' of the Prophets. In the first station of 'pure abstraction and essential unity',[23] the Manifestations are expressions of divine Will, are indistinguishable in their essential purposes, and are perfectly harmonized in their plan of enlightenment:

In this respect, if thou callest them all by one name, and dost
ascribe to them the same attribute, thou hast not erred from
the truth. Even as He hath revealed: 'No distinction do We
make between any of His Messengers!' For they one and all
summon the people of the earth to acknowledge the Unity of
God, and herald unto them the Kawthar of an infinite grace
and bounty. They are all invested with the robe of Prophethood, and honoured with the mantle of glory.[24]

Of course, inasmuch as each Manifestation is a distinct
individual and is constrained both by the exigencies of the
age in which He appears and by the capacity of the people
to whom He ministers, each Prophet and each Revelation
is distinct from every other. Therefore, each religion, or,
more accurately, each stage in the ongoing religion of
God, contains laws and guidance specifically appropriate
for a particular social and historical context and for a finite
duration.

If we see in this a parallel to the parental guidance or
gradual education of an individual, we can infer several
other obvious but nevertheless useful conclusions. For
example, since it would be unwise, unjust and counter-
productive to enforce the rules and guidance appropriate
for an individual of five years of age on one who is ten or
twelve years old, we can well appreciate how in due time
the laws and guidance that were once a source of enlightenment and justice for one revelation can become a
pernicious source of retardation and injustice when applied
to people living in later dispensations. In this same vein,
we can understand that however much a teacher or a
parent might long to impart the ultimate wisdom and long
term effects of some spiritual course of action, human
beings progress incrementally and gradually. Therefore,
the student can only comprehend and utilize the increment
of knowledge appropriate to his or her present experience,
insight and capacities.

Progressive Revelation and the Covenant

An integral part of the Bahá'í paradigm of history is the concept of a twofold pact or covenant between God and man which corresponds to the twofold station of the Prophets. Corresponding to the station of essential unity is the idea of an eternal covenant between man and God which designates the process by which God will never leave humankind without guidance.* Mankind's part in this agreement is synonymous with the twin duties enunciated in first chapter – to seek out and follow the Manifestation. The function of the Manifestation in this agreement is that each provides guidance regarding the Prophet who will appear after him:

> The divine Prophets are conjoined in the perfect state of love. Each One has given the glad tidings of His successor's coming and each successor has sanctioned the One Who preceded Him. They were in the utmost unity, but Their followers are in strife. For instance, Moses gave the message of the glad tidings of Christ, and Christ confirmed the Prophethood of Moses. Therefore, between Moses and Jesus there is no variation or conflict. They are in perfect unity, but between the Jew and the Christian there is conflict. Now, therefore, if the Christian and Jewish peoples investigate the reality underlying their Prophets' teachings, they will become kind in their attitude toward each other and associate in the utmost love, for reality is one and not dual or multiple. If this investigation of reality becomes universal, the divergent nations will ratify all the divine Prophets and confirm all the Holy Books.[25]

The second sort of covenant corresponds to the station of distinction among the Manifestations and alludes to the

---

* This covenant is variously designated in the Bahá'í writings as the 'Great Covenant', the 'Eternal Covenant', and the 'Ancient Covenant'.

particular guidance given by each Manifestation whereby
the followers are provided with a succession of authoritative
guidance for that dispensation. That is, the Manifestation
designates individuals or institutions to organize and
safeguard the religion from contention and discord.

In a letter written in 1975 the Universal House of Justice
further clarified the use of these terms with the following
definitions of *covenant* in the context of religious history:

> A Covenant in the religious sense is a binding agreement
> between God and man, whereby God requires of man certain
> behaviour in return for which He guarantees certain bless-
> ings, or whereby He gives man certain bounties in return for
> which He takes from those who accept them an undertaking
> to behave in a certain way. There is, for example, the Greater
> Covenant which every Manifestation of God makes with His
> followers, promising that in the fullness of time a new
> Manifestation will be sent, and taking from them the under-
> taking to accept Him when this occurs. There is also the
> Lesser Covenant that a Manifestation of God makes with His
> followers that they will accept His appointed successor after
> Him. If they do so, the Faith can remain united and pure. If
> not, the Faith becomes divided and its force spent.[26]

Stated simply, the Greater Covenant alludes to the Bahá'í
concept of progressive revelation, the gradual and incre-
mental enlightenment of humanity through the process of
divinely appointed emissaries. In this context, the Greater
Covenant alludes to the entire cycle of human progress on
this planet, whereas the Lesser Covenant alludes to the
chain of authority which, when upheld and protected,
unites all the religions in one process of human education
and safeguards the individual religion until the advent of
the next dispensation.

The importance of this concept to the Bahá'í concept of
religion as an eternal educational process is obvious. If this
is an accurate description of history, it means that all

human social progress wheels around these integral cycles. It demonstrates that the unity of religion enunciated throughout the Bahá'í teachings is not a pious hope, but the underlying reality of all religious history. Or stated conversely, by failing to grasp the allusions of the Prophets to their essential unity of purpose and coordination of human education, humanity has rather consistently in the past perverted or distorted what was intended as a logical and subtle plan of enlightenment and made it a source of discord, contention and strife.

Well aware of this strategic problem, the Manifestations devote an important part of their teachings to educating their followers about the historical relationship among the Prophets of the past and preparing their followers for the appearance of the succeeding Manifestation:

> Each One [Prophet] has given the glad tidings of His successor's coming and each successor has sanctioned the One Who preceded Him. They were in the utmost unity, but their followers are in strife.[27]

> His Holiness Abraham, on Him be peace, made a covenant concerning His Holiness Moses and gave the glad-tidings of His coming. His Holiness Moses made a covenant concerning the Promised One, i.e. His Holiness Christ, and announced the good news of His Manifestation to the world. His Holiness Christ made a covenant concerning the Paraclete [Muḥammad] and gave the tidings of His coming. His Holiness the Prophet Muḥammad made a covenant concerning His Holiness the Báb and the Báb was the One promised by Muḥammad . . . The Báb made a Covenant concerning the Blessed Beauty of Bahá'u'lláh and gave the glad-tidings of His coming . . . Bahá'u'lláh made a covenant concerning a promised One who will become manifest after one thousand or thousands of years.[28]

Of course, the inextricable relationship between these two covenants parallels the inextricable relationship between the twin stations of the Prophets. That is to say, the main reason the followers of one Manifestation reject and even persecute the succeeding Manifestation and His followers (thereby violating the Greater Covenant) is that the Lesser Covenant has itself become vitiated so that the teachings of the Prophet have become distorted and the believers are thus unprepared.

Here again the critical linkage between the twin duties becomes apparent. The believers may in some sense have recognized the station or power of the Revelator, but they have failed or fallen short of obedience to His guidance. And as we observed in the first chapter, one part of this paradigm cannot work without the other because they are expressions of one dynamic process.

Independent Prophets and 'Minor' Prophets

Viewing the Bahá'í paradigm of religious history as a whole, then, we see that if we view human history as an unending succession of progressive cycles of growth, each building on what has gone before, the smallest cycle of time is the dispensation of an individual Manifestation, which usually endures approximately five hundred to a thousand years. And yet within that dispensation, there may be discernible periods of development that might likewise be described in terms of organic or cyclical growth. With some religions, like Judaism, for example, we note the appearance of what the Bahá'í writings designate as 'minor' Prophets. In explaining the station and purpose of these prophetic figures, as opposed to a Manifestation, 'Abdu'l-Bahá states that where the Manifestations are 'followed', the minor prophets 'are not independent and are themselves followers'.

The independent Prophets are the lawgivers and the founders of a new cycle.

Through Their appearance the world puts on a new garment, the foundations of religion are established and a new book is revealed.[29]

The minor Prophets may have an important influence in revitalizing and reinvigorating the dispensation in which they appear, but they fully acknowledge that their purpose is not to found a new religion or inaugurate a new cycle of religious history; it is rather to advance the teachings of the Manifestation whose light they reflect:

> [They] are followers and promoters, for they are branches and not independent; they receive the bounty of the independent Prophets, and they profit by the light of the Guidance of the universal Prophets. They are like the moon, which is not luminous and radiant in itself, but receives its light from the sun.[30]

Thus we may distinguish between those independent Prophets or Manifestations (i.e. Noah, Húd, Ṣáliḥ, Abraham, Moses, Zoroaster, Buddha, Christ, Muḥammad, the Báb and Bahá'u'lláh) and those who are 'followers and promoters', such as 'Solomon, David, Isaiah, Jeremiah and Ezekiel'.[31] Therefore, when in history we discover evidence of social and religious reform, we may be witnessing evidence of an impetus promulgated by a minor or lesser Prophet rather than the advent of a new Manifestation. Likewise, in the Qur'án when Muḥammad states that 'every people hath had its apostle',[32] He may well have been alluding to these lesser Prophets, or He may have been describing a period in human spiritual and social evolution when, because of the constraints of travel and communication, more than one Manifestation was at work in the world at the same time, each one ministering to the needs and capacities of a relatively narrowly-defined culture or region.

It is the very ambiguity about what we presently know

regarding the ascent of human civilization in relation to
the process of revelation that should excite the students of
history and of religion alike. For it is abundantly clear
from these observations that if the Bahá'í hypothesis about
the relationship between the cycles of religious history and
the evolution of the human body politic prove true, then
we have not really begun the study of ancient cultures and
their part in this ongoing process. Future studies bode
infinitely more portentous jewels of insight than all we
may have learned from the accumulated archaeological
discoveries unearthed since Heinrich Schliemann first
came upon the site of ancient Troy in 1868.*

The Gradual Unification of the Process

We have already observed that the parallel in development
between the individual and society as a whole dictates that
the evolving or gradually more inclusive sense of self that
signals individual fulfilment of spiritual purpose is
also a valid index to the progress of society in general.
Therefore, we might assume that as cycles unfold and
encompass vaster regions, they will likewise bring forth
ever more inclusive social structures to express the essential unity of the human race.

In this connection, Shoghi Effendi states that the distinguishing characteristic of our present age is that we
have arrived at a point where the collective sense of self
can incorporate the entire planet:

> Unification of the whole of mankind is the hall-mark of the
> stage which human society is now approaching. Unity of
> family, of tribe, of city-state, and nation have been success-

---

* Through his unrelenting travels and discoveries, Schliemann became the
father of modern archaeology by helping to establish it as a science.

ively attempted and fully established. World unity is the goal towards which a harassed humanity is striving.[33]

Stated even more clearly, if we consider human social evolution on this planet as the life cycle of a single organism (i.e. the human body politic), we can observe that after the foundational sorts of physical, social and intellectual preparation have occurred, the organism will achieve a sort of maturity. It will reach its full potential for expressing spiritual principles in social structures.

But such a condition does not in any way imply that the cycle of human development ends. Certainly we do not consider an individual human being having arrived at the age of maturity to be finished with his or her development. Rather such a one is said to have acquired all the powers and faculties needed to achieve full potential. In effect, the journey to fulfilment as a process of wilful ascent via the artistic process we enunciated in the first chapter can now be said to have begun in earnest.

Thus, the arrival of the human body politic at its own maturation signifies not the end of development, but the beginning of its most meaningful sort of progress. Where before the educational process had been only partially understood and utilized by a few, and where our common identity was only vaguely appreciated, the essential universal identity and purpose of human life on this planet can now become commonly recognized, acknowledged, upheld and nourished.

The Bahá'í writings thus assert that the process of education set in motion at the inception of the planet itself has with the advent of the Báb in 1844 reached the point of fruition and maturity. The earth as a seed planted in the matrix of the universe is ready to bring forth its most cherished fruit, a united human family going about the business of constructing an 'ever-advancing civilization'.

And like a youth who suddenly understands the patience, wisdom and love that have been the motive force for his parents' persistence, humankind will now come to understand and appreciate the benignity and boundless grace with which God has been guiding human history. At such a point, confusion about the relationships among religions will evaporate and the spiritual education of humanity will be enthusiastically embraced. The now mature youth, suddenly aware that it is his own well being he is pursuing, will no longer need the urging of parents and teachers; he will see the end in the beginning.

The Cyclical Paradigm of Human History

The Cyclical Nature of Individual Dispensations

The cyclical nature of a single dispensation is evident in the pattern by which most religions have developed. The Manifestation appears, and with the dawning of this advent, three sorts of influence are spread: spiritual verities are restated; the laws, daily regimen and social structures are updated; and a revitalizing spiritual energy reinvigorates the entire planet, even though the generality of humankind may be unaware of the source of this influence.

In this context, Christ clearly affirms that He has not come to abolish the law but to fulfil it.* Similarly, Muḥammad in the Súrih of Houd explicates the divine process whereby successive Manifestations have been sent to assist human advancement. Bahá'u'lláh reveals a lengthy exposition on the same cyclical process in the *Kitáb-i-Íqán* when he employs the metaphor of a rebuilt or renewed city:

---

* 'Think not that I am come to destroy the law, or the prophets: I am not come to destroy, but to fulfil' (Matt. 5:17).

Once in about a thousand years shall this City be renewed and re-adorned . . .

That city is none other than the Word of God revealed in every age and dispensation. In the days of Moses it was the Pentateuch; in the days of Jesus the Gospel; in the days of Muḥammad the Messenger of God the Qur'án; in this the Bayán; and in the dispensation of Him Whom God will make manifest His own Book – the Book unto which all the Books of former Dispensations must needs be referred, the Book which standeth amongst them all transcendent and supreme.[34]

In explaining essentially the same cyclical process of renewal and return or resurrection, 'Abdu'l-Bahá employs the analogy of a tree:

From the seed of reality religion has grown into a tree which has put forth leaves and branches, blossoms and fruit. After a time this tree has fallen into a condition of decay. The leaves and blossoms have withered and perished; the tree has become stricken and fruitless. It is not reasonable that man should hold to the old tree, claiming that its life forces are undiminished, its fruit unequalled, its existence eternal. The seed of reality must be sown again in human hearts in order that a new tree may grow therefrom and new divine fruits refresh the world. By this means the nations and peoples now divergent in religion will be brought into unity, imitations will be forsaken, and a universal brotherhood in the reality itself will be established.[35]

As the influence of the new cycle spreads, civilization is advanced and revitalized until, in due course, the power of that religion to guide and advance the human condition wanes and declines, like the sun setting at the end of the cycle of a day.*

---

* In this connection, the scriptures often allude to a dispensation as a day.

The Grouping of Dispensations in Universal Cycles

Each Dispensation, however, operates within a larger sort of cycle, what 'Abdu'l-Bahá calls a 'universal cycle'. These more encompassing cycles of development, we may presume, relate to particular phases of human development:

> . . . cycles begin, end and are renewed, until a universal cycle is completed in the world, when important events and great occurrences will take place which entirely efface every trace and every record of the past; then a new universal cycle begins in the world, for this universe has no beginning . . .
>
> Briefly, we say a universal cycle in the world of existence signifies a long duration of time, and innumerable and incalculable periods and epochs.[36]

We may well guess what sorts of human development characterized universal cycles of the past. Since traces of those cycles have been obliterated, however, we can only speculate about the sort of growth that has occurred in the Adamic or Prophetic cycle (the Prophets who have appeared over the past six thousand years), the one cycle we know much about, and the sort of progress that is about to occur in the Bahá'í Era. Simply to understand that numerous cycles have occurred in the past and that others will occur in future is to glimpse the vast scope of the history of our planet, and to become awed by what the future holds.

In this context, of course, a third cycle is evident, the overall evolution of human society from the dust, which can be viewed as a single organic process with definable stages of achievement. But we should not conclude from this paradigm that at some point there will be no further development in the form of more encompassing cycles beyond our planet. In effect, we can infer that, given an infinitely expandable universe, there are doubtless successively more encompassing cycles of development which will necessitate a further expansion of our identity beyond a global sense of self.

Possibly, as our understanding of this process increases in the future, we will be able to understand better that even the quantum leaps forward signalized by the use of the opposing thumb, the development of basic tools, the discovery of fire, and other sorts of advancement to which we find allusions in ancient mythologies, resulted from the specific guidance of an ancient Manifestation in some early cycle. Was it possibly a Manifestation that urged our earliest progenitors from the sea, or to try to stand upright?

In considering the various ramifications of the Bahá'í view of history in terms of a cyclical paradigm, we are lead to intriguing questions like this. One of the most fascinating of these, for example, is to consider at what point in the evolution of the human species divine intervention in the form of explicit religious instruction begins. As we have already noted, if we employ the analogy of individual human development as a paradigm for the collective evolution of humankind, we would infer that in some form or another, external guidance has been from the beginning. But even with the individual, parental assistance is expressed in a variety of ways. There may be no direct intercourse between the child in the womb and the parents who await the emergence of the infant, but we are now discovering how much the physical condition of the mother and even her spiritual and mental attitude may affect healthy growth of that embryonic human being, even though the foetus may not be conscious of that influence.

Certainly overt assistance begins as soon as birth occurs, even though the child is in no sense physically mature or even cognitively aware that it is being assisted. By analogy, then, we can assume that divine assistance existed in even the most primitive forms of human evolution and advancement. Therefore, while those earliest forms of our species may not have been consciously aware of a decision to leave the water, external influence was nonetheless being exerted. But at what point in human evolution does the two-part process begin to occur? At what point does spiritual development become a conscious process, a moral choice? Might we infer, for example, that the Adamic myth is portraying the point in human development when we became aware of our Evian self, our moral or spiritual nature, when we were first held accountable for our moral choices?

The Bahá'í writings assert that prior to the Adamic cycle, there were 'many universal cycles preceding this one in which we are living. They were consummated, completed and their traces obliterated'.[37] Therefore, while we are assured that the purpose of those earlier Manifestations was ever the same, 'the evolution of spiritual man',[38] we cannot know at what primitive levels they had to operate in order to achieve this purpose:

> Though we cannot imagine exactly what the Manifestations of the remote past were like, we can be sure of two things: They must have been able to reach Their fellowmen in a normal manner – as Bahá'u'lláh reached His generation, and They were sent from God and thus Divine Beings . . .[39]

It is conceivable, then, that in the earliest stages of human development, there may have been many Manifestations on the planet at the same time teaching very fundamental sorts of ideas: how to fashion tools, make fire, fashion a wheel, domesticate animals. If this paradigm is valid, it is quite conceivable that we will in due time understand more completely how this force has been at work in history. Possibly we will then be better able to piece together a clearer picture of our own becoming. What we can already observe in the paradigm of gradual enlightenment is a sequence of organic cycles of growth, each operating within some more encompassing organic process, and all of these cycles integral parts of the overall cycle of the life of the planet itself.

The Special Significance of the Present Age

The Birth of a New Universal Cycle

It is in the context of the most expansive of these three types of cycles (the overall planetary evolution) that we find in the Bahá'í paradigm the most significant implications about the special importance of the Bahá'í Revelation and about the progress of humanity in general. That is, while the advent of a new dispensation inevitably unveils a more complete vision of who we are and how we can more effectively utilize the untapped human resources latent within us, the Bahá'í writings assert that humanity has with the advent of the dispensation of Bahá'u'lláh entered a new universal cycle, and, even more significantly, has achieved the point of maturity for the organic planetary evolution of the species as a whole.

As we have mentioned, the Bahá'í scriptures allude to the sequence of dispensations begun approximately six thousand years ago with the appearance of Adam as the 'Adamic' or 'Prophetic' cycle, a period which, in one sense, might be seen to achieve completion with the dispensation of Muḥammad. Indeed, one interpretation of Muḥammad's statement that He was the 'Apostle of God, and the seal of the prophets'[40] is that Muḥammad completed a sequence of instruction intended to lead humanity from a very primitive sense of morality to a fundamental appreciation of religion as a coordinated and coherent expression of divine grace and guidance revealed to humankind throughout history. Consequently, the fundamental theme of Muḥammad's ministry is the oneness of God and the unity of the process by which God assists humanity by sending these 'Apostles'.*

Attaining Planetary Maturation

In this same context, the Bahá'í writings designate the new universal cycle inaugurated by the advent of the Báb in 1844 as the beginning of the 'Bahá'í Era' or the 'Cycle of Fulfilment'.[41] As we have noted, the term 'fulfilment' in this context does not mean completion or termination, but the period of maturation.

History has long awaited this transition, because the energy of all previous dispensations within the Adamic cycle, as well as all cycles prior to the Adamic cycle, were in preparation for the point at which humanity as a whole would realize its essential nature, appreciate the divine process which has provided external assistance in rearing this child, and respond appropriately by establishing those institutions designed to utilize the now mature human body politic:

> Great indeed is this Day! The allusions made to it in all the sacred Scriptures as the Day of God attest its greatness. The soul of every Prophet of God, of every Divine Messenger,

---

* The Súrih of Houd, for example, is very similar to the initial passages of Bahá'u'lláh's the *Kitáb-i-Íqán* in its recitation of the advent of the Prophets and the subsequent rejection and mistreatment of those same figures by the people they are sent to assist, a clear demonstration of God's grace. However, there are other equally sound explanations for what Muḥammad means by this passage.

hath thirsted for this wondrous Day. All the divers kindreds of the earth have, likewise, yearned to attain it.[42]

The whole human race hath longed for this Day, that perchance it may fulfil that which well beseemeth its station, and is worthy of its destiny.[43]

In terms of our previously discussed goal of achieving an ever-more expanding or inclusive identity, this point of maturation for humanity implies the achievement of a thoroughly global identity and the expression of that understanding in the artifice of human society. This is why the Bahá'í writings laud the importance of this 'Day', because it is the Bahá'í thesis that humankind is about to enter a stage in which human potential will be unleashed, a stage that all previous growth and development has carefully prepared us to pursue. Indeed, it is in this context that the Bahá'í writings speak of this period as fulfilling prophecies about 'the long-awaited advent of the Christ-promised Kingdom of God on earth'[44] and the biblical allusions to the advent of the 'new Jerusalem'.[45]

From a Bahá'í perspective, then, the significance of revelation of Bahá'u'lláh is not solely that it restates eternal verities and provides a new set of laws appropriate to this age, though these are obviously not minor or insignificant accomplishments. Neither does the primary significance of this revelation lie in the fact that it ushers in a new cycle. According to the Bahá'í vision of history, the advent of this revelation marks the turning point in the entire cycle of human development on this planet.

Given such a perspective, it is natural that we would want to know exactly how this transition will occur and what methods Bahá'u'lláh has revealed to fashion in artistic form the fully evolved sense of ourselves as members of one global community.

What the Future Holds

According to Bahá'í texts, the initial stages of the transition to this maturity are well under way and will be substantially in place before the end of the twentieth century, an assertion we will later examine in more detail. For our present purposes, it is sufficient to note that however naive or idealistic such expectations may presently seem, they are certainly no less astounding than has been the exponential change that has taken place in virtually every arena of human endeavour during the course of the last century. If we could imagine ourselves living a hundred years ago and having the opportunity to witness the present state of human society, we would be utterly dumbfounded.

In the same way that the scientific or material advancement of the last century would astound the imagination of the most imaginative genius of previous centuries, so it is conceivable that an equally radical transformation of our global community could take place, as events of the past several years clearly indicate. Yet, we must remember that the impending transformation of human society from ostensibly disparate, fragmented and uncoordinated enclaves into a coherent, organized and spiritually unified commonwealth, which might have seemed unthinkable a few years ago, will not be a process of unexpected, random or circumstantial change but rather the end result of a process set in motion from the earth's beginnings.

In this regard, 'Abdu'l-Bahá notes that in the unfolding of a universal cycle there appears a Manifestation whose advent clarifies or galvanizes or consummates the thematic purpose for that cycle. This Manifestation 'Abdu'l-Bahá designates as the 'universal Manifestation' for that cycle:

> In such a cycle the Manifestations appear with splendour in the realm of the visible until a great and supreme Manifes-

tation makes the world the centre of His radiance. His appearance causes the world to attain to maturity, and the extension of His cycle is very great. Afterward, other Manifestations will arise under His shadow, Who according to the needs of the time will renew certain commandments relating to material questions and affairs, while remaining under His shadow.[46]

He further notes that, even though the Bahá'í cycle has barely begun, the universal Manifestation for that period of fulfilment is Bahá'u'lláh:

Concerning the Manifestations that will come down in the future 'in the shadows of the clouds' . . . know, verily, that in so far as their relation to the Source of their inspiration is concerned, they are under the shadow of the Ancient Beauty [Bahá'u'lláh]. In their relation, however, to the age in which they appear, each and every one of them 'doeth whatsoever He willeth'.[47]

Thus, humankind on this planet will never reach some final point of spiritual attainment, some plateau where no further spiritual or social development is possible. According to the Bahá'í writings, the remainder of this universal cycle of five thousand centuries will be a refining of this transformation of human society accomplished during the dispensation of Bahá'u'lláh.

This leads us to several intriguing considerations. Will there be other universal cycles with universal Manifestations who accomplish comparable sorts of transformation of human awareness, further vast expansions of human identity comparable in scope to the emergence of a global consciousness?

The discussions of these cycles in the Bahá'í writings sometimes seems perplexing. In one instance Shoghi Effendi describes the appearance of the Báb 'as standing at the confluence of two universal prophetic cycles, the Adamic Cycle stretching back as far as the first dawnings of the world's recorded religious history and the Bahá'í Cycle destined to propel itself across the unborn reaches of time for a period of no less than five thousand centuries'.[48] Yet in other instances, the Adamic and Bahá'í Cycles are linked together: 'We are in the cycle which began with Adam, and its supreme Manifestation is Bahá'u'lláh.'[49]

The answer to the first of these questions is that the point of transition and transformation we as a species are now experiencing is unique in the evolution of this particular planet. For while there will no doubt be other milestones of advancement in the future, there is only one period of maturation for a given organism. Or stated another way, however more refined and expansive we become, we will never again on this planet experience so momentous a transformation as occurs at the point of self-awareness associated with attaining maturity. For however much certain insightful individuals may in the past have understood this process and the potential of humankind to become united, it would have been impossible for these learned ones to implement that understanding universally in social or political form.

In this connection, the Báb observed that 'every religion of the past was fit to become universal'.[50] He was clearly referring to acceptance among the generality of the populace to whom that Manifestation came, since, as 'Abdu'l-Bahá notes, physical and material constraints of the past meant that 'understanding and unity amongst all the peoples and kindreds of the earth were unattainable' when the world was 'widely divided'.[51] But Bahá'u'lláh observes that in this Day, it is the clear intention that the revelation reach all peoples:

> The summons and the message which We gave were never intended to reach or to benefit one land or one people only. Mankind in its entirety must firmly adhere to whatso-ever hath been revealed and vouchsafed unto it. Then and

only then will it attain unto true liberty. The whole earth is illuminated with the resplendent glory of God's Revelation.[52]

This concept of our age as the point of maturation for the human race does not mean that there will never be another cycle of crucial importance or another universal Manifestation with so significant a mission as that of Bahá'u'lláh. Shoghi Effendi notes that 'There will . . . be [a Prophet] similar to Him in greatness after the lapse of 500,000 years . . .'[53] What becomes further apparent is that the terms designating cycles are general appellations employed for our benefit, not scientifically constraining definitions of structure. For example, we might well wonder how the six thousand years of the Adamic cycle could be compared with the five hundred thousand years of the Bahá'í cycle, a ratio of approximately 83 to 1.

Conceivably, the initial stages of understanding witness a quality of change that makes it relatively comparable in the scope of change that is accomplished. Yet the Bahá'í writings often link the Adamic cycle together with the Bahá'í cycle as part of one coherent expression of cyclical evolutionary change:

The Bahá'í cycle is, indeed, incomparable in its greatness. It includes not only the Prophets that will appear after Bahá'u'lláh, but all those Who have preceded Him ever since Adam. These should, indeed, be viewed as constituting but preliminary stages leading gradually to the appearance of this supreme Manifestation of God.[54]

In this same context, 'Abdu'l-Bahá designates 'this Holy Dispensation' as 'the crowning glory of bygone ages and cycles'.[55] Shoghi Effendi alludes to the advent of Bahá'u'lláh as 'marking the culmination of the six thousand year old Adamic Cycle'.[56] And in another passage he states:

The Revelation of Bahá'u'lláh, whose supreme mission is none other but the achievement of this organic and spiritual unity of the whole body of nations, should, if we be faithful to its implications, be regarded as signalizing through its advent the coming of age of the entire human race. It should be viewed not merely as yet another spiritual revival in the ever-changing fortunes of mankind, not only as a further stage in a chain of progressive Revelations, nor even as the culmination of one of a series of recurrent prophetic cycles, but rather as marking the last and highest stage in the stupendous evolution of man's collective life on this planet.[57]

At the same time, Shoghi Effendi makes it clear that this pre-eminent position of crucial transformation being ushered in by the dispensation of Bahá'u'lláh does not imply the superiority of Bahá'u'lláh over other Manifestations nor of the Bahá'í Faith over those religions that have preceded it or that will succeed it in the future:

> Nor does the Bahá'í Revelation, claiming as it does to be the culmination of a prophetic cycle and the fulfilment of the promise of all ages, attempt, under any circumstances, to invalidate those first and everlasting principles that animate and underlie the religions that have preceded it.[58]

The conclusion of any consideration of the Bahá'í overview of history as an organic, evolutionary, cyclical and essentially spiritual process does not, therefore, depend on the exactitude of terms. In a general sense, it provides a perspective on the process by which the human species proceeds through various kinds of development to achieve a condition of maturity whereby further understanding may be acquired about how humanity can effect social structures to give artistic expression to spiritual forms. Possibly the most significant value of the Bahá'í paradigm of human social evolution is its treatment of how this transformation will proceed, what social and governmental structures must needs be developed, what immediate changes will be required to transform our present system so that it befits our newly emerged identity, and what foundations will be laid for future progress.

Before we can examine or appreciate fully the salutary remedies enunciated in the Revelation of Bahá'u'lláh as a demonstration of this perspective and a synthesis of the twin duties of knowing and worshipping, we would first do well to understand more precisely why, if the Bahá'í paradigm of history is accurate, the process does not seem to have worked as we might suppose it would have. When we consider that an all-powerful and omniscient Deity designed a plan whereby humanity is to be educated and guided step by step, why is it that so far only a relatively few have recognized and understood that educational process? Even more to the point insofar as matters of theodicy are concerned, if God intended that humanity turn to these successive Manifestations in order to learn spiritual lessons by degrees, why is it that more often than not there seems to have been a failure in these religions to accomplish their goals? In fact, why is it that so often the advent of new guidance has resulted in the very opposite of the intended result, in warfare instead of peace, contention instead of continuity, regression instead of advancement? Or stated in terms more relevant to our own precarious situation, if we are presently in the midst of a glorious and long-awaited transition to the universal maturation of humankind and the establishment of a global community, why do we appear to be on the brink of destroying the very organism that has served to bring us forth – our mother the earth?

4

New Wine and Old Skins
The Divine Art of Progressive Revelation

Then the disciples of John came to him, saying, 'Why do we and the Pharisees fast, but your disciples do not fast?' And Jesus said to them, 'Can the wedding guests mourn as long as the bridegroom is with them? The days will come, when the bridegroom is taken away from them, and then they will fast. And no one puts a piece of unshrunk cloth on an old garment, for the patch tears away from the garment, and a worse tear is made. Neither is new wine put into old wineskins; if it is, the skins burst, and the wine is spilled, and the skins are destroyed; but new wine is put into fresh wineskins, and so both are preserved.'[1]

Matthew

If the Bahá'í paradigm of history implies that the pattern of human failure to appreciate divine guidance will soon change with the onset of our collective maturation, we might reasonably question what will cause such a difference. But before we can appreciate the Bahá'í assertion that human response to divine guidance will change, we first need to assess what heretofore has been the source of our collective failure. Stated more bluntly, if humankind has repeatedly failed to respond appropriately to divine instruction, why can we not assume that the guidance is inadequate or faulty, especially if religion itself, the very tool devised as a means of human education, consistently seems to become a source of iniquity, strife and in-humanity. As we noted in the previous chapter, one would presume that an omnipotent and omniscient Deity could devise a plan that would work better.

The Relationship of the Wineskin to the Wine

At the heart of the answer to this question is the subtle relationship between the revealed wisdom of the Manifes-tation and the institutionalization of that insight into some religious edifice. For if we can generalize about why religion as a force in history has fallen short of its intended objectives, the most obvious response would be that the benign motives and spiritual wisdom once in the hands of fallible human authorities most often become lost to dogmatism and the attempt of ecclesiastics to maintain their own status.

There are other important related sources of this schism between revelation and implementation, between the knowing and the doing, this inevitable need to put the new wine in a new skin, to fashion a vessel sufficient to contain the new wisdom and convey it to a thirsting human society. For example, there is the immediate problem on the part of the followers of the previous Prophet of ostensibly having to transfer their allegiance from one personality to another. There is an even more strenuous problem on the part of those in authoritative control of the previous religion who, if they accept the new revelation, must relinquish their authority, their profession, their social status. Consequently, it has been a common pattern in religious history that those charged with leading the faithful to the recognition of the 'returned' Manifestation are the very ones who most fervently reject the new Prophet and persecute those who would follow Him.

Among the most weighty problems afflicting this process, the one which has caused the most damage to our modern perception of religion and its relation to our attempt to deal meaningful with the complex world we live in, is the emergence of a profound conflict between these twin aspects of revelation, between the statement of spiritual principles and the translation of those principles into law, ordinance and institution. Yet, though this is a problem endemic to religious history, we have inherited a fragmented view of ourselves that derives in large part from the origins of this schism in Christianity. To see how we can escape from this dichotomized sense of self, therefore, we would do well first to examine how we got here.

The Origins of this Schism in Christianity

At the Last Supper, when Christ has His disciples participate in the symbolism of drinking the wine and eating the bread, He gives them subtle insight into the meaning of this act. The wine represents His blood, which 'is the new covenant', and the bread represents His body 'which is given for you'.[2] What He leaves for them to figure out is the more expansive implications. What are they doing symbolically when they ingest these symbols? If the wine and bread symbolize the blood and the body of Christ, what do the blood and body themselves represent?

Inasmuch as the blood is the life-giving source of nourishment for the body, we must presume it is primary in this relationship. As such, it represents the Holy spirit which vitalizes Christ as Manifestation and will sustain His teachings after His physical martyrdom. The body of Christ, therefore, most probably represents the edifice that is sustained by this spirit, that gives outer form to this unseen energy as the human body dramatizes the soul's progress. Thus the 'body of Christ' early in the evolution of Christian exegesis came to represent the Church itself as institutional channel through which the teachings of Christ were conveyed to humanity.

We may also recognize in this two-part symbol the same paradigm we have been discussing variously as the twin duties of human purpose, the dual aspects of the artistic process, the female and male components of the Adamic myth, the twin stations of the Manifestations, and the two categories of guidance brought by each Manifestation. Or on a more general level, we may recognize in these symbols the inextricable relationship in this life between the soul and body, between the spiritual laws of the universe and the physical metaphorization or implementation of those laws in concrete analogues – into forms or names. But what we also may recognize in these twin symbols as we familiarize ourselves with religious history, especially with the succession of religions in terms of the Bahá'í paradigm of cyclical and progressive revelation, is an allusion to the delicate relationship between the revealed teachings of the Manifestation and the attempt after the death of the Prophet to institutionalize His revelation.

The sacrament of the Eucharist, the most central and sacred rite for the majority of Christendom, has a variety of meanings for the different branches of Christian belief. For purposes of our discussion, however, it can be seen as a poignant attempt by Christ to explain what is in many ways the focal point of any dispensation because this act symbolizes the alliance or conjoining of the unseen world with the physical world of perceptible forms. It also focuses on how God's progressive guidance of humanity through explicit intervention in human affairs often seems

to fail or falter when the converts from the previous
revelation do not appreciate the need to establish a new
identity, a new institution, a new name to signalize a
radically altered and expanded vision of human purpose.

Thus, when Christ speaks of putting the new wine in a
new wineskin He is clearly alluding to the necessity of
establishing a new religious institution to sustain the new
revelation. Included with such an establishment would
necessarily be new laws, a new way of life, a new name
and a new identity for the followers. He is with this
allegorical act, in other words, trying to make clear that
His revelation is not an attempt to renovate Judaism or
replenish what had become the hollow vessel of Judaic
ecclesiastical structures with a new spirit. He is not merely
speaking of the abrogation of a few laws, the addition of
others, nor the purification of a past and now outmoded
dispensation; rather He is speaking of a totally new 'skin'
or edifice to contain the new covenant and the newly
released wine of spiritual insight and power.

Yet He is equally clear about portraying this revolutionary change as a fulfilment, as a continuity, not as a
destruction: 'Think not that I have come to abolish the law
and the prophets; I have come not to abolish them but to
fulfil them.'[3] Therefore, He seems to imply that without
something to contain the wine and convey it to the
faithful, their personal religious experience of Christ's
reality might temporarily inspire and transform them as
individuals, but such an experience would hardly serve to
assist the rest of humanity in any meaningful way.

In this sense, the laws and institutions revealed or
instigated by the Prophet are the primary and essential
means through which the renewed outpouring of the Holy
spirit is given meaningful form. Otherwise, the revelation
would become little more than an inspirational lesson in

theology.* Nevertheless, virtually at the moment of Christ's death, major difficulties arose as to how radically different this institution would be from what had preceded it, how the institution should be formed, how administered, how sustained. And because Christ left little explicit guidance about how these tasks should be accomplished, it is not hard to trace in the early history of the Christian church how the good intentions of the apostles and the patristic fathers, coupled with the confusion about the question of Christology (the nature and station of Christ), almost immediately distracted and perverted the essential teachings of Christ to the extent that by the fourth century, the Christian institution as the body of Christ was irreparably severed from the spiritual verities that constituted the soul of Christ's ministry. The wineskin, mutilated beyond repair, allowed the wine to trickle upon the earth and thus become mixed with baser stuff.

Some Inferences about this Schism

The problem of the schism between the spiritual truth of a revelation and the attempt to contain and express that truth in an effective edifice is hardly unique with Christianity. One of the major themes of Christ's ministry was His attempt to enunciate to His Jewish audience how their religion had become a rigorous canon of law that was largely devoid of meaningful and effective spiritual content – it had become a lifeless body. In fact, it is for this reason that Christ so often employed metaphorical allusions to resurrection as a process of reanimating lifeless flesh.

After Christianity, the same pattern of schism occurred

---

* Since 'Abdu'l-Bahá assures us that the transforming spiritual force unleashed by the advent of a Prophet is not dependent for its effect on human recognition, this is obviously a hyperbolic assertion.

in Islam. In fact the seeds of that schism were planted as
the Prophet lay on His deathbed. According to Shí'í belief,
Muḥammad had clearly designated 'Alí as His successor
and head of the Faith.[4] On His deathbed Muḥammad then
asked for writing materials that He might officially so
indicate His intentions in a will.[5] The subsequent division
between Sunní Islam, which avowed allegiance and
ascribed authority to the elected Caliphate, and Shí'í
Islam, which ascribed authority to the Imámate, thus
effectively initiated the schism between the authority of
the revealed words of the Prophet in the Qur'án and the
institutionalization of those teachings by ecclesiastics and
the institutions they devised for safeguarding and conveying the wine of this new revelation to the generality of
humanity.

Some Muslim clerics would doubtless argue that the
twofold aspects of the Revelation are intact: the Qur'án
contains the spiritual teaching and the Sharí'at* contains
the written law. But there is little agreement on this
among Muslims or Islamicists, and no clear guidance for
establishing this division in the authoritative utterances of
the Manifestation:

> On the very day that Muḥammad passed out of this mortal
> world and before His body was laid to rest, winds of
> dissension blew through the edifice of His Faith. Having
> created a coherent nation out of an agglomerate of contending,
> restless tribes and having founded a state with a framework of
> laws, it is inconceivable that He would not have envisaged
> who should succeed Him. Moses had conferred authority
> upon Joshua, Christ had put the keys of Heaven and Earth in
> the hands of Peter; yet neither of them had in His lifetime

---

* The Sharí'at or Sharí'a is the 'religious law including parts of the Qur'án
as well as other laws. The Sharí'at was abrogated by the laws revealed by
the Báb and Bahá'u'lláh' (Momen, *A Basic Bahá'í Dictionary*, p. 207).

established a realm demanding an administration. But this was exactly what Muḥammad had done.[6]

As we have noted, then, this division between the wine and the wineskin (between the teachings of the Manifestation and the edifice of the religious institution raised to promulgate and safeguard those teachings) is, more often than not, the pattern of religions, not the exception. At the very least it is a major symptom of the demise of a dispensation, and most certainly it is at the heart of the perversion and chauvinism that so often comes to typify the intransigence and stagnation of religious institutions. Furthermore, once severed from the clear sense of its purpose, the institution often comes to hold its highest duty to be in securing and perpetuating its own existence rather than in educating and assisting the followers.

What will make a Difference?

If we can assume that it is an historical pattern for revealed religions to fail consistently to accomplish all of their intended goals in large part because of the schism between these dual aspects of divine guidance, we still have not begun to deal with the heart of this matter. Again we are left to pose obvious sorts of questions regarding theodicy. Why do the Manifestations not give more specific guidance for erecting the institutions and why exactly do the followers seem doomed to failure when they establish them? That is, if we accept at face value the Báb's statement that the intended course of religion has become waylaid because of the 'incompetence of their followers',[7] we need to understand more exactly what that inadequacy is, especially if we are to accept the Bahá'í assertion that for some reason that record of past failure will come to an end with this dispensation.

Stated in terms of a simple analogy, if I as a teacher repeatedly give a test to students and they seem inevitably to fail, and fail in a somewhat similar and predictable fashion, might I not reasonably assume that either the instruction has been inadequate or else that the test is beyond the students' capacity? Or even if I am satisfied that the test is fair and within the range of the students' abilities – that indeed the fault lies with the students – what might cause me to believe that this same pattern will at some point change and the students will someday be blessed with perception?

Anyone who has raised children with a relative degree of success may take consolation in recalling the occasions when any sort of propitious outcome to a child's upbringing and development might have seemed absolutely bleak in spite of the parents' most heartfelt, altruistic, repeated and selfless expressions of love and dedication, what Bahá'í poet Robert Hayden termed 'love's austere and lonely offices'.[8] Or those of us whose own parents persisted in bestowing love and guidance in spite of our own ingratitude and malfeasance may recall how in time we ourselves emerged from a condition of wilful disobedience and heedlessness of their noble efforts to become aspirants to nobility and fully appreciative of their parental gifts, most especially when we too had to endure the selfsame tribulations of parenthood.

In short, we might respond to this fundamental question of theodicy by observing that we as human beings often seem to need to learn things gradually, empirically and sometimes painfully until we reach an age when we are capable of putting it all together, often because we have come to experience firsthand the wisdom and beneficence of restraint, moderation and obedience. Along these same lines, we may consider that, once having come of age, humanity will at long last come to appreciate the utter justice, benignity and simple logic underlying the eternal plan of God as enunciated by Bahá'u'lláh in the *Kitáb-i-Íqán*. By this means, perhaps humanity will acquire a clarity of perception that could not have been coerced or enforced. Or we may similarly comfort ourselves by realizing that it is impossible to judge the outcome of the educational process by witnessing the sometimes faltering stages of its genesis, even as 'Abdu'l-Bahá advises:

> Do ye not look upon the beginning of the affairs; attach your hearts to the ends and results. The present period is like unto the sowing time. Undoubtedly it is impregnated with perils and difficulties, but in the future many a harvest shall be gathered and benefits and results will become apparent.[9]

Indeed, we can see in such advice the very definition of knowledge that Bahá'u'lláh implies in *The Seven Valleys* – seeing the end in the beginning: 'Yet those who journey in the garden land of knowledge, because they see the end in the beginning, see peace in war and friendliness in anger.'[10]

Therefore, we might be tempted to acknowledge the past failures of humanity to use well the gift of divine guidance bestowed through the Manifestations and to rejoice that such will not be the case after humanity comes of age. In fact, Bahá'u'lláh states that one of the results of humanity's transition to adulthood will be that after the universal recognition of progressive revelation which will occur in this dispensation, humankind will never again reject or persecute succeeding Revelations. Or stated another way, the advent of a new Revelation will not imply that the previous dispensation has become corrupt, convoluted or counter-productive: this is a 'Day which shall never be followed by night', a 'Springtime which autumn will never overtake'.[11]

But such an assurance by itself is not particularly comforting if we must accept on faith alone that whatever in the past deterred or hindered humanity from recognizing the Manifestation and following His advice will not similarly afflict the body politic again. To accept the idea that such a change will result from the maturation of humankind is rather like asking a teenager who has never witnessed others go through puberty to believe while in the midst of adolescent confusion that the present emotional and physical turmoil and consternation will have a fortuitous outcome.

In order to be more fully assured and comforted, in other words, we require a clearer understanding of how this divine plan of education has in the past become diverted, and, more importantly, what provisions are made so that the same sort of schism and distortion will not occur in the future.

The Problem of Recognizing the Manifestation

Prior to the schism between ecclesiastical authority and the untrammelled teachings of the Manifestation, but intimately associated with and causally related to that same problem, is the difficulty of recognizing the Prophet in the first place, or, having recognized Him, to understand with any degree of clarity the spiritual station of the Prophet or His relationship to the divine plan by which God is educating humanity. For while the Manifestation may bring two sorts of revelation as the most important proof or fruit of His authority, it is hardly a simple thing for one to ascertain if such revealed guidance derives from an authoritative source.

Since to outward seeming the Manifestation is but another human being, the process of discerning in His character or words some sign of an other-worldly authority is subtle and enigmatic, exactly what one might expect in a spiritual test that at once judges and instructs humankind. Therefore, we might expect that if God truly intended for His Prophets to be recognized, He would have provided some obvious clues to their identities; but motive is everything in this. If one were to recognize and follow a Manifestation because of His physical appearance or His ability to perform superhuman deeds, the basis for faith would be circumstantial, not spiritual.

Consequently, the Manifestations are seldom what most people expect. They rarely appear in obvious circumstances, and, according to Bahá'u'lláh in the *Kitáb-i-Íqán*, they are purposefully concealed so that only individuals whose motives are sincere will see and understand. In short, while humanity as a whole has consistently failed the test of recognizing the Manifestations, the test or judgement implicit in their appearance is not intended to be easy. In this sense, the test of discovering the Manifestation is itself an essential part of human spiritual education, because recognition implies an understanding of the distinguishing attributes of these beings and a willingness to accede to their guidance. Therefore, a cursory review of the parallels associated with the recognition of the Manifestations will help demonstrate why their appearance induces such a test or judgement, and why that judgement almost inevitably sets the stage for the eventual schism between the wine and the wineskin.

The Criteria for Recognition

The Manifestations, though veritable emblems of humility, unashamedly and forthrightly proclaim their station, not as a tribute to themselves, but as an enunciation of the power of God working through them. Therefore, each of them proclaims at some point in His ministry that to reject

His guidance is tantamount to a rejection of God. Yet, because the proof of their authority is their own immaculate character and the spiritual content of what they say, the Prophets have initially been rejected by all but a handful of the followers of the previous Manifestation. Bahá'u'lláh describes this as a general pattern of human response when He observes that 'whensoever the portals of grace did open, and the clouds of divine bounty did rain upon mankind, and the light of the Unseen did shine above the horizon of celestial might, they all denied Him, and turned away from His face – the face of God Himself'.[12]

The first reason that people fail to recognize 'the face of God Himself' is that the people to whom the new Manifestation appears have inherited a religious tradition that is in a state of decline. That is why a new Revelation is needed. Consequently, the people have generally lost touch with their spiritual sensibilities and tend to judge others by outward circumstance. But the Manifestation may not be physically or socially impressive according to the standards of people to whom He appears, especially when we consider that the Manifestations have appeared in societies which were in a state of moral decline, even decadence.

Commenting on this dilemma, Muḥammad remarks in the Qur'án as to why the people rejected Noah:

We sent Noah heretofore unto his people, and he said, 'O my people! serve God: ye have no other God than He: will ye not therefore fear Him?

But the chiefs of the people who believed not said, 'This is but a man like yourselves: he fain would raise himself above you: but had it pleased God to send, He would have sent angels: We heard not of this with our sires of old; –

Verily he is but a man possessed; leave him alone therefore for a time.'[13]

Bahá'u'lláh similarly comments in the beginning of the *Kitáb-i-Íqán* that

> . . . man can never hope to attain unto the knowledge of the All-Glorious, can never quaff from the stream of divine knowledge and wisdom, can never enter the abode of immortality, nor partake of the cup of divine nearness and favour, unless and until he ceases to regard the words and deeds of mortal men as a standard for the true understanding and recognition of God and His Prophets.[14]

Thus, when Christ instructs His disciples about how to distinguish between a true prophet and a false, He gives them the following simple but profound guidance:

> Beware of false prophets, who come to you in sheep's clothing but inwardly are ravenous wolves. You will know them by their fruits. Are grapes gathered from thorns, or figs from thistles? So, every sound tree bears good fruit, but the bad tree bears evil fruit. A sound tree cannot bear evil fruit, nor can a bad tree bear good fruit. Every tree that does not bear good fruit is cut down and thrown into the fire. Thus you will know them by their fruits.[15]

However, He leaves it to them to figure out exactly what the fruit of a Prophet is, and that is the key to the problem. Unless one understands (even if intuitively) what distinguishes the Manifestation from human beings, he or she is not likely to recognize the spiritual station of such a figure, but will instead look for phenomenal attributes and powers (miracles), will adjudge them by social or moral standards common to the social norms, or else will attempt to discover some literal fulfilment of prophecy, much as the Pharisaic Jews expected a literal king on the throne of David and some Christians in turn wait expectantly for the descent of the returned Christ through the clouds.

Because the Manifestation is not human but is forced to assume human guise in order to communicate on a level understandable to human beings, we can sometimes sense in their words the frustration they feel at trying to express the nature of the unseen spiritual world to beings who have no empirical knowledge of that reality. To a certain extent, their dilemma might be compared to the difficulty a human being would experience in putting on an animal skin and trying to communicate with creatures of the animal kingdom the most fundamental sorts of human knowledge.

It is in this context that the Manifestations speak despairingly of those who desire for them to demonstrate authority through some phenomenal sign:

> Then some of the scribes and Pharisees said to him, 'Teacher, we wish to see a sign from you.' But he answered them, 'An evil and adulterous generation seeks for a sign; but no sign shall be given to it except the sign of the prophet Jonah. For as Jonah was three days and three nights in the belly of the whale, so will the Son of man be three days and three nights in the heart of the earth.'[16]

In one sense, Christ is forewarning them that there will be a sign (the resurrection), and yet, as Bahá'u'lláh notes in His explication of prophetic imagery in the *Kitáb-i-Íqán*, only those with spiritual perception will be able to decipher such signs.

In the same way, Muḥammad frequently notes in the Qur'án how the people inevitably desire some physical evidence of His spiritual station. He notes that when the Prophet informs the people, 'I truly am your trustworthy Apostle',[17] the people inevitably respond:

> Thou art but a man like us, and we deem thee liar –
> Make now a part of the heaven to fall down upon us, if thou art a man of truth.[18]

The same circumstance occurs in the life of Bahá'u'lláh in

Baghdad when, after becoming jealous because of the growing respect and reputation Bahá'u'lláh has acquired among the citizenry of the area, as well as from the learned and dignitaries from far off, the assembled 'ulamá demand that Bahá'u'lláh perform some miracle to prove His station. Bahá'u'lláh states that though they 'have no right to ask this' since 'God should test His creatures, and they should not test God', He will accede, but only under the condition that they choose one miracle to which they all agree and that, should He perform the miracle, they will 'acknowledge and confess the truth of My Cause'.[19] After three days, an envoy from the Shí'í divines brought a message that they were unable to decide on a miracle and had decided to drop the matter.

It is in this same context that Bahá'u'lláh, in discussing the true proof or 'fruit' of the Manifestation in the *Kitáb-i-Íqán*, affirms that the verses revealed by the Prophet constitute the most obvious and abiding proof of the Prophet's station to those endowed with spiritual perception. He observes ironically that the majority of people 'clamour for guidance' even while that guidance is being proffered to them:

> Gracious God! how strange the way of this people! They clamour for guidance, although the standards of Him Who guideth all things are already hoisted. They cleave to the obscure intricacies of knowledge, when He, Who is the Object of all knowledge, shineth as the sun. They see the sun with their own eyes, and yet question that brilliant Orb as to the proof of its light.[20]

He then concludes succinctly that the 'proof of the sun is the light thereof'.[21]

Thus, while one might intuit from their demeanor or sense in the exemplary moral character of the Manifestations that they have spiritual power or an other-worldly eloquence, it is the revealed word, the choice wine, that is the clearest proof, precisely because the sort of proof people desire, and which the Manifestation is fully capable of demonstrating, would attract those who, while sensing some demonstration of a power beyond human ken, do not really know what it is they have discovered.

But the primary reason the revealed teachings are a sufficient sign relates not so much to the spiritual station of the Manifestations as it does to the source of their words. For while words are the property of all alike, the Manifestations each claim that nothing they say by way of unfolding the new revelation is from themselves. Each with unmistakable clarity attributes the authority of His utterance to the power of God speaking through Him.

Thus, God assures Moses, 'I will be with your mouth and teach you what you shall speak.'[22] Therefore when Moses speaks to His followers, He tells them that His utterance is the law of God spoken through Him. Likewise, when Christ enunciates the new law, the people are astonished, 'for he taught them as one who had authority, and not as their scribes'. But after He tells Philip, 'He who has seen me has seen the Father', He immediately cautions, 'The words that I say to you I do not speak on my own authority; but the Father who dwells in me, does his works'.[23]

Muḥammad also forthrightly states that He is an Apostle of God come with authority: 'Muḥammad is not the father of any man among you, but he is the Apostle of God, and the seal of the prophets: and God knoweth all things.'[24] At the same time, He makes it absolutely clear that He is not the only Apostle that has been endowed with this authority: 'Muḥammad is no more than an apostle: other apostles have already passed away before him.'[25]

This same dual perspective is evident in the statements of the Báb. When He is examined by the assembled ecclesiastical dignitaries in Tabríz prior to His being

sentenced to death, He responds to their questions about
His station and authority by enunciating in resounding
tones that He is the Qá'im:

> I am, I am, I am the Promised One! I am the One Whose
> name you have for a thousand years invoked, at Whose
> mention you have risen, Whose advent you have longed to
> witness, and the hour of Whose Revelation you have prayed
> God to hasten. Verily, I say, it is incumbent upon the peoples
> of both the East and the West to obey My word, and to
> pledge allegiance to My person.[26]

He further clarifies the distinction between Himself as an
Apostle of God and the station of other men:

> The substance wherewith God hath created Me is not the clay
> out of which others have been formed. He hath conferred
> upon Me that which the worldly-wise can never compre-
> hend, nor the faithful discover . . . I am one of the sustaining
> pillars of the Primal Word of God.[27]

At the same time, He clearly attributes all His accomplishments to the Will of God working through Him and
states, 'In truth I Myself am the first to bow down before
God and to believe in Him.'[28]

Bahá'u'lláh in His letters to the kings and rulers
similarly speaks with the voice of absolute authority: 'O
Kings of the earth! Give ear unto the Voice of God, calling
from this sublime, this fruit-laden Tree . . .'[29]; and in the
Kitáb-i-Aqdas He states, 'Ye are but vassals, O kings of
the earth! He Who is the King of Kings hath appeared
. . .'[30] At the same time, Bahá'u'lláh acknowledges that all
He says and does is but the Will of God working through
Him:

> This thing is not from Me, but from One Who is Almighty
> and All-Knowing. And He bade Me lift up My voice
> between earth and heaven . . . Not of Mine own volition

have I revealed Myself, but God, of His own choosing, hath manifested Me.[31]

Why Humanity Must Struggle to Understand

Thus, there is an enigmatic quality, an ostensible paradox, a fine subtlety to this process of recognizing divine guidance and authority as conveyed to humanity through the Prophets. Each appearance, however benign its intent, is fraught with its peculiar tests or judgements for the people to whom the Prophet appears, even though that judgement is neither capricious nor arbitrary. Like the testing of students by any competent educator, this judgement has as its animating purpose not solely to determine who has achieved enlightenment and growth, but to assist the student in acquiring those attributes. Thus, in His letter to Muḥammad Sháh, the Báb states, 'If it were My will, I would disclose to Your Majesty all things; but I have not done this, nor will I do it, that the Truth may be distinguished from aught else beside it . . .'[32]

A teacher of mathematics withholds the answers to a problem not to be cruel nor to determine who is already knowledgeable, but to induce students to learn the process by which the answer can be obtained; not to have the students memorize the answers to specific problems, but to acquire the tools for solving subsequent problems. Similarly, the test imposed by a coach or trainer by which an athlete is challenged to exceed his or her present capacity, though sometimes a painful process, is not intended as punishment or even to see how capable the athlete is at present, but to increase and expand the athlete's capacity by stressing the body beyond its present condition.

Therefore, Bahá'u'lláh notes throughout the *Kitáb-i-Íqán* that there is a wisdom and a justice in the concealment of the Manifestations. One example He cites of such divine ingenuity by which God challenges us is the virgin birth of Christ. Bahá'u'lláh describes the consternation of Mary when she discovered that, though sinless, she had conceived a child out of wedlock. Bahá'u'lláh then exhorts us to 'meditate upon this most great convulsion, this grievous test',[33] both for Mary and for those who would be challenged to recognize the Messiah in the personage of one born from questionable circumstances. Bahá'u'lláh then concludes, 'Behold how contrary are the ways of the Manifestations of God, as ordained by the King of creation, to the ways and desires of men!'[34] And elsewhere in the same discussion He exhorts us to 'ponder in thy heart the commotion which God stirreth up. Reflect upon the strange and manifold trials with which He doth test His servants.'[35] He also assures us that as we come 'to comprehend the essence of these divine mysteries', we will appreciate the subtle wisdom in this educational process and 'grasp the purpose of God, the divine Charmer, the Best-Beloved'.[36]

We might suppose that this distinction between the spiritual station and powers and the ostensible physical limitations of the Prophet would be a problem only for those who attain the physical presence of the Manifestation, particularly family members and others who see the Prophet as vulnerable to the various misfortunes that befall human beings – illness, injury, grief, pain, suffering. But even for those who must accept the station of the Prophet after His passing, this distinction is also important. For example, any consideration of the authority of the laws and admonitions of a Manifestation depends on the spiritual station one attributes to the Prophet.

The point is that while phenomenal events associated with the lives of the Prophets may substantiate their station by fulfilling ancient prophecies or traditions or by demonstrating to those present some other-worldly power, the principal abiding proof of the Manifestation is the Revelation itself, the word made flesh. Any other proofs, while important clues to some, may just as easily be deterrents to others.

Recognition and Ecclesiastical Authority

If the judgement or testing of the individual in recognizing the Manifestation is difficult, it is a sublime irony of religious history that it is an infinitely more grievous test and judgement for the ecclesiastics who function as guardians of the previous dispensation.

We might suppose that these scholars, as students of religion and as spiritual guides to their people, would have all the more reason to be informed, to be wary about the prophecies, the attributes and the traditions that would distinguish the Prophet. Furthermore, since they should be well versed in the history of their own religion, we might suppose they would be particularly cautious about repeating the same sort of errors that the learned ones of the previous dispensation committed in rejecting the Manifestation they presently follow. But having a vested interest in the status quo, in the perpetuity of their own institutionalized authority, the ecclesiastics usually find it more difficult than any of the rest of the populace to be receptive.

Consequently, it has been a consistent pattern in the continuity of religion that the ecclesiastics of every dispensation are most often at the forefront in persecuting the next Manifestation during His lifetime and in deterring the birth of the new Revelation:

> Leaders of religion, in every age, have hindered their people from attaining the shores of eternal salvation, inasmuch as they held the reins of authority in their mighty grasp. Some

for the lust of leadership, others through want of knowledge and understanding, have been the cause of the deprivation of the people.[37]

Thus it was the learned Pharisees and Sadducees who scoffed at Christ, while a lowly illiterate fisherman became His first follower and the standard bearer of His Faith. Likewise, the most vituperative denunciation of Islam as a pagan movement came from the ecclesiastics and scholars of the Christian Faith. In recent history, the most vehement persecutors of the Bábí and Bahá'í religions have been the Muslim clergy. There is no doubt that, apart from His statement that the scriptures are now available to all, Bahá'u'lláh's abolition of a professional clergy responds to this persistent problem.

Of course, the clergy of past dispensations are faced with a particularly difficult decision. If the one before them truly is an Apostle come in fulfilment of their own prophecies and expectations, they are obliged to discard their own authority and follow Him. If He is not, it is their duty, as they understand it, to deter the claimant as a blasphemer, a perverter of the true Faith of God. Perhaps what is most challenging to the ecclesiastics, however, is that the Manifestation, though duly respectful, shows no obeisance to their authority since He is well aware that it is they who should be helping Him prepare the believers for the new Revelation. Therefore, the Manifestation does not await their approval before He begins to institute the new law. Furthermore, because the new law may abrogate or radically alter the old, the ecclesiastics may well perceive the new Revelation as striking at the heart of their own beliefs, something Bahá'u'lláh alludes to as the 'cleaving of the heaven' of the previous religion:

In like manner, strive thou to comprehend from these lucid, these powerful, conclusive, and unequivocal statements the

meaning of the 'cleaving of the heaven' – one of the signs that
must needs herald the coming of the last Hour, the Day of
Resurrection. As He hath said: 'When the heaven shall be
cloven asunder.' By 'heaven' is meant the heaven of divine
Revelation, which is elevated with every Manifestation, and
rent asunder with every subsequent one. By 'cloven asunder'
is meant that the former Dispensation is superseded and
annulled. I swear by God! That this heaven being cloven
asunder is, to the discerning, an act mightier than the cleaving
of the skies! Ponder a while. That a divine Revelation which
for years hath been securely established; beneath whose
shadow all who have embraced it have been reared and
nurtured; by the light of whose law generations of men have
been disciplined; the excellency of whose word men have
heard recounted by their fathers; in such wise that human eye
hath beheld naught but the pervading influence of its grace,
and mortal ear hath heard naught but the resounding majesty
of its command – what act is mightier than that such a
Revelation should, by the power of God, be 'cloven asunder'
and be abolished at the appearance of one soul? Reflect, is this
a mightier act than that which these abject and foolish men
have imagined the 'cleaving of the heaven' to mean?[38]

Christ tries to prepare His own followers for such a test
when He alludes to the judgement that will occur with the
advent of the 'Son of Man': 'the sun will be darkened, and
the moon will not give its light, and the stars will fall from
heaven, and the powers of the heavens will be shaken'.[39]
Similarly, Muḥammad uses the same symbolism regarding the Day of Resurrection when each soul will recognize
the divine Reality:

When the Earth with her quaking shall quake
And the Earth shall cast forth her burdens,
And man shall say, What aileth her?
On that day shall she tell out her tidings,

Because thy Lord shall have inspired her.
On that day shall men come forward in throngs to behold
their works.
And whosoever shall have wrought an atom's weight of
good shall behold it,
And whosoever shall have wrought an atom's weight of
evil shall behold it.[40]

Therefore, for those to whom religion has become but superstition or an outworn code of law, the standard by which they necessarily shall judge the advent of a new Manifestation will be the extent to which such an event seems to confirm their own interpretation and expectations, standards which, because the previous dispensation is in a state of decline, will often be faulty. Consequently, their own comfortableness with the new teachings will almost inevitably become the gauge by which they assess the veracity of the Manifestation's claim to Prophethood.

Continuity after the Passing of the Manifestation

While the problems associated with recognition of the Manifestation persist after His passing, though perhaps less encumbered by matters of physical appearance or social circumstances, the most crucial problem afflicting the promulgation of the new revelation involves the succession of authority.

Related to the establishment of an administrative order and a religious edifice are several dilemmas: How are the believers to define their new identity? How are they to create and maintain some authority to safeguard the integrity of the new teachings? How are they to interpret, implement and administer the new law? How are they to respond to conditions not specifically alluded to by the teachings of the Prophet?

Examples from Recent Revelations

In a most general sense, the inherent nature of these problems relating to the creation of a new skin to contain the new wine is demonstrated by what happened when Moses ascended the mountain to converse with God and left the believers under the authority of Aaron. By the time the Manifestation returned, Aaron had acquiesced to the whims of the people, who, deprived of the authoritative presence of Moses, had reverted to their old religious traditions.

Certainly this event dramatically presaged the problems the Jewish people would later encounter in maintaining fidelity to their Covenant, but the episode also calls to mind one of the Hidden Words of Bahá'u'lláh as He considered what problems may befall His own believers after His passing: 'O My Children! I fear lest, bereft of the melody of the dove of heaven, ye will sink back to the shades of utter loss, and, never having gazed upon the beauty of the rose, return to water and clay.'[41] Both the appellation 'children' and the description of them as 'never having gazed upon the beauty of the rose' seem to indicate believers in a primary state of enthralment and attraction. They may have some sense of the authority and station of the Prophet, but they have not as yet become intellectually and spiritually confirmed in this belief. Consequently, like the initial infatuation associated with the Valley of Love as depicted in *The Seven Valleys*, this emotional attraction to the Revelation is liable to error or declination once the sensually perceived source of that attraction is removed – they may return to their former base condition of attraction to 'water and clay', their material or appetitive desires.

In fact, we can, without going into much detail, note the basis for Bahá'u'lláh's fears when we examine the conditions that obtained immediately after the passing of the three Manifestations prior to Bahá'u'lláh. When Christ died, the Apostles were utterly dispirited, confused and lost until they were exhorted to action by Mary Magdalene and confirmed in their beliefs by the vision of the holy spirit among them. Even so, they soon fell to debating what laws they should keep, what identity they had, who had authority to make such decisions, and, not too much later, who or what Christ really was.

As we will discuss in the next chapter, the resulting debates among the disciples marked the beginning of various theological and ecclesiastical divisions within what was to become the Christian church. Consequently, by the time of the advent of Muḥammad, Christianity as a body of belief and as a religious institution bore little resemblance to anything Christ had taught and even less to the spirit of his admonitions regarding His return. Indeed, the Christian church by the time of Muḥammad had much the same sort of dogmatism, orthodoxy, theological confusion, obstinacy and chauvinism that Christ had found so reprehensible in the religious institutions and attitudes of the Pharisaic Jews.

The problem facing Islam was somewhat different. The explication of theological doctrines and the fundamentals of Islamic law were laid out with sufficient clarity in the Qur'án that there was less room for debate about the spiritual station of Muḥammad or the essential laws that should be followed. But the contention over the succession of authority served effectively to distort or pervert much of what Muḥammad had made clear. Furthermore the addition of *ḥadíth*,* sometimes authentic and some-

---

* In Islam *ḥadíth* are 'oral traditions about things which Muḥammad said or did which were handed down for generations before being written. In

times not, together with a body of law derived from the supposedly authoritative utterance of the clergy, in time superseded whatever clarity Muḥammad might have intended for the Qur'án to have or whatever authoritative decisions might have derived from His lesser covenant had it remained intact.

This same pattern persisted after the execution of the Báb in 1850 with the attempt of Mírzá Yaḥyá, at the instigation of Muḥammad 'Alí of Isfahan, to usurp the station of Bahá'u'lláh. Likewise, after the passing of Bahá'u'lláh, Mírzá Muḥammad 'Alí attempted to usurp the authority of 'Abdu'l-Bahá. But because the succession of authority in Bahá'í history is linked by means of authoritative documents, and because the institutions themselves are laid out by the Manifestation Himself, these attempts at usurpation, while causing mischief, did not divert the chain of conferred authority or pervert the designed evolution of the religious edifice.

Has the Plan of God become Diverted?

To cite these examples of how consistently the new wine gets poured into wineskins that are somehow not as new or as fit as they might be, is not to imply in any way that the power and influence of these Revelations is lost or wasted or that the plan of God is somehow altered or diverted. As 'Abdu'l-Bahá points out in *Some Answered Questions*, the reformation of human history and the revitalizing of the planet unleashed with the appearance of these other-worldly beings is not contingent on human response. New ideas and concepts, innovative social structures, advances in learning and in material civilization are

---

Shí'ih Islam, *ḥadíth* about the Imáms were also transmitted (Momen, *A Basic Bahá'í Dictionary* p. 93).

set in motion regardless of how well or poorly the followers of the Prophet construct the religious edifice as the Prophet's poem: '. . . at the time of the appearance of each Manifestation of God extraordinary progress has occurred in the world of minds, thoughts and spirits.'[42]

Stated more accurately, we should not infer from the consistent failure of humanity to utilize to the optimum extent the advent of the new revelation that the revelations of God have been ineffective or that the overall plan of God has been weakened or injured. The failure of the student to use well a plan of education does not injure the educational system; it impedes the progress of the student who chooses not to benefit from the bounties that system might bestow. The well-planned system will eventually succeed in its objectives because, whether we wish it so or not, humanity will come of age and will in time come face to face with the utter pragmatism implicit in the divine guidance of the Prophets.

Nevertheless, there is a short term effect in that the duration of the influence of an individual dispensation and the extent to which the power of a revelation will transform human society are both related to the degree of care and fidelity the followers have in constructing the religious edifice that will give social expression to the spirit of the Prophet's teachings. Bahá'í historian Hasan Balyuzi notes the dual aspects of this historical force as it pertains to the historical influence of Christ and Muḥammad:

> . . . so overwhelming was the power of the spirit released by Jesus of Nazareth and the Arabian Prophet that their Faiths reared and sustained civilizations of untold splendour. We cannot avoid the horrendous chronicles of fratricidal warfare, nor overlook the stained records of oppression, tyranny and intolerance. Of such stuff is history made. Over them, however, shines the devotion of countless millions, who,

through suffering, led mankind in its unceasing march to view more spacious horizons.[43]

What exactly is lost or abused, then, if the followers are not precisely clear about what they should do or how they should do it? Furthermore, how can we judge them harshly if the Manifestation does not give them explicit guidance? Or even more to the point, why did the Manifestations of the past not leave behind documents about succession or a blueprint for the institution, as Bahá'u'lláh did? Surely as divine emissaries they had the capacity to foresee what events would take place after their passing. We can hardly attribute the absence of such guidance to chance or circumstance since, we must presume, these beings who claim to function at divine behest were capable of surmounting whatever circum-stantial obstacles might have seemed to impede their leaving a will or contriving a plan.

Obviously there is a single answer to these questions – that the time in human history had not yet arrived when it was best to do so. Of course, it is equally obvious that this answer is somewhat rhetorical, assuming as it does that God in His justice always does what is best for human education. Therefore, if Manifestations of the past did not give more explicit guidance, it was because somehow humanity would in time benefit from the lessons learned by not having such instruction. In short, it was a test.

And what indeed have we learned, or might we learn in the future, from having collectively experienced those tests and having failed? No doubt a myriad lessons about ourselves and about the divine process which impels us forward. For one thing, we see that without such guidance, we manage to take the gift of divine assistance and change it from a means of human advancement and the attainment of justice to a machine for perpetrating some of the most onerous sorts of injustice, something Bahá'u'lláh notes in the *Hidden Words*:

> Wings have I bestowed upon thee, that thou mayest fly to the realms of mystic holiness and not the regions of satanic fancy. The comb, too, have I given thee that thou mayest dress My raven locks, and not lacerate My throat.[44]

For another, we come to appreciate that however intelligent, eloquent and autonomous we may think we are, without reliance on a divine system of organization we become utterly incapable of knowing what to do with all this subtle learning. Indeed, at the peak of the foremost expression of secular humanism in terms of material and technological advancement, we also find ourselves on the very brink of irreparably damaging the very tree of our existence.

In sum, we learn complete and utter humility regarding our own capacity for self-governance without divine assistance and moral principle, and, most important of all, we learn how absolutely careful we must in the future be in safeguarding the institutions when they are infallibly devised. For we have seen what happens when we make them up as we go along – we consistently poison the well of our advancement so that religion can in time become a pernicious source of evil rather than a source of sustenance and well-being.

This almost inescapable result of religious institutions devised by human invention is perhaps nowhere more apparent than in the historical fact that inevitably the most vehement persecutors, detractors, defamers and impediments to the new Manifestation and the progress of His Revelation are the ecclesiastical authorities of the man-made institution which avows to uphold the previous dispensation. The irony of this, as we have mentioned, is hardly lost on the Manifestations, who inevitably direct their harshest criticism at those who by title and profession are charged with leading the people to truth. Christ, for example, refers to the scribes and Pharisees as 'blind guides',[45] and Bahá'u'lláh addresses those 'that are foolish, yet have a name to be wise!' in the following manner:

> Wherefore do ye wear the guise of shepherds, when inwardly ye have become wolves, intent upon My flock? Ye are even as the star, which riseth ere the dawn, and which, though it seem radiant and luminous, leadeth the wayfarers of My city astray into the paths of perdition.[46]

But of all the unfortunate results that have occurred as a result of the past inadequacies of the religious edifice to safeguard and convey the wine of the new revelation, perhaps the most grievous problem we have inherited results from the problem of antinomianism.

Though most familiar as a Christian doctrine enunciated in the letters of Paul, antinomianism (anti-law) is the idea prevalent in various religions that faith, belief and salvation cannot be induced or sustained by obedience to regulation or to religious authority or through deeds in general. As this idea has been perpetrated through the past centuries of Western Christendom, this same attitude has come to represent the separation of the moral aspect of our lives from the material or practical or social aspects of our existence.

As a result of the present dominance of the world by concepts of materialism spawned by this attitude, a cancerous disease threatens to devour our physical environment as it has already eaten away at the vitals of our cultural heritage, and we now struggle haphazardly to impose some moral perspective on the social and political affairs of a world in which no commonly accepted moral assumptions can now be made.

Because the evolution of this pervasive attitude derives

directly from the influence of the schism between the wine
and the wineskin that takes place in Western European
Christian thought, we might benefit from examining that
evolution in order to understand the Bahá'í perception
about how future events will counteract or cure that
disease and bring about a reunion in the factionalized and
disjointed parts of the human psyche.

5

Adam and Eve Get Divorced

How Christian Antinomianism Begets Western Materialism

To dissociate the administrative principles of the Cause from the purely spiritual and humanitarian teachings would be tantamount to a mutilation of the body of the Cause, a separation that can only result in the disintegration of its component parts, and the extinction of the Faith itself.[1]

Shoghi Effendi

If the revealed truth of the Christian religion is represented as the new wine and the Christian laws and institutions the wineskin intended to contain and convey that wine to the believers, the emergence of antinomianism early in Christian thought might well represent the initial tear in that skin. In part an understandable reaction against the rigid orthodoxy and attention to law which had become the heart and soul of Judaism, this Christian orientation eventually disparaged the belief in any sort of causal relationship between deeds and salvation. In time, this attitude became compounded and confirmed by non-Christian influences, such as Manichaeism and gnosticism. Much of Christian theology came to perceive physical reality as injurious to spiritual development. Social concerns became regarded as largely irrelevant to the preparation for the life to come.

While there were various attempts in the evolution of Christian thought to find some synthesis between one's earthly life and one's spiritual aspirations, none was lastingly successful, and the end result was that modern Western Christendom inherited a perception of the human condition as a constant war between the higher spiritual self and the lower bestial or appetitive self. Instead of perceiving the interplay between belief and action that we have thus far discussed so extensively as delineating human purpose (or at least as fostering the goal of an expanded sense of self), the pervasive outlook that established the foundation of contemporary European and American attitudes perceived an antipathy between these twin aspects of self. This antipathy became expressed overtly in the schisms between science and religion, between church and state, between social reform and moral perspective.

The long-range effect of this process has been the emergence in Western civilization of a cancerous materialism that has metastasized to infect and afflict the entire fabric of the global community. Related to this condition, this unplanned child of Christian thought, is the present schism between morality and any system capable of managing the practical affairs of the human social reality. It would seem, then, that if we are to have a reunion of what have become the disjointed parts of ourselves, it will result not from some abstract notion of goodness, but from our coming to appreciate in the most fundamental ways that such a synthesis is necessitated by the exigencies of our own survival.

To understand how we came to this state of disintegration and fragmentation is to discover that this schism was not the natural course of events. This sequence of causality was, in fact, an aberration of our natural condition brought about by centuries of ever more entrenched dogma, by the perversion of religious truth, not through the unwisdom of applying religious truth to practical reality or the incursion of theocracy.

Consequently, before we presume to examine the Bahá'í contention that the Revelation of Bahá'u'lláh contains divine guidance about how to re-integrate the twin forces of revealed truth with social action by conveying a choice new wine in a carefully wrought new skin, we would do well to review how civilization became disintegrated in the first place. For only by understanding how this disease occurred can we avoid its recurrence and appreciate the efficacy of the cure.

The Origins of Christian Antinomianism

The Foundation for Contention

In his book *The Light Shineth in Darkness*, Udo Schaefer adds his perspective as a Bahá'í to the long-standing debate in Christianity about the dispute between Paul and the Apostles regarding the law as it applied to newly-converted Christians. This debate centres around the so-called antinomian (anti-law) portions of Paul's epistles which can be interpreted to imply the complete irrelevance of one's actions to one's spiritual condition, especially as this condition pertains to salvation. Certainly it was this interpretation that inspired St Augustine (354–430) to pen his influential *De Doctrina Christiana*, upholding the concept of the monastic or ascetic life as the most appropriate method for practising the Christian ideal. It was this same interpretation of Pauline doctrine that gave theological credence to Luther's rebellion against various beliefs and practices of the Roman Church, but particularly against the notion that 'justification' or salvation was possible only through the sanctioned or authoritative acts of atonement as prescribed by the Church.

To a great extent, therefore, the entire issue of antinomianism in Christianity revolves around the figure of Paul, so that for those who have come to believe there is no relationship between deeds and salvation, he has become the infallible spokesman. But for some who uphold the doctrine of the inextricable relationship between belief and action, he is perceived as the perverter of true Christianity, much as Shí'í Muslims stigmatize 'Umar as having usurped the conferred authority of the Imáms.

Schaefer espouses the latter attitude when he states, 'Jesus conferred authority on Peter, Paul usurped it.'[2] Schaefer asserts that the Christian religion has become based not on the Gospel of Jesus but on a 'gospel about Jesus' which emphasizes the teachings of Paul as they concern the 'the babe in the cradle and the Redeemer on the Cross'.[3] Schaefer then explains how most of the central doctrines of Christianity have their basis in Paul's perversion or diversion of the intended purpose of Christ's ministry. He further attests that as a result of this unfortunate usurpation by Paul, Christianity opposes the fundamental verities that Christ's ministry was intended to uphold and clarify.

> Measured by the standard of Bahá'u'lláh's revelation, the Pauline doctrine of Justification, the doctrine of Original Sin, the doctrine of the Holy Trinity, the sacramentalization of the Christian religion, the whole Church plan of salvation – which not only contradicts the Jewish understanding of God but was also strongly repudiated by the revelation of God which succeeded Christianity – these are a deformation of Jesus's teaching.[4]

Of central concern to Schaefer is the antinomian theme of Paul's letters which, Schaefer contends, effectively destroys the vital relationship between Judaism and Christianity so that the continuity of revelation (perhaps the major theme of the Qur'án six hundred years later) was effectively ignored or obliterated. For while the Apostles were attempting to keep intact those Judaic laws not altered by Christ, Paul was undermining this effort.

But though the contradictions between the Bahá'í concept of continuous or progressive revelation and what has become a standard Christian belief in the uniqueness of Christ are undeniable, it does not necessarily follow that these distinctions result from Paul's perversion of true Christianity. For one thing, if Schaefer's contention is correct, it is extremely curious that there is no hint of condemnation of Paul anywhere in the authoritative writings of the Bahá'í Faith. On the contrary, every mention of Paul is either laudatory or else ascribing to him authoritative utterance.*

We might accept that Bahá'u'lláh or 'Abdu'l-Bahá could have omitted mentioning the ill-advised or corrupt inclinations of a prominent religious figure of note, but it is extremely difficult to accept that they would praise someone who had served to pervert the course of Christianity from its intended goal, much less allude to him as a 'most faithful servant'.

If Paul is not blameworthy, then one of two things must

---

* In *Epistle to the Son of the Wolf* Bahá'u'lláh cites St Paul's letter to the Romans in order to impress upon the Muslim cleric of Isfahan, Shaykh Muhammad-Taqíy-i-Najafí (the Son of the Wolf), the verity that all earthly power derives from the power of God: 'In the Epistle to the Romans Saint Paul hath written: "Let every soul be subject unto the higher powers. For there is no power but of God; the powers that be are ordained of God"' (p. 91).

Less inferential is 'Abdu'l-Bahá's lofty praise of Paul. In explaining how we should not presume to judge the spiritual condition of others, 'Abdu'l-Bahá in *Paris Talks* states: 'How many men who have seemed saint-like to follow. Either the antinomian tenor of Christianity is not at odds with Bahá'í belief, or else the sort of anti-nomianism which is at odds with Bahá'í belief derives not from Paul's intended meaning, but from erroneous inter-pretations of Paul's words.

As we have already noted, because the relationship of physical and social action to spiritual transformation is such a major theme in the Bahá'í writings, it might seem we could dismiss the first of these two possibilities fairly quickly. Expressed in Christian terminology, the Bahá'í response to what is espoused as the Pauline doctrine of salvation by faith in Christ's martyrdom might be stated as follows: it is insufficient to accept Christ as Lord and Saviour unless one also obeys the laws and exhortations Christ revealed, since these two responses are inter-dependent and inextricable. As we noted in the first chapter, Bahá'u'lláh enunciates this theme throughout His revealed writings, stating that 'the essence of faith is fewness of words and abundance of deeds . . .'[5]

Christ's Statements to the Contrary

Perhaps Christ's most powerful treatment of this same theme is to be found in the Sermon on the Mount, the preamble to which are the beatitudes and His rather emphatic allusion to progressive revelation. Here He indicates His function in advancing the law of the previous Manifestation and the imperative that those who profess to be a follower must demonstrate fidelity by obedience to the law:

---

their friends have fallen into the greatest humiliation. Think of Judas Iscariot; he began well, but remember his end! On the other hand, Paul, the Apostle, was in his early life an enemy of Christ, whilst later he became His most faithful servant' (p. 147).

Think not that I have come to abolish the law and the prophets; I have come not to abolish them but to fulfil them. For truly, I say to you, till heaven and earth pass away, not an iota, not a dot, will pass from the law until all is accomplished. Whoever then relaxes one of the least of these commandments and teaches men so, shall be called least in the kingdom of heaven; but he who does them and teaches them shall be called great in the kingdom of heaven. For I tell you, unless your righteousness exceeds that of the scribes and Pharisees, you will never enter the kingdom of heaven.[6]

There are at least two possible interpretations here. Christ is admonishing His hearers to be faithful to the Judaic law until 'all is accomplished' (i.e. His ministry is complete), or He is referring to law in the generic sense of the eternal and changeless laws of God. In either case, one implication is apparent – it is all well and good for them to recognize the Messiah, but unless their personal behaviour is changed by this experience, they have not really accomplished much. In fact, salvation itself ('the kingdom of heaven') will be available only to believers who have manifested 'righteousness' (spiritualized actions) in daily action to the degree that their conduct is superior to that of the scribes and Pharisees, the upholders of the old law.

Most important, however, Christ then explains what their new behaviour is to be, comparing His new directives with the old laws as He does so. Some of the Judaic laws He intensifies. Where it had been illegal to kill, He forbids them to be angry with others. Where before adultery had been forbidden, He indicts lustful thoughts. Some laws He abrogates or modifies: where before divorce was allowed, Christ permits it only 'on the ground of unchastity'.[7] Some laws He adds: in place of Mosaic tribal retributive justice (an eye for an eye), He admonishes His followers to turn the other cheek.

He concludes this lengthy discourse by cautioning that

it is not sufficient to profess faith in order to achieve salvation: 'Not every one who says unto me, "Lord, Lord", shall enter the kingdom of heaven, but he who does the will of my Father who is in heaven.'[8] Even more specifically, He describes what will happen to their faith should they not follow His commandments regarding personal conduct:

> And every one who hears these words of mine and does not do them will be like a foolish man who built his house upon the sand; and the rain fell, and the floods came, and the winds blew and beat against that house, and it fell; and great was the fall of it.[9]

In the context of our previous discussion, Christ's allusion here to deeds as the foundation for building a strong edifice would seem to symbolize clearly that deeds or a changed behaviour (clothing the hearing of spiritual truth with the garment of action) will become the basis by which the new religion will be established.

As one of the most weighty and well-known confirmations of Christ's admonition regarding the relationship between moral comportment and salvation, James also explicates the relationship between deeds and faith. In fact, the animating theme of his epistle is that the followers of Christ should be 'be doers of the word, and not hearers only':

> But be doers of the word, and not hearers only, deceiving yourselves. For if any one is a hearer of the word and not a doer, he is like a man who observes his natural face in a mirror; for he observes himself and goes away and at once forgets what he was like. But he who looks into the perfect law, the law of liberty, and perseveres, being no hearer that forgets but a doer that acts, he shall be blessed in his doing.[10]

After reminding them of some of the specific laws of Christ and exhorting them to be exemplars of this revealed instruction, James issues what is the most memorable and powerful statement about works and faith. Here James refers to the 'royal law' (by implication the eternal laws of God as revealed through Christ), and describes works not as simply an embellishment or demonstration of faith, but as an organic and integral part of faith:

> If you really fulfil the royal law, according to the scripture, 'you shall love your neighbour as yourself', you do well . . . What does it profit, my brethren, if a man says he hath faith and has not works? Can faith save him? . . . So faith, if it has no works, is dead.[11]

James further emphasizes this theme by implying that they should pay heed to exemplifying their beliefs more through action than through words: 'Who is a wise man and understanding among you? By his good life let him show his works in the meekness of wisdom.'[12]

Misunderstandings of Paul's Meaning

Since these pronouncements of the inextricable relationship between action and salvation, between knowing and worshipping, are unmistakably clear, we must presume that Christian antinomianism derives from a misunderstanding of Paul, together with other influences outside Christianity. Indeed, Peter indicates that confusion about Paul's sometimes abstruse doctrinal discourses was already occurring, and he cautions the believers to be wary of those who were using Paul's writings to support their own ambition or licentiousness:

> So also our beloved brother Paul wrote to you according to the wisdom given him, speaking of this as he does in all his letters. There are some things in them hard to understand, which the ignorant and unstable twist to their own destruction, as they do the other scriptures.[13]

Peter goes on to warn the followers to 'beware lest you be carried away with the error of lawless men and lose your own stability'.[14] Here he implies, as does James, that some converts were taking Paul's antinomian statements as a licence to abdicate moral behaviour.

Of course, the importance of this issue centred around whether or not the followers of Christ were reformed Jews or founders of a new religion. In effect, at the heart of the controversy about the relationship between law and salvation was their perception of the relationship between Christianity and Judaism. Therefore, when Paul came to the second conference at Jerusalem, some of the Pharisaic converts resisted Paul's liberality in allowing Gentiles to become Christian without being circumcised, saying, 'It is necessary to circumcise them, and to charge them to keep the law of Moses.'[15] Peter, who through a trance had already been informed about changes in the law,[16] and who had further been given the authority to teach the Gentiles, confirmed Paul's modification of the requirements:

> Now therefore why do you make trial of God, by putting a yoke upon the neck of the disciples which neither our fathers nor we have been able to bear? But we believe that we shall be saved through the grace of the Lord Jesus, just as they will.[17]

James as president of the church also rendered judgement that 'we should not trouble those of the Gentiles who turn to God, but should write to them to abstain from the pollutions of idols and from unchastity and from what is strangled and from blood'.[18]

Paul later saw fit to liberate converts even from some of these constraints, affirming, 'What God hath cleansed, you must not call common.'[19] But Paul also condemned as unnecessary the whole concept of compliance with law as the basis for salvation, stating that the law is neither a sufficient nor a necessary means for attaining 'justification' or salvation. His corollary to this assertion is the often repeated notion of the sufficiency of faith, though he never defines the term *faith* very decisively or exactly. For example, Paul affirms that 'a man is justified by faith apart from works of law',[20] that 'no man is justified before God by the law',[21] and that 'Christ redeemed us from the curse of the law'.[22]

Taken as a whole, then, Paul's antinomian polemics might seem to imply the exact opposite of what Christ and James describe when they portray works as both a sign of faith and an integral part of faith, the 'completion' of faith, as James calls it. It is for this reason that the writings of Paul would later be employed by reformers such as Luther and Calvin to refute the idea of deeds as causally related to salvation.

Paul himself never states that deeds have no relevance to faith or conviction. His point inevitably relates to the Judaic (really the Pharisaic) approach to 'justification', the idea that simply following a code of behaviour without recognition of the Manifestation would be sufficient to bring about spiritual transformation. His point in this context would seem to confirm Bahá'u'lláh's own statement that 'Neither is acceptable without the other'.[23] For example, Paul notes that Abraham's willingness to sacrifice Isaac was a dramatic demonstration of righteousness – without His belief in God, Abraham would never have considered such an action. In short, recognition of divine authority preceded the deed.

A noteworthy point is that Paul's own life testifies eloquently to his belief in the relationship between belief and action – how actions confirm and complete faith. As Joseph Fitzmyer observes, Paul's concept of faith clearly implies service as an inextricable part of the process of being Christian:

. . . his full sense of faith demands that the Christian manifest in his conduct his basic commitment to Christ through deeds of love. 'In union with Christ Jesus neither circumcision nor the lack of it means anything, but only faith action through love' (Gal 5:6). This is why Paul continually exhorts his Christian converts to the practice of all sorts of good deeds.[24]

Another worthwhile observation in this connection is that after one discussion on the principle of works,[25] Paul asks rhetorically if by these observations he is implying that they should 'overthrow the law by this faith?' 'By no means! On the contrary, we uphold the law.'[26] Nor does Paul ever imply that the justification through 'faith' is a blind inductive leap; rather he portrays a process of justification which involves understanding and accepting the station, authority and sacrificial martyrdom of Christ.

Thus Paul never dissevers deeds from belief, whether as an index to one's spiritual transformation or as a means of acquiring certitude. Most generally he is announcing a radically new orientation towards spiritual enlightenment, a religion that is not legalistic. He is also restating what Christ so often affirmed, that belief or faith is, first of all, a matter of attraction to spiritual attributes, an attraction which, if it is confirmed, will result in changed behaviour. Therefore, when Paul explains that the deeds without the recognition of the Manifestation are not sufficient, he would seem to imply that faith is possible only through God's grace in sending His Apostle in spite of human perversity.

Like Paul, the Bahá'í writings, while exalting the ordinances of God as the means by which 'the sweet-smelling savour of My garment can be smelled' and as one means by which 'the standards of Victory will be planted upon the highest peaks',[27] never imply that salvation is earned, that one is saved by virtue of some quantity of acts done 'under the law'. The inextricable relationship between belief and action is operant in this life, but one's spiritual transformation is always the end result of the beneficence, forgiveness and assistance of God.

There is another noteworthy point in this. When Paul refers to the 'law' and 'works of the law', he is using connotatively-loaded terms. His audience was well aware that Paul was alluding to the Judaic law, not to Christ's own directives nor to the concept of deeds as relevant to spiritual transformation. Paul makes this clear in one sense when he refers to the law as the tools of the Judaic religion that served to prepare followers for the coming of the Messiah. He explains that the old law had a vital function in the progressive enlightenment of humanity; it was 'added because of transgressions'[28] and thereby safeguarded religious people from a waywardness that would have prevented them from recognizing the Messiah: 'the law was our custodian until Christ came.'[29]

So it is that when Paul calls Christ 'the end of the law', he means that Christ is the 'goal' or 'objective' of the law. The old law has completed its function by guiding the faithful to the Messiah. Now the new law is operant.

The Contention between Paul and the Apostles

The contention between Paul and the 'pillars' of the church regarding what constraints should be laid upon new converts cannot be so easily explained away. Here we cannot dismiss differences as a matter of interpretation. The debate between Paul and Peter at Antioch was real and, as Schmithals describes the confrontation, at times 'unfortunate'.[30]

> But when Cephas [Peter] came to Antioch I opposed him to his face, because he stood condemned . . . But when I saw that they were not straightforward about the truth of the

gospel, I said to Cephas before them all, 'If you, though a Jew, live like a Gentile and not like a Jew, how can you compel the Gentiles to live like Jews?' We ourselves, who are Jews by birth and not Gentile sinners, yet who know that a man is not justified by works of the law but through faith in Jesus Christ, even we have believed in Christ Jesus, in order to be justified by faith in Christ, and not by works of the law, because by works of the law shall no one be justified.[31]

There are at least two possible explanations for what is occurring in these confrontations. The first is that these debates were a difficult period of working out a new identity and the fundamental doctrines for the new faith. Whether Paul travelled to Jerusalem[32] to obtain sanction for his ministry or for the sake of church unity as Schmithals believes,[33] the end result seems to be a vindication of Paul's activity. Were Paul trying to wreck the church, establish his own special brand of Christianity, or pervert the proper course of the new Faith, we can presume his methods and doctrines would not have been sanctioned.

But Paul had already been granted authority to spread his gospel among the 'uncircumcised' by Peter, John and James, the so-called pillars of the church. Furthermore, when the Apostles reconsidered what requirements should be made for new converts, they themselves ultimately acceded to Paul's wisdom. 'Abdu'l-Bahá likewise vindicates Paul's alterations to the law when He explains how religious laws must change to befit that changed nature of the human organism to which religion ministers:

> For example, in the time of Moses, His law was conformed and adapted to the conditions of the time; but in the days of Christ these conditions had changed and altered to such an extent that the Mosaic Law was no longer suited and adapted to the needs of mankind; and it was, therefore, abrogated. Thus it was that Christ broke the Sabbath and forbade

divorce. After Christ four disciples, among whom were Peter and Paul, permitted the use of animal food forbidden by the Bible, except the eating of those animals which had been strangled, or which were sacrificed to idols, and of blood. They also forbade fornication.[34]

'Abdu'l-Bahá further observes that later Paul even relented on the first three of these laws and 'only maintained the prohibition of fornication'.[35] He concludes that 'these alterations and this abrogation are due to the impossibility of comparing the time of Christ with that of Moses. The conditions and requirements in the later period were entirely changed and altered. The former laws were, therefore, abrogated.'[36]

But lest we consider Paul's confrontation with the Apostles as inappropriate and unbecoming behaviour, given Christ's ordinances regarding the spirit of Christian fellowship, we might find useful an analogous situation in Bahá'í history which also illustrates the dramatic events that accompany the transition from one dispensation to another.

The scene was the conference at Badasht in the year 1848. The Báb was imprisoned in Chihríq, and Bahá'u'lláh, then a follower of the Báb and one of the most revered leaders of the Bábí Faith, 'unobtrusively yet effectually presided over that conference, and guided and controlled its proceedings'.[37] The assemblage of eighty-one disciples from various provinces included the most prominent Bábí teachers and had as its primary purpose the discussion about what was to be the relationship between this new revelation and the Islamic dispensation that preceded it. Their most specific concern had to do with how they should respond to Islamic law and tradition.

Though unknown to the other believers, Quddús and Ṭáhirih, two of the 'Letters of the Living' and prominent

Bábí teachers, under the direction of Bahá'u'lláh feigned a severe quarrel focused on the question of whether they were to uphold the 'sanctity of the ordinances of Islám'[38] or sanction the 'annulment of the fundamental statutes of the Islámic Faith'.[39]* Quddús enunciated the conservative view, that they should continue observing Islamic law. In opposition to this position was Ṭáhirih, who advocated a break with the Islamic past as a dramatic recognition of the Báb's station as a Manifestation of God equal in rank to Muḥammad.

The dramatic climax of the conference occurred one day when Bahá'u'lláh invited these two exponents of opposing factions to His tent, ostensibly to continue their debate. Suddenly, to the utter dismay and consternation of the believers, Ṭáhirih entered unveiled before the assemblage, a severe violation of Islamic law. Quddús appeared so angered by this affront that he gestured with his sword as if he might strike her down. Undeterred, Ṭáhirih arose, and, without the least premeditation and in a language strikingly resembling that of the Qur'án, delivered a fervid and eloquent appeal to the remnant of the assembly, ending it with this bold assertion: 'I am the Word which the Qá'im is to utter, the Word which shall put to flight the chiefs and nobles of the earth!'[40]

Though some were unable to withstand the shock of this revolutionary act, the premeditated purpose of the conference was dramatically achieved. The remaining believers now understood that this Faith was not a purification of Islam, not a revision of past laws and tradition, but a new revelation with new laws, new expectations, and imposing on them a new identity, something each of them acknowledged by receiving a new name.

---

* For a confirmation of this pre-arranged drama, see Shoghi Effendi, *The Dawn-Breakers*, p. 294, n. 1.

Whether or not the conferences at Jerusalem and Antioch were also premeditated drama to allow the followers to examine their new identity and to break with the restrictions of their past traditions and attitudes, the situations are strategically the same. Therefore, we can derive from the points of similitude several crucial observations about the nature of continuity which the concept of progressive revelation dictates.

First, continuity and fulfilment imply not a reworking of the old laws and institutions, but a dramatic break with the old law, an entirely new wineskin for the new wine. It is for this reason that the advent of the new Manifestation so severely tests the expectations of those who are faithful to the old law.

Another related observation we can make regarding this process of transition is that Schaefer's claim that the sort of Jewish Christianity which he describes as being destroyed by Paul's altering of Christ's intended fulfilment of Judaic law seems unfounded. When Christ broke the law of the Sabbath, He was committing an act that the Jewish community would have found as shocking as Ṭáhirih's removal of her veil. Such dramatic expressions of change and transition were not accidents, but tests and judgements intended to force the followers of the previous dispensation to examine their beliefs.

For example, discussing the consternation caused when Muḥammad changed the Qiblih from Jerusalem to the Ka'bih, Bahá'u'lláh states that this was not a strategically necessary action in any common sense, not really a logical decision, but a dramatic test for those who might profess belief:

> God caused not this turmoil, but to test and prove His servants. Otherwise, He, the ideal King, could easily have left the Qiblih unchanged, and could have caused Jerusalem to remain the Point of Adoration unto His Dispensation,

thereby withholding not from that holy city the distinction of acceptance which had been conferred upon it.[41]

Each new revelation, in other words, necessarily departs from the outmoded symbols, methods and institutions that have become associated with the previous stage of human development. For Paul, the most detrimental and odious remnant of the dead or ineffectual past was the mechanical nature of Judaic law. It is in this same vein that Christ, Muḥammad and Bahá'u'lláh so often employ the image of resurrection (the reanimation of dead bodies or institutions) to refer to the process of spiritual awakening that occurs with the advent of a new dispensation.

How much Paul was influenced in his thinking or in his style of argumentation by his own past, as many have noted, is for our purposes largely irrelevant. Neither can we fault him for what has been done with his teachings by others. Certainly we cannot attribute to Paul responsibility for the parade of theologians who gradually made Christianity unrecognizable from anything Christ or the Apostles might have had in mind. Therefore it is to other influences we must turn if we are to discover in the evolution of Christian antinomianism the seeds of contemporary attitudes about the division between the spiritual and material world, this divorce between the Evian self and the Adamic self.

The Further Development of the Schism between the Twin Duties

By itself, Paul's emphasis on salvation as a thing of the spirit might not have fostered the later chauvinism in Christianity which interpreted the advent of Christ as a unique and unparalleled divine intervention in human history, thereby severing Christian beliefs from the more inclusive perspective that exists in Judaism and Islam. But as Schaefer notes, Paul's apologetics were also used (or abused) in what became the pivotal theological dilemma of Christianity, Christology – the argument about the spiritual station of Christ.

The Problem of Christology

The book of John begins enigmatically, 'In the beginning was the Word, and the Word was with God, and the Word was God.'[42] This Johannine idea of Christ as divine Logos, pre-existent and eternal, was coupled with Paul's emphasis on Christ's redemptive martyrdom and resurrection as sufficient recompense to justify a fallen humanity. Many Christian thinkers further inferred that Christ was divine essence incarnate. In effect, the two ideas became causally linked in the following manner: if God had become incarnate this one time to redeem humanity, then any presumption that our own meagre deeds are also necessary or relevant should be deemed complete hubris.

Neither Christ nor His apostles ever asserted that Christ was God. This inference took several hundred years to evolve into doctrine, one of the most significant milestones in that process being the Council of Nicaea in 325 AD. The so-called Antiochene school (the church at Antioch) had followed the interpretation suggested in the Gospel according to Mark that Christ was inspired, filled with the Holy Spirit beginning with His baptism in the Jordan. According to this view, Christ was essentially human but made aware, given a mission by God and empowered by the Holy Spirit.

An opposing view followed by the so-called Alexandrian school (the church and theologians at Alexandria) was based in large part on the description of Christ in the Gospel of John, that Christ was the Eternal Word of God become flesh. Thus, Christ was not a human receptacle filled with divine inspiration but heavenly power assuming a human form. A third alternative of some intermediary station or creation – Christ as Apostle or Manifestation – was largely ignored.*

As the controversy grew, the first ecumenical council of the Christian Church was called in 325 AD by the Emperor Constantine I who hoped the synod would put an end to this noisome quarrel so that he might adopt the church for his political purposes of unifying the Roman Empire.† But almost as soon as he had seized upon the religion as a source of unity, he realized that the religion he had adopted was itself divided, especially regarding the crucial matter of Christology. Accordingly, Constantine convened and presided over the Council of Nicaea in an effort to reconcile these differences, though he himself was not yet a Christian.

The synod proceeded as follows. An Alexandrian presbyter named Arius had asserted that the Lord Christ who had suffered and wept and died could not logically be the same as the First Cause of all creation who is clearly beyond such limitations. Opposed to his view was the Trinitarian doctrine, particularly as espoused by Athanasius, a doctrine that the Father, the Son and the Holy Ghost are

---

* Some interpretations of the Trinitarian doctrine may be employed to imply such an intermediary station, but this interpretation was not in the mainstream of Christian thought.

† With the Edict of Milan in 313, the severe persecution of Christianity had come to an end, and when Constantine became sole ruler in 324, he saw in Christianity (which had been a *de facto* force of rebellion and destruction for a pagan Rome) a potentially unifying and organizing force: it could provide a solidarity that breached so many boundaries of ethnicity. Constantine in his fight for the Milvian Bridge outside Rome placed the

three distinct Persons, but one God. To express this concept, the council, against the strong objections of some, adopted the non-scriptural term *homo-ousios* (of one, or of the same essence) to signify the absolute equality of Christ with God.

At one point the debate became so heated that the aged Arius was struck in the face when he arose to speak. Others ran out of the chamber rather than hear what they considered to be heretical doctrine. But in time the Antiochene forces prevailed, and the emperor, anxious to preserve the Empire, sustained the Trinitarian position.

The ecclesiastical authority of the Church thus became permanently fused forever with political aims, controversy and agenda. The Church fathers were no longer concerned primarily with ministering to the needs of the faithful or discovering how the religious life as enunciated by Christ could best be understood and implemented. But more significantly, the fundamental idea of Christ as fulfilling and continuing the teachings of Moses, as being part of a continuous divine process, was replaced by a chauvinistic and esoteric notion of the Advent of Christ as a unique expression of divine intervention and grace to save the fallen race of humankind. In addition, the very theology that Christ had tried to disentangle and clarify became instead a thing of mystery, the resolution of which was left in the hands of ecclesiastical scholars and authorities. The religion which Christ had entrusted to a simple unlearned fisherman had thus become the exclusive property of an elite and often self-serving coterie of ecclesiastics who, in their own way, were no less rigid or dogmatic than the Pharisees who had condemned Christ to death.

Christian monogram on the shields and banners of his troops and claimed that the God of the Christians had assisted his cause.

The Seeds of Asceticism

In addition to the subtle but profound way in which the question of Christology seemed to confirm the antinomian tenor of Pauline Christianity, there were several other forces which further severed the Church edifice from the spirit and substance of Christ's revelation. Among the most important of these were Gnosticism and Manichaeism.*

Gnosticism, which derived its name from the Greek word *gnosis* (knowledge), was a syncretistic philosophy that replaced the orthodox Christian notion of faith with a belief in the individual's ability to acquire a specialized knowledge of divinity. According to the gnostics, the soul of man dwells in a physical body that is alien to his spiritual purposes and antithetical to his spiritual development. Highly individualistic, dualistic and pessimistic (believing that matter itself is evil), the gnostics rejected the notion of the Gospel as the fulfilment of prophecy and the idea of the historical disclosure of God. Marcion of Pontus (died *c.* 160) in particular adopted Paul's statements about justification (salvation) through grace, as opposed to the Old Testament notion of obedience to law. He also taught that the Old Testament derived from an inferior and vengeful God of justice, and He further held that the idea of the Old Testament as disclosing a continuous divine revelation was a distortion and corruption of the texts.

Another influence on this evolving schism was Manichaeism, which takes its name from Mani, a third century Iranian prophet. A form of Gnosticism, Manichaeism also perceived the physical condition as contrary to the essentially spiritual nature of man. It affirmed that as we come

---

* Interestingly, both of these philosophies may have their roots in traditions derived from Zoroastrianism in Persia.

to know our true selves, we perceive ourselves as strangers to the physical environment, and we also come to realize that God, as truth and goodness, is also alien to this condition and could not have created it. Consequently, there must necessarily have been an opposing evil force which created this corrupt environment.*

Here we find the beginnings of a great emphasis on the notion of Satan and a kingdom of evil. For unlike some philosophies (such as the concepts of Taoism or the various native American religious concepts of the universe as constituted of opposing but complementary ingredients and forces that fashion an organic whole), Manichaeism affirms that one of the two equal opposing forces is purely good, the other purely evil. Therefore, Manichaeism perceives a parallel in the antipathy between good and evil in the human struggle between spirit and matter. Consequently, our best response to this life, according to this view, is to escape it as best we can. Accordingly, instead of being perceived as an instrument for expressing spiritual understanding in metaphorical forms, the body becomes perceived as part of the degenerate material reality and therefore antithetical to spiritual development.

Related to this attitude, and, inferentially, as confirmation of such ideas, was the fact that Christ never married. Furthermore, Paul not only remained unmarried but advised others to refrain from marriage if they could. Consequently, asceticism emerged early as an ideal in Christianity and the gnostic influences corroborated this position. Salvation came to be perceived as an internal condition and the material world was believed to be of the devil. The antinomian tenor of Christianity became further entrenched with the emerging view of the Old

---

* This thought demonstrates elements of both Zoroastrianism and neo-Platonism.

Testament as a period of spiritual darkness totally un-related to the advent of Christ.*

Another major force in continuing and amplifying the evolving antinomian tenor of Christianity is the influence of St Augustine. A Manichaean before converting to Christianity in 387, Augustine is generally acknowledged to have been the greatest thinker of Christian antiquity; certainly he is the most influential. In his extensive writings he attempted to combine his love of philosophy with his Christian beliefs, and he found in Neo-Platonism a way of coming to terms with the nature of God and the existence of evil. Of importance to our present discussion, he was also a mighty force in preparing the way for Luther because he propagated the belief in salvation by grace apart from deeds or obedience to law. His teachings also set the stage for Calvin because he asserted in *The City of God* the doctrine of predestination, a belief that further supported the idea that one's physical life is largely irrelevant to one's spiritual condition or eternal destiny.

As a Manichaean, Augustine had perceived the material world as an emanation of an evil force, whereas in reconciling Christian thought through Neo-Platonism, he came to believe that evil was essentially non-existent, the absence of good. The world and the flesh were not inherently evil, only lower expressions of divine reality, as darkness is the absence of light.† Thus, although con-verted through a mystical vision, Augustine attempted

---

* One main distinction between the teachings of Mani and that of the other gnostics should be noted – belief in an historical disclosure of God. Mani taught that he was a messenger from God in the line of Zoroaster, Buddha and Jesus. He further taught that while the truth had been partially revealed in these predecessors, it was his mission to bring together the essential truth of these revelations. Sometime between the year 274 and 277, he was executed for these beliefs by Zoroastrian authorities.

† This is discussed most significantly in Book Seven of *The Confessions*.

through his writings to synthesize faith with reason, the material world with the spiritual world.

But this attitude did not long sustain him, possibly because of the lingering influence of his initial Manichaean perspective. Consequently, instead of perceiving the material world as a metaphorical expression of the spiritual world, as a means of gaining access to the spiritual world, Augustine began to uphold the ascetic notion of abandoning the lower or physical self in order to gain admission into the upper reaches of pure spirit. Likewise, instead of perceiving deeds done in the physical world as a means of understanding spiritual relationships (the essence of Platonic thought), Augustine came to construe Platonism as implying a rejection of things physical and as confirming the ascetic ideal of *contemptu mundi*.*

So it was that in time Augustine came to discern an important difference between Neo-Platonic thought and Pauline Christianity, a distinction made plain in Augustine's struggle against the Pelagian heresy, a doctrine affirming the idea that individuals attain salvation through moral rectitude and that unless one is free to avoid sin and change one's behaviour, God's punishments and rewards would be unjust. Augustine, however, especially in his old age, linked sin to the fall of man – to 'primal sin'. Furthermore, he attributed that initial failure to human sexuality. Accordingly, Augustine affirmed that Adam fell freely, but that the human soul, now subject and slave to the flesh, no longer has power to extricate itself. Salvation can now come only through the descent of divine love in

---

* As discussed in *The Purpose of Physical Reality* (p. 21), this phrase meaning 'disdain for the world' was the title of a seminal work by Pope Innocent III. The phrase also came to connote an attitude common in the mediaeval Roman Church as a part of the whole theme of mutability so common in mediaeval literature.

the heart of the sinner. In effect, faith and belief are attained through a recognition of Christ's redemption and not through any material action on the part of the believer.*

As Augustine came to emphasize the Pauline notion of divine grace as the sole source of human movement towards the good, he also came to see in Paul's writing the idea of God's foreknowledge, especially as it regards individual human response. He concluded that if God foreknows who will and will not be saved, then one's salvation must be predestined.† Consequently, those who respond to belief are the chosen ones, the 'elect'.

This belief that one's spiritual destiny is predetermined further entrenched the attitude that physical life and one's performance in it are inconsequential to one's spiritual destiny. Such a belief also upholds the perception that human social or material progress is largely unrelated to any divine purpose because history itself is perceived as irrelevant to the process of human redemption. In effect, redemption or salvation becomes an event rather than a process.

The Influence of Anti-Feminism

No where does Christ command or even praise celibacy or asceticism, and nowhere does Christ hint that women are

---

* In fact, these two views are not as diametrically opposed as they might seem. Pelagius argued that the 'right path' became apparent to the Christian through the example of Christ, thereby unifying the acceptance of Christ with wilful morality; and Augustine believed that one's love of God derived from free will, even though the initial spark of faith enters the heart as a gift of the Holy Spirit – it is not earned.

† This traditional problem obviously ignores the distinction between foreknowledge and predestination. Instead, it presumes that if God foreknows one's salvation or damnation, then no action on the part of an individual can alter that condition because God is omniscient. Since one's

spiritually inferior to men. Yet one of the most powerful forces in confirming and exacerbating the antinomian tenor of Christianity is the early emergence of blatant anti-feminism, an attitude which served as a corollary to the idealization of celibacy. Inextricably related to this view, consequently, was the increasingly more severe disen-franchisement of women, the condemnation of sexuality, and, symbolically, the schism between the male and female aspects of the human body politic (the relationship between the spiritual principles and the dramatizing of these in action).

While it is difficult to be certain about all the sources of this anti-feminism, some are evident. As we have noted, Christ never married, nor did Paul. Marriage thus became for the Roman Church a sacrament whose sole purpose was procreation. Furthermore, the idea emerged that the true marriage for the Christian is the mystical conjoining of one's soul with Christ. Since celibacy, not marriage, is the ideal state, the greatest threat to such a condition is sexuality. And because the Church fathers were the progenitors and promulgators of such doctrine, naturally the greatest temptation to sexuality for these men was women.

Perhaps the most significant source of anti-feminism was the literal interpretation of the Adamic myth. Eve was, according to such belief, the source of human sin and downfall, for while Adam also fell, it was his uxorious-ness* that led to his failure. Eve fell because of her pride – she aspired to a station beyond that to which she was consigned. Therefore, inseparable from the notion of

---

destiny cannot be altered, then there is no free will. This is essentially the same argument used later by Calvin and the Puritans who followed Calvin's theology.

* Being excessively devoted to or indulgent with one's wife.

primal sin was the corollary belief that woman was the cause of that sin.

Anti-feminism was obviously enigmatic and ironic since Christianity, as we infer it from Christ's teachings, significantly enhanced and expanded the role of women in religion and in society. For example, Christ forbade divorce, formerly a means by which women were at the disposal of men in Jewish society. Furthermore, women played an integral part in Christ's ministry. Paul himself states 'there is neither male nor female; for you are all one in Christ Jesus'.[43] Even more ironically, as this anti-feminism increased in intensity, there emerged in Christianity a veneration of the figure of the Virgin Mary, a tendency sometimes alluded to as 'maryolotry', wherein the figure of the Virgin as mother of God assumed a spiritual station virtually superior to that of Christ Himself.

But the adoration of the Virgin did little to abate the denigration of women, who were, from such a view, relegated to one of two conditions – the mother/saint or the seductress/whore – both of which were equally de-humanizing since neither allowed for an acceptable middle ground or synthesis of dual realities, some human condition. Of particular importance to our own theme, such extreme views paralleled the failure of Christian theologians to discover some middle ground or synthesis about the human condition in general. The spiritual or rational self (Eve) was effectively divorced from the physical or sensual self (Adam).

The Schism between Science and Religion – Ockham's Razor

Thomas Aquinas (1225?–74) made a noble attempt to repair this ever-widening schism in Christian thought by trying to synthesize the Platonic view of the physical world as a metaphorical image of the spiritual world with the newly-introduced scientific methodology of Aristotelianism. Long veiled from Western thought until conveyed to the West by Muslim scholars, Aristotelianism affirmed that one can learn about spiritual reality through a methodical study of the physical world and its laws. By this means, Aquinas thought to synthesize what were becoming two distinct areas of intellectual interest: theology as a study of the spiritual reality and naturalism as a study of the phenomenal world.

The discovery, or rediscovery, of Aristotle's use of logical argument (syllogism, etc.) had now become nurtured by the translations and interpolations of Aristotle's work, largely by Muslim scholars such as the Persian scholar Avicenna (980–1037) and Averroes (1126–c. 1198), a Muslim who lived in Cordova, Spain. The reason for this primacy of Muslim scholars over the Western European thinkers was the fact that the Islamic culture in all its aspects was during the ninth through the twelfth centuries significantly ahead of Western Europe in science, philosophy and theology. In his history of philosophy *Socrates to Sartre*, Samuel E. Stumpf notes additionally:

> Moreover, the Moslem world had access to the chief works of Aristotle centuries before Western Europe finally received them. Many texts of the Greek philosophers had been translated into the Arabic, from which later Latin translations were made in the West. By 833, philosophy was well established in Baghdad, where a school had been established for translating Greek manuscripts on philosophy and science, and for creative scholarship as well.[44]

Though Aristotelianism found favour among many Western European thinkers, Christian writers such as Bonaventura found the Aristotelian focus on the physical world (and on the rational mind as the means of establishing and confirming one's beliefs) objectionable and antithetical to the major premise of Christian thought as elucidated by Augustine.*

Nevertheless, Aquinas was able to synthesize the merits of Aristotelian logic with the spiritual implications of the traditional neo-Platonism of patristic Christianity. Aquinas asserted that the individual through his own wilful intellect could gain belief (or at least confirm faith) by examining the laws and relationships of the natural or phenomenal world. The objection to Aquinas' ideas by traditional scholastic theologians went as follows: if one's faculties are tainted by sin and the physical world is likewise corrupt, then how could faith be affirmed or confirmed by using a defective instrument to examine a corrupt edifice.

But there was another objection. Platonism as an epistemological system had come to imply for the Church fathers a spiritual/emotional search within oneself for that godly spark of intuitive understanding, that spark of faith – something closely akin to the mystical process we discussed earlier. Aristotelian epistemology, on the other hand, implied a belief contracted by the application of intellect and reason. To the scholastic thinker, Christian

---

* According to Stumpf, part of this perception of Aristotelianism as antithetical to Christian thought resulted from the fact that Aristotle's work was translated from the interpretations of his work by Muslim scholars. While such an observation is worth noting, it is quite clear that the same objections would have been lodged regardless of how faithful the translation had been, because the objection was more to the nature of methodology than to the method itself. That is, shifting emphasis away from the ascetic ideal and from faith to a reliance on observation and logic flew in the face of the increasingly Pauline orientation of Christian theology.

theology was in danger of becoming a science rather than a personal spiritual experience, an approach to religious truth that threatened the so-called authoritative glossing (interpretation) of scripture by the Church fathers.* For if interpretation was meaningful only if it could be proven in an objective way, then the concept of authority could be perceived as invalid.

A further objection to Thomism was Aquinas' assertion that the physical world was a metaphorical reflection of spiritual reality, a view that hardly seemed confirmed by the conditions of mediaeval life. Understandably, emphasis on the next world by the Church fathers seemed justified in light of the political injustice and general chaos of the so-called Dark Ages, one reason, as we noted in the first volume, that the stoicism of Boethius (480–524) in his *Consolation of Philosophy* had such a strong appeal. In such a context, it was hard to accept the humanistic and existential orientation of Aristotelianism, which emphasized the perfection and beauty of the natural world as a vehicle through which humanity might gain insight into the perfection of the spiritual world.

For Aquinas, such antithesis was unnecessary. For him, belief involved the inextricable union of faith with reason, of this world with the next, and he objected to the Augustinian tradition which implicitly condemned both physical reality and deeds performed in that milieu. Aquinas believed that once having achieved belief through faith, reason could operate to confirm and uphold that belief, that theology could and should be logically consistent, and that the revelation of God, because it is expressed

---

* 'Glossing' of scripture by recognized scholars of the Church was accepted as authoritative interpretation of biblical text, and elaborate arguments might be established by accepting these interpretations as proven doctrine.

in human terms and human language, could likewise be studied by means of the scientific method.* Aquinas thus viewed the phenomenal world as an expression of divine creation, but its value for him did not lie solely in its ability to lead one intuitively to a contemplation of the spiritual world which it reflected. Aquinas believed that even a purely rational and intellectual examination of the natural world would eventually lead one to a discovery of God.

Aquinas objected to the radical Averroists† and to nominalists like William of Ockham. Ockham (1280–1349) was a strict empiricist who denied the existence of universals except as a human contrivance. He affirmed instead that all we can know with certainty in this life are particular things or individual names (hence the term *nominalist*). Therefore, universal terms do not in fact refer to a reality beyond things themselves. Where Aquinas believed that one could infer a universal harmony as a concrete or artistic expression of divine reality or of the mind of God, Ockham believed that people are what they are because God chose to make them that way, not because of an eternal pattern or divine plan. Ockham did not deny the validity of studying both science and theology, but he affirmed that where scientific truth is accessible through reason, theological truth is accessible only through revelation (faith). He further asserted that a

---

* Aquinas still safeguarded theology from philosophy as being a matter of faith derived from authoritative revelation, whereas philosophy 'begins with the immediate objects of sense experience and reasons upward to more general conceptions until, as in Aristotle's case, the mind fastens upon the highest principles or first causes of being, ending in the conception of God. Theology, on the other hand, begins with a faith in God and interprets all things as creatures of God' (Stumpf, *Socrates to Sartre*, p. 180).

† They believed that religious knowledge was sometimes incompatible with rational knowledge, one being the product of faith, the other the product of reason.

truth confirmed from one source does not necessarily correlate to or corroborate the inference about that truth from the other source. In fact, he asserted that truths may in some instances contradict each other.

While Ockham did not intend it, his notion of the separation of these methods for examining and formulating truth ('Ockham's razor') had the effect of severing rather than coordinating or synthesizing these two sorts of human capacity. Therefore, where Aquinas might employ the Aristotelian method to arrive at his several proofs of the existence of God, Ockham would applaud the use of such faculties only when applied to their proper purview, the natural world, and not such universal concerns which were properly approached through the tools of theology (faith and inspiration).

This crucial debate was not confined to these two figures or to a brief span of time. Coming as it did immediately prior to the expanding horizons of the known world and the equally dramatic expansion of human understanding regarding the natural world that occurred in the Renaissance, Ockham's enunciation of this principle helped establish and formalize the schism in Christianity between science and religion.

The Copernican Revolution

One benefit of this schism was the liberation of science from theocratic tyranny – human reason and scientific discovery could advance unencumbered by the constraints of theological implications, though figures such as Galileo (1564–1642) would help pay the price for that freedom. In effect, the religious experience came to be accepted in Western Christianity largely as a personal emotional condition. Religious conviction might be confirmed by a kind of logic, but it was often a specious form of reasoning in which the believer was asked to accept as given the whole foundation of established belief and authoritative interpretation of scripture.

The schism between reason and faith so acutely symbolized in Ockham's razor likewise symbolized the increasing difficulty of accepting the authority of the Church as the sole means by which salvation and justification might be achieved, especially in light of the increasing abuses of authority on the part of officers of the ecclesiastical courts. The result of this perception of the distinction between the spirit of the Christian faith and the institution charged with channelling that spirit to the laity was the emergence of various reformers and reformation movements. In England in the fourteenth century there was John Wyclif (1320?–84) and the Lollard movement. Most important, of course, was Martin Luther (1483–1546) in Germany who initiated the Reformation and the birth of Protestantism.

Luther, who called Ockham 'my beloved Master William',[45] agreed that knowledge of God was a gift of grace gained by faith, not something reason could discover or even assist. Luther called reason 'that all-cruelest and most fatal enemy of God'.[46] Invoking the authority of St Paul's antinomian statements, Luther asserted that one 'needs no works to justify him'.[47] Likewise, continuing in the vein of Augustine's Manichaeism, Luther paid little heed to the importance of physical life or the practical affairs of governance. Luther believed that social and political affairs were not relevant to religious conviction. He asserted that 'to suffer wrong destroys no one's soul, nay it improves the soul, although it inflicts loss upon the body and property . . .'[48]

But neither the Protestant nor the Catholic Church could long remain impervious to or unconcerned with the findings and theories of science. As the heliocentric theories of Copernicus (1473–1543) became confirmed by the findings of scientists like Galileo and Kepler (1571–1630), the Church tried ferociously to restrain science, and the gulf widened between science and religion as the further advances in scientific investigation seemed to contradict the fundamental assumptions of formalized Christian theology: the later theories of Newton (1642–1727), for example, implied a mechanistic universal system without need of divine assistance or intervention. Even less could Christian thought abide the affront to its literalistic assertion of biblical infallibility implied in what has been called the Second Copernican Revolution of Charles Darwin (1809–82), whose theory of evolution seemed diametrically opposed to the view of a creation brought into being instantaneously by an all-powerful Creator.

The end result of this schism between science and religion was that, as the industrial revolution took hold in the middle of the nineteenth century, the entire issue of human spirituality and morality become increasingly superfluous to the more rampant and visible evidence of a science, a technology, a materialism that seem sufficient to account for all human realities.

Children of Divorce: The Modern Heritage of the Schism

The Effect on World Politics

It might be valid to observe that the more rapidly science advanced, the more tenaciously Western Christian thought and other world religions felt the need to dig in their heels against the onslaught of a world view which relegated spiritual matters to the privacy of the church, the synagogue, the mosque or the temple, and left the management of human society to the amoral world of politics, armaments and high finance.

Some of the overt attempts to extricate governance from the purview of religion were quite understandable. After Henry VIII severed the Church of England from the Catholic Faith in 1533, England had experienced over two centuries of bloody civil wars between the Catholics and Protestant factions. Consequently, some of the initial settlements in America resulted from the attempt of Puritan emigrants to escape the religious constraints imposed by this same strife. Indeed, the whole revolutionary atmosphere in Europe and America at the end of the eighteenth and beginning of the nineteenth centuries was also closely linked with the attempt to cast off the restraints of archaic and traditional notions of governance as the tool of entrenched systems of aristocracy and morality. As a result, the founding fathers of American governance, while protecting the freedom of worship, were equally careful to sever any possible collusion or official alliance between religion and governance.

This separation of church and state was even more emphatic in revolutionary Russia a century later. The Bolshevik revolution against the blatant injustices of monarchical systems was also a rejection of religion as a part of that established authority. Religion was, according to Karl Marx, 'the opium of the people'.[49] The more overt theocracies of the Middle East have experienced highs and lows. The once invincible Ottoman Empire eventually disintegrated, but we witness now an upsurge in pan-Islamic movements and Islamic fundamentalism, in spite of secularized reforms in most Muslim countries.

With the spectacular advances in technology, science and material civilization that have occurred in the last one hundred and fifty years, religion as a political or social force in world affairs has been largely forgotten or purposely cast aside. In its stead are matters of raw power, pure and simple. Since the middle of the nineteenth century, formal religious movements and ecclesiastical authority have had an increasingly tangential role to play in the arena of world affairs.

This is not to say that questions of morality, of social and political justice have not been crucial in shaping the world in which we now reside; but more and more rapidly, even fundamental assumptions have been shorn away under the weight of sheer expediency and self-interest on the part of those in power. What began as the schism between religion and science has in time evolved into a schism between religion and all practical matters regarding human society. The result is that, with few exceptions, there is presently worldwide little correlation or connection between religion, religious principles or moral perspective, and the daily administration of human society.

The New Science and the New Hope

Beginning in the early part of the twentieth century with the foundations of new physics, theorists like Albert Einstein, instead of further disentangling themselves from any religious tenor to their activity, came increasingly to be aware of and fascinated by the mysterious harmony and inscrutability of universal systems. More recently there have emerged among such inquisitive minds a new breed of mystic and a rapidly growing body of literature which advocates a spiritual basis for universal scientific realities and human social relationships.

Instead of diminishing the need for the belief in a higher power or a spiritual dimension, these studies seem to confirm Aquinas' beliefs by discovering in the infinitely complex nature of universal physical science metaphorical expressions of a spiritual reality. Stated more simply, while religion in Western Christian thought has abandoned science, science has begun to discover or rediscover religion, at least in a theoretical sense.

Until the rapid influence of Western materialism in this century, this same sort of schism between materiality and spirituality had not occurred in most Eastern thought. It is not surprising, therefore, that it is in Eastern philosophy and religious perspectives that science found a synthesis of perspectives that seemed to vindicate and explain science as complementary to religion. For example, in his overview of the evolution of the 'new physics', Gary Zukov in his work *The Dancing Wu Li Masters* states that the mysticism and mystery of Eastern religions actually express metaphorically an awareness of the same principles that contemporary scientists are only beginning to infer:

These powerful metaphors have applications to the developing drama of physics. Although most physicists have little patience (professionally) with metaphors, physics itself has become a powerful metaphor. Twentieth-century physics is the story of a journey from intellectual entrenchment to intellectual openness, despite the conservative prove-it-to-me nature of individual physicists. The realization that the discoveries of physics *never* will end has brought physicists, as well as those who have followed the story of physics, to an extremely fertile plateau. This realization invites the intellect to leap forward, although at great risk to its present hegemony.[50]

Similarly, in discussing the extraordinary revision in our world view that the modern age is suddenly bringing into focus, Marilyn Ferguson concludes that the moral imperatives explicit in ostensibly outworn and discarded religious beliefs are now becoming the practical imperatives of pure expediency:

The wider paradigm of relationships and family transcends old group definitions. The discovery of our connection to all other men, women, and children joins us to another family. Indeed, seeing ourselves as a planetary family struggling to solve its problems, rather than as assorted people and nations assessing blame or exporting solutions, could be the ultimate shift in perspective.[51]

More specifically she observes that our contemporary experience, rather than further fragmenting us, has produced instead a rapidly coalescing sense of ourselves as a global community:

> We have had a profound paradigm shift about the whole Earth. We know it now as a jewel in space, a fragile water planet. And we have seen that it has no natural borders. It is not the globe of our school days with its many-coloured nations . . . All countries are economically and ecologically involved with each other, politically enmeshed.[52]

Guy Murchie in his work *The Seven Mysteries of Life* also observes in the analogues from scientific laws operant in material world the spiritual principles applicable to human realities. Yet he views these metaphors from the laws of the phenomenal world not as objective examples only, but as demonstrating how the physical universe is inextricably related to and bound up in our own existence and purpose:

> All of us beings here are cells of the unknown essence of our world, nodes of flesh that could as well be notes of melody. We are part of something infinite and eternal. There is no boundary between us and the world.[53]

More recently, others have continued to discover in the laws and relationships governing the phenomenal world a vindication of the same essential principles of correlation between the spiritual and physical world that Aquinas was attempting to enunciate in a synthesis of Aristotelian approaches to neo-Platonic assertions.*

Since we concluded in the first volume of this work that moral principle and spiritual law have the weight of physical law,[54] and that spiritual reality and the phenomenal reality are but different aspects of one creation, it should not be surprising that human learning applied to one aspect should discover the other:

> Religion and science are the two wings upon which man's intelligence can soar into the heights, with which the human soul can progress. It is not possible to fly with one wing alone! Should a man try to fly with the wing of religion alone he would quickly fall into the quagmire of superstition, whilst on the other hand, with the wing of science alone he would also make no progress, but fall into the despairing slough of materialism. All religions of the present day have fallen into superstitious practices, out of harmony alike with the true principles of the teaching they represent and with the scientific discoveries of the time. Many religious leaders have grown to think that the importance of religion lies mainly in the adherence to a collection of certain dogmas and the practice of rites and ceremonies! Those whose souls they profess to cure are taught to believe likewise, and these cling tenaciously to the outward forms, confusing them with the inward truth.[55]

As we have already noted, the discovery of moral and spiritual principles demonstrated or metaphorized by the phenomenal world is hardly confined to the study of physics. Daily we encounter to an ever greater extent the practical implications of the principles enunciated a hundred years ago by Bahá'u'lláh. For example, Bahá'u-

---

* In his work *Quantum Questions: The Mystical Writings of the World's Greatest Physicists*, Ken Wilbur examines this same process of synthesis, as do Elizabeth Sartour in her work *Gaia: The Journey from Chaos to Cosmos* and James Gluck in *The Science of Chaos*.

'lláh cautioned that 'the civilization, so often vaunted by the learned exponents of arts and sciences, will, if allowed to overleap the bounds of moderation, bring great evil upon men'.[56] As we now struggle to save our environment and protect ourselves against our own inventiveness, we can well appreciate the wisdom of this exhortation. Likewise, as we are now faced with the immediate necessity of creating global plans to deal with issues of economic disparity, social injustice, environmental disaster and global lawlessness, we can readily appreciate Bahá'u'lláh's succinct pronouncement that

> The day is approaching when all the peoples of the world will have adopted one universal language and one common script. When this is achieved, to whatsoever city a man may journey, it shall be as if he were entering his own home. These things are obligatory and absolutely essential. It is incumbent upon every man of insight and understanding to strive to translate that which hath been written into reality and action . . . That one indeed is a man who, today, dedicateth himself to the service of the entire human race. The Great Being saith: Blessed and happy is he that ariseth to promote the best interests of the peoples and kindreds of the earth. In another passage He hath proclaimed: It is not for him to pride himself who loveth his own country, but rather for him who loveth the whole world. The earth is but one country, and mankind its citizens.[57]

But while it is essential to recognize the necessity of reinvesting in social action, in governance, in our daily lives, the spiritual dimension that has been so sadly neglected, understanding alone cannot bring about needed change. Neither is there apparent some readily available force capable of bringing about a reunion of science and religion, social order with moral issues, our spiritual aspirations with our daily lives.

The Bahá'í writings assert that such reunion is possible,

even inevitable. However, this coalescing of the disjointed limbs of the human body politic will not be easy or instantaneous. Instead, the Bahá'í texts describe an evolutionary process by which there will emerge in due time a world commonwealth capable of expressing in human social and material structures the spiritual realities that underlie phenomenal creation. The Bahá'í scriptures also affirm that this process is well under way.

6

The Choice Wine at the Family Reunion

Take heed lest anything deter thee from extolling the greatness of this Day – the Day whereon the Finger of majesty and power hath opened the seal of the Wine of Reunion, and called all who are in the heavens and all who are on the earth.[1]

Bahá'u'lláh

From our analysis of the evolving schism between science and religion and the broader implications of that sundering in terms of our contemporary world, we can begin to appreciate the far-reaching effects of what happens when the most powerful force for human advancement (divine revelation) becomes abused or misapplied. As we have also noted, a major portion of this dilemma derives from two major sources: the persistent failure on the part of humanity to appreciate and thereby utilize the continuity of divine revelation, and the likewise persistent failure on the part of believers to fashion an institution capable of channelling the spiritual power of a new revelation into meaningful patterns of daily life and social programmes.

There is little wonder, then, that a significant portion of Bahá'u'lláh's exposition of progressive revelation in the *Kitáb-i-Íqán* dwells on the problems arising out of the transition that occurs with the advent of a new Manifestation. Of special value to our study is Bahá'u'lláh's explication of the symbolic terms associated with these

points of transition or judgement as they relate to the
continuity of religion. After examining His treatment of a
few of these terms, we can better appreciate the poetic
language Bahá'u'lláh employs in alluding to the Bahá'í
revelation as demarcating a turning point in the education
of humankind after which there will never again on this
planet be a lethal severing of the twin forces of human
progress.

Symbolic Terms Associated with a New Dispensation

Resurrection

Because the advent of a new revelation implies a renewal
of divine guidance, the revealed teachings of the Manifestations often employ such terms as 'rebirth' and
'resurrection' to designate the process by which humanity
is revived and revitalized. Indeed, the first and perhaps
most difficult task of the new Manifestation is to reawaken
those followers of the previous Prophet who have become
ritualized, lethargic or otherwise diverted from their
purpose of coordinating social action with spiritual
purpose in order to expand the sense of human identity. In
effect, the 'body' of the previous revelation, the institution
and its leaders, has become spiritually dead.

Christ tried to explain this same concept of resurrection
to the cynical Sadducees.* Likewise Muḥammad used the
term 'resurrection' in several contexts, sometimes alluding
to individual spiritual awakening, sometimes to the after-

---

* The Sadducees pose to Christ what they believe to be a real puzzler about
a theoretical case of several brothers marrying the same woman after each
dies in succession. Their question is whose wife will she be after the
resurrection, to which Christ replies that they are ignorant of 'the
scriptures' and 'the power of God' because 'in the resurrection they neither
marry nor are given in marriage . . .' (Matt. 22: 23–30).

life of the individual soul, and at other times to the 'Day of
Resurrection' as a particular turning point in history
wherein humankind will be judged.[2] Of particular interest
for our purposes is Muḥammad's explanation of the
figurative significance of the concept of spiritual rebirth as
it is exemplified in physical analogues, all of which serve
to remind humanity of God's relentless grace:

> O men! if ye doubt as to the resurrection, yet, of a truth, have
> We created you of dust, then of the moist germs of life, then
> of clots of blood, then of pieces of flesh shapen and unshapen,
> that We might give you proofs of our power! And We cause
> one sex or the other, at our pleasure, to abide in the womb
> until the appointed time; then We bring you forth infants;
> then permit you to reach your age of strength; and one of you
> dieth, and another of you liveth on to an age so abject that all
> his former knowledge is clean forgotten! And thou hast seen
> the earth dried up and barren: but when We send down the
> rain upon it, it stirreth and swelleth, and groweth every kind
> of luxuriant herb.[3]

Bahá'u'lláh in the *Kitáb-i-Íqán* further elucidate the symbolic use of the term 'resurrection' when He observes that
with every appearance of a Manifestation these same terms
become appropriate: 'In every age and century, the purpose
of the Prophets of God and their chosen ones hath been no
other but to affirm the spiritual significance of the terms
"life", "resurrection", and "judgement".'[4] Bahá'u'lláh explains these 'symbolic terms'[5] as relating to the spiritual
rebirth of people with every new dispensation, but He also
explains that the particular allusions in previous dispensations to the 'Day of Resurrection', or a particularly
important renewal, designates the advent of the Báb and
the inauguration of the Bahá'í Era, the age or cycle of
fulfilment in which human purpose will be universally
understood and implemented.

From such a perspective, therefore, Muḥammad fulfilled

Christ's allusion to a resurrection in a general sense: '. . . the Day of Resurrection was ushered in through the Revelation of Muḥammad.'[6] But as Bahá'u'lláh goes on to explain in this same Tablet, the 'Day of Resurrection' referred to in the 'well-known tradition' is the time when 'the Qá'im riseth'.[7] According to Bahá'í belief, the Báb is the Qá'im. Therefore, the Báb's declaration of His station in 1844 signalized the beginning of a new cycle and a process of reviving the dead and lifeless body of the human body politic. In fact, as the Báb Himself repeatedly acknowledges in His own writings, the sole purpose of His nine-year dispensation was to prepare the way for a global unity by awakening the custodians of the previous revelation to the dawn of this new age.

Reunion

Closely related to the term 'resurrection' and thematically integral to our discussion so far about the inextricable relationship between the dual aspects of human reality is the use of the term 'reunion' in relation to the advent of the Bahá'í revelation. On the simplest level, the term connotes the spiritual proximity of people to God when the Manifestation as God's emissary appears among them. Bahá'u'lláh thus uses the term as an allusion to the emphatic expression of God's grace among men. More particularly, Bahá'u'lláh employs the term to designate this age as a period of fulfilment which the advent of this dispensation inaugurates:

> Take heed lest anything deter thee from extolling the greatness of this Day – the Day whereon the Finger of majesty and power hath opened the seal of the Wine of Reunion, and called all who are in the heavens and all who are on the earth.[8]

> Let all eyes rejoice, and let every ear be gladdened, for now is the time to gaze on His beauty, now is the fit time to hearken

to His voice . . . Turn the anguish of your separation from Him into the joy of an everlasting reunion, and let the sweetness of His presence dissolve the bitterness of your remoteness from His court.[9]

This is the Day, O my Lord, whereon every atom of the earth hath been made to vibrate and to cry out: 'O Thou Who art the Revealer of signs and the King of creation! I, verily, perceive the fragrance of Thy presence. Methinks Thou hast revealed Thyself, and unlocked the door of reunion with Thee before all who are in Thy heaven and all who are on Thy earth.[10]

The phrase 'this Day' combined with the concept of 'reunion' in these passages alludes at once to a dramatic transition in the historical progress of humanity as a social organism and to the emergence of a universal consciousness – the reunion of the disjointed members of the body politic into one harmonious family. For even though the evolution of a world social order has not previously occurred on this planet, it is a 'reunion' in the sense that humanity originated from the same physical substance, has the same spiritual purpose, and, after aeons of separated and isolated or disjointed development of the various constituent parts, can now recognize its common heritage, its essential organic unity. Once this insight is gained, humanity can wilfully participate in constructing a social system suitable to this common identity:

Know ye not why We created you all from the same dust? That no one should exalt himself over the other. Ponder at all times in your hearts how ye were created. Since We have created you all from the same substance it is incumbent on you to be even as one soul, to walk with the same feet, eat with the same mouth and dwell in the same land, that from your inmost being, by your deeds and actions, the signs of oneness and the essence of detachment may be made manifest.[11]

In this context, the reunion fosters on a collective level the same expanded sense of self delineated in our discussion of individual spiritual ascent depicted in *The Seven Valleys*.

Insofar as the term 'reunion' alludes to the coalescing of the twin duties of the human purpose (the knowing and the doing), Bahá'u'lláh is in these and other passages enunciating and celebrating the reunion of spiritual vision with social ordinance and edifice, the healing of the schism that has for so long plagued our planet.

The New Wineskin

Since the edifice of the Bahá'í revelation (its laws and institutions) are themselves an integral part of the revelation of Bahá'u'lláh rather than an *ipso facto* product of fallible human invention or contrivance, the wine of this revelation comes with its own wineskin, perfectly conceived and therefore precisely capable of channelling the renewed outpouring of divine bounty to each and every citizen of the body politic. In this sense, the Bahá'í institutions represent what Shoghi Effendi calls 'that Divine Polity which incarnates God's immutable Purpose for all men'.[12]

But before we sample the new wine, we need to be aware of one subtle point about the transition implicit in this process. The transformation of a fragmented world into a coherent social and spiritual organism is, from the Bahá'í perspective, a natural and inevitable part of human evolution and of the evolution of the planet itself. In this sense, the transformation of human society is preordained and divinely empowered:

> The principle of the Oneness of Mankind, as proclaimed by Bahá'u'lláh, carries with it no more and no less than a solemn assertion that attainment to this final stage in this stupendous

evolution is not only necessary but inevitable, that its realization is fast approaching, and that nothing short of a power that is born of God can succeed in establishing it.[13]

Furthermore, the Bahá'í writings assert that this transformation, though, resulting from spiritual laws and principles, naturally finds its overt expression in the form of human social structures and institutions:

> That mystic, all-pervasive, yet indefinable change, which we associate with the stage of maturity inevitable in the life of the individual and the development of the fruit must, if we would correctly apprehend the utterances of Bahá'u'lláh, have its counterpart in the evolution of the organization of human society. A similar stage must sooner or later be attained in the collective life of mankind, producing an even more striking phenomenon in world relations, and endowing the whole human race with such potentialities of well-being as shall provide, throughout the succeeding ages, the chief incentive required for the eventual fulfilment of its high destiny.[14]

However, if this reunion, this process of achieving a world social and political edifice based on spiritual principles, is a natural and inevitable part of human destiny, to what extent do we collectively or individually have a part to play? If the process is divinely ordained, does it matter whether or not we assist it or even become aware of it?

The clear but subtle response to this, as we will later study in more detail, is that while the overall destiny of human social evolution is an inherent property of our creation, the progress towards that shore still is influenced by human volitional effort. For example, Shoghi Effendi makes it clear that the rapidity and ease with which this transformation will be effected in social form is dependent to a large extent on the degree to which humanity utilizes the specific tools for change provided by Bahá'u'lláh:

The Most Great Peace, on the other hand, as conceived by Bahá'u'lláh – a peace that must inevitably follow as the practical consequence of the spiritualization of the world and the fusion of all its races, creeds, classes and nations – can rest on no other basis, and can be preserved through no other agency, except the divinely appointed ordinances that are implicit in the World Order that stands associated with His Holy Name.[15]

Thus, the foundation and securing of a world commonwealth are the 'divinely appointed ordinances' revealed by Bahá'u'lláh, yet even these cannot be imposed. They can only be implemented and effected by the freely chosen and coordinated actions of humanity. Therefore, we need to appreciate that even when the Manifestation Himself provides the specific blueprint for the receptacle that will contain the wine of His revealed truth, there still persists the subtle interplay between divine guidance and human free will.

Unsealing the Choice Wine

Vineyard Imagery

As we have mentioned, Christ speaks of the 'new wine' which must needs be placed in a new wineskin as an allusion to the relationship between spiritual teachings and the implementing of those teachings in social and ecclesiastical structures. In keeping with this same poetic imagery, He later explains divine justice in relation to the kingdom of heaven through the parable of the workers in the Vineyard – those who labour to help produce and gather the fruit that will become the wine.[16] Later, in attempting to explain His relationship to His followers and to God, He again employs vineyard imagery:

I am the true vine, and my Father is the vinedresser. Every

branch of mine that bears no fruit, he takes away, and every branch that does bear fruit he prunes, that it may bear more fruit.[17]

This idea of the purging or pruning of the branch seems to allude to the testing to which a follower will be subjected that he or she might bring forth the fruit of good deeds. Furthermore, the analogy implies that meaningful action or deeds can only be accomplished when one is aware of the source of those deeds by being faithful to the covenant. Every follower is but a branch of the 'true vine', the Manifestation, but a branch cannot prosper or produce fruit unless it remains connected with the vine: 'the branch cannot bear fruit by itself, unless it abides in the vine . . .'[18]

Vineyard imagery is similarly employed in Bahá'í scripture. In *Epistle to the Son of the Wolf*, Bahá'u'lláh states that 'Carmel, in the Book of God, hath been designated as the Hill of God, and His Vineyard. It is here that, by the grace of the Lord of Revelation, the Tabernacle of Glory hath been raised'.[19] Likewise, 'Abdu'l-Bahá employs such epithets as 'celestial Vineyard'[20] and 'Vineyard of God'[21] when referring to the Bahá'í Faith. In the same vein, He may address an individual Bahá'í as a 'gardener of Truth' in the 'divine vineyard'[22] or as 'skilful labourer in the vineyard of God'.[23]

The usefulness of this image has to do with its capacity to render in comprehensible poetic terms a complex spiritual relationship, though it may seem an ironic metaphor since Bahá'u'lláh, like Muḥammad before Him, proscribes the drinking of wine. Perhaps some degree of the reliance on this metaphor derives from Christ's use of this symbol in the sacrament, but the use of it also has to do with the capacity of wine to produce intoxication, the same sort of carefree joy and detachment that one en-

thralled with the love of God exhibits. Bahá'u'lláh thus
explains the use of this imagery by stating,

> think not that the wine We have mentioned in Our Tablet is
> the wine which men drink, and which causeth their intelli-
> gence to pass away, their human nature to be perverted, their
> light to be changed, and their purity to be soiled. Our
> intention is indeed that wine which intensifieth man's love for
> God, for His Chosen Ones and for His loved ones, and
> igniteth in the hearts the fire of God and love for Him, and
> glorification and praise of Him.[24]

He further explains the specific meaning of this metaphor
as it appears in His own writings as well as in the Qur'án:

> We meant by this Wine, the River of God, and His favour,
> the fountain of His living waters, and the Mystic Wine and its
> divine grace, even as it was revealed in the Qur'án, if ye are of
> those who understand. He said, and how true is His utter-
> ance: 'A wine delectable to those who drink it.' And He had
> no purpose in this but the wine We have mentioned to you,
> O people of certitude![25]

Therefore, even though Christ did not specifically pro-
scribe the drinking of wine, it is equally clear that His use
of the metaphor is precisely the same. Wine symbolizes
divine sustenance, a source of inspiration capable of
exhilarating and transforming whoever imbibes it. Perhaps
even more relevant to our previous chapter, this wine is
made from the fruit of the branches, a fruit that is picked
by the labourers working in the vineyard. If the branches
are the believers, their fruit would be their spiritual
understanding translated into deeds. The gathering of that
fruit by the labourers might signify some cumulative
effect of those deeds, such as the coalescing of such effort
that occurs in the unified social edifice of a community
organized around religious principles.

The Choice Wine

We have mentioned the twofold nature of the revelation as relating to the distinction between the wine and the wineskin. For example, we have discussed how the Manifestations 'speak a twofold language', the one 'devoid of allusions', is 'unconcealed and unveiled', and the other 'veiled and concealed, so that whatever lieth hidden in the heart of the malevolent may be made manifest and their innermost being be disclosed'.[26] As we have noted, this distinction parallels the language employed by the Manifestation in conveying spiritual, ethical or mystical matters, as opposed to the Manifestation speaking as lawgiver and designer of social edifice.

Bahá'u'lláh confirms such an interpretation in *Epistle to the Son of the Wolf* when He states, 'At one time We spoke in the language of the lawgiver; at another in that of the truth-seeker and the mystic . . .'[27] Yet Bahá'u'lláh penned well over a hundred works and employed a variety of styles, only a few of which can be easily classified into one of these two categories. How, then, can we distinguish between the 'wine' and the 'wineskin' from these revealed writings?

According to Shoghi Effendi, among all the hundreds of works of Bahá'u'lláh, two works stand out as the most significant, the *Kitáb-i-Íqán (The Book of Certitude)* and the Kitáb-i-Aqdas (the Most Holy Book), the one an exposition of the essential unity of the divine process whereby God systematically assists His creation; the other a repository of laws and a blueprint for the institutions designed to guide and sustain humanity for at least the next thousand years. Since the *Kitáb-i-Íqán* is the heart of Bahá'u'lláh's explanation of spirituality as expressed in terrestrial terms, it might well be considered the wine of the revelation. Likewise, since the Kitáb-i-Aqdas translates that truth into a daily regimen and a social structure, it could well be viewed as the wineskin capable of conveying the new wine to humankind.

But a further examination of the fundamental contents of these works and their relationship to each other reveals yet a further and more expansive use of the wine imagery. Written 'in defence of the Bábí Revelation',[28] the *Kitáb-i-Íqán* was revealed 'within the space of two days and two nights'[29] as a response to questions posed by the as yet unconverted uncle of the Báb, Hájí Mírzá Siyyid Muhammad. These questions, which concerned the 'Shí'ih expectations of the advent of the Qá'im of the House of Muhammad',[30] were categorized by the uncle under four headings:

1. The Day of Resurrection. Is there to be corporeal resurrection? The world is replete with injustice. How are the just to be requited and the unjust punished?

2. The twelfth Imám was born at a certain time and lives on. There are traditions, all supporting the belief. How can this be explained?

3. Interpretation of holy texts. This Cause does not seem to conform with beliefs held throughout the years. One cannot ignore the literal meaning of holy texts and scripture. How can this be explained?

4. Certain events, according to the traditions that have come down from the Imáms, must occur at the advent of the Qá'im. Some of these are mentioned. But none of these has happened. How can this be explained?[31]*

---

* These are cited by Balyuzi from papers recently discovered in the uncle's own hand.

Bahá'u'lláh responds to each of these particular questions, and He also elucidates in this logically structured treatise the major ingredients of the divine plan by which God gradually educates humanity through a succession of divinely-guided messengers or Manifestations. In the course of this discussion, Bahá'u'lláh also explicates the meaning of various Christian and Islamic prophecies regarding the 'return' which the advent of the Báb fulfils, and He renders a general discourse on the methodology of prophecy itself.

Beginning with the observation about the supreme irony of how humanity has consistently persecuted the very ones empowered by God to assist and educate humankind, Bahá'u'lláh then proceeds to demonstrate how each Prophet came with clear proofs of His identity. He further explains how these proofs became misinterpreted or misapplied. The second part of the essay focuses on the station, methodology and nature of the Manifestations themselves, how they are in their 'twofold station'[32] both individual beings responding to the exigencies of a particular stage in human organic growth, relinquishing their own will to become a divine instrument, and how, at the same time, they function as dramatic expressions of God Himself:

> They are the mirrors that truly and faithfully reflect the light of God. Whatsoever is applicable to them is in reality applicable to God, Himself, Who is both the Visible and the Invisible . . . By attaining, therefore, to the presence of these holy Luminaries, the 'Presence of God' Himself is attained.[33]

The overall effect of this apologia is a justification for the process of progressive revelation, a vindication of God's indirection and subtlety in this, and a clear explication of how humanity has, by abusing this process, deprived itself of the very source of its own comfort. Shoghi Effendi states that 'by sweeping away the age-long barriers that have so insurmountably separated the great religions of the world', the *Kitáb-i-Íqán* has 'laid down a broad and unassailable foundation for the complete and permanent reconciliation of their followers'.[34] Furthermore, serving as it does to coalesce the previously veiled or necessarily incomplete explications of progressive revelation enunciated by previous Manifestations, the work 'broke the "seals" of the "Book" referred to by Daniel, and disclosed the meaning of the "words" destined to remain "closed up" till the "time of the end"'.[35]

In addition to unveiling the eternality, unity and coherence of the divine process which has ever been at work in the course of human evolution, the revelation of the *Kitáb-i-Íqán* represents for the purposes of our discussion another most interesting fulfilment of prophecy. In the Qur'án Muḥammad alludes to 'the great day', 'the day when mankind shall stand before the Lord of the worlds'. He states that at that time the unfaithful shall be 'shut out as by a veil from their Lord' and then they shall be told, 'This is what ye deemed a lie'; whereas the righteous shall be greatly rewarded:

> Thou shalt mark in their faces the brightness of delight;
> Choice sealed wine shall be given them to quaff,
> The seal of musk. For this let those pant who pant for bliss . . .

In view of the scope of the work, it not surprising that Shoghi Effendi designates the *Kitáb-i-Íqán* as having 'pre-eminence among the doctrinal' works of Bahá'u'lláh.[37] But of particular interest is the possibility that this same Tablet is that same pure wine with the seal of musk alluded to by Muḥammad. Indeed, Shoghi Effendi confirms that this is the case when he notes that the *Kitáb-i-Íqán* itself 'proffered to mankind the "Choice Sealed

Wine", whose seal is of "musk".'[38]* In effect, the righteous ones mentioned in the Qur'án are those who recognize the new Manifestation and are consequently rewarded by being given to understand the justice and benignity of God's ways to man. From the title Bahá'u'lláh bestows on this crucial work – *The Book of Certitude* – we can infer that the lucid insight into theodicy which the work proffers is capable of inducing a confirmation of faith and acquiescence to the Will of God.

The unsurpassed power and weightiness of this work does not mean that the sum total of the spiritual teachings of Bahá'u'lláh are contained in the *Kitáb-i-Íqán*. The vintage bequeathed by Bahá'u'lláh is also found in numerous other spiritual or doctrinal works. However, the essential thesis of these other doctrinal works is a further explication of this same theme – the unity of the human family and the integrity of the divine plan by which that family attains understanding of the unity of God.

Unsealing the Wine at the Family Reunion

It is appropriate to our previous discussion about the inextricable relationship between knowledge and action that the choice wine in this metaphor is bestowed with the revelation of the *Kitáb-i-Íqán*, but its contents are still withheld because the wine is still sealed, albeit with an attracting perfume, a musk.

We might presume that the seal alludes to the fact that the explication of divine justice which induces certitude is,

---

* 'Revealed on the eve of the declaration of His Mission, it proffered to mankind the "Choice Sealed Wine", whose seal is of "musk", and broke the "seals" of the "Book" referred to by Daniel, and disclosed the meaning of the "words" destined to remain "closed up" till the "time of the end".'

while enticing, insufficient without some means of implementing that insight into some form of action. In effect, we are allowed to behold the wine, to detect its fragrance, but we still need a means of unsealing the wine and a receptacle to contain it that we might partake of this choice vintage.

We should not be surprised, therefore, when Bahá'u'lláh Himself alludes to the revelation of the laws, exhortations and administrative order in the Kitáb-i-Aqdas as the unsealing of the choice wine:

> Think not that We have revealed unto you a mere code of laws. Nay, rather, We have unsealed the choice Wine with the fingers of might and power.[39]

As further confirmation of this interpretation, we may take note that in works penned after 1873, that is after the revelation of the Kitáb-i-Aqdas, Bahá'u'lláh frequently employs this same metaphor by way of implying that the synthesizing, or reunion, of spiritual insight with social guidance conveys the choice wine to the faithful in a new wineskin:

> Whoso faileth to quaff the choice wine which We have unsealed through the potency of Our Name, the All-Compelling, shall be unable to discern the splendours of the light of divine unity or to grasp the essential purpose underlying the Scriptures of God, the Lord of heaven and earth, the sovereign Ruler of this world and of the world to come. Such a man shall be accounted among the faithless in the Book of God, the All-Knowing, the All-Informed.[40]*

In His final Tablet, *Epistle to the Son of the Wolf* penned in

---

* According to Balyuzi in *Bahá'u'lláh, the King of Glory* (p. 381), this Tablet belongs to what Shoghi Effendi in *God Passes By* (p. 205), terms one of three 'distinct categories' of Bahá'u'lláh's writings during this period, the category of Tablets which 'partly enunciate and partly reaffirm the fundamental tenets and principles underlying that Dispensation'.

1891, Bahá'u'lláh alludes to the 'Sealed Wine' as a symbol of God's Revelation in five different passages. In one of these He states:

> Ponder upon the things which have been mentioned, perchance thou mayest quaff the Sealed Wine through the power of the name of Him Who is the Self-Subsisting, and obtain that which no one is capable of comprehending.[41]

In summary, then, the revelation of the *Kitáb-i-Íqán* represents the 'choice sealed wine' given to humanity as the means by which the mysteries can be unveiled and true understanding gained (and, thereby, certitude and confirmation as well). And yet, though the wine be given, it cannot be quaffed until the vintage is unsealed and placed in a wineskin, something that is accomplished when the laws and institutions are revealed in the Kitáb-i-Aqdas. Furthermore, we can presume that the pouring of the wine into the new wineskin is something accomplished with the completion of the Bahá'í administrative order in 1963 with the election of the Universal House of Justice. Yet, we might also correctly infer that this process is dynamic and not fully accomplished until in due course the secular world adopts the system devised by Bahá'u'lláh to effect the just administration of human affairs.

A Family Reunion

This pouring of wine into the wineskin thus symbolizes the same sort of reunion or revitalization or resurrection that occurs historically whenever a Manifestation ushers in a new revelation, thereby advancing human understanding, instigates social reform and generally reinvigorates the phenomenal world with a fresh outpouring of spiritual energy. Yet, as we have implied, coming at this turning point in human social and spiritual evolution, this particular reunion symbolizes something more permanent than the binding of old wounds. Heralding and signalling the advent of a general understanding of human unity and purpose resulting from humanity's coming of age, this reunion will thus cause a permanent healing of the baseless and unnecessary antipathy between science and religion, between complementary components of ourselves, between our spirituality and our materiality, between the female and male aspects of ourselves.

It is in this context that the Bahá'í writings allude to Bahá'u'lláh as a 'Divine Physician' who, well aware of the afflictive disease sundering the peoples of the world and impeding the divinely ordained course of human progress, has prescribed the only efficacious remedy:

> The All-Knowing Physician hath His finger on the pulse of mankind. He perceiveth the disease, and prescribeth, in His unerring wisdom, the remedy. Every age hath its own problem, and every soul its particular aspiration. The remedy the world needeth in its present-day afflictions can never be the same as that which a subsequent age may require. Be anxiously concerned with the needs of the age ye live in, and centre your deliberations on its exigencies and requirements.[42]

Therefore, while all new revelations effect a resurrection of divine purpose and a renewed integrity to the process of human education, the particular milestone in the unfolding of collective human development that the Bahá'í revelation signals is made unmistakably clear:

> 'This', He furthermore declares, 'is the king of days', the 'Day of God Himself', the 'Day which shall never be followed by night', the 'Springtime which autumn will never overtake', 'the eye to past ages and centuries', for which 'the soul of every Prophet of God, of every Divine Messenger,

hath thirsted', for which 'all the divers kindreds of the earth have yearned', through which 'God hath proved the hearts of the entire company of His Messengers and Prophets, and beyond them those that stand guard over His sacred and inviolable Sanctuary, the inmates of the Celestial Pavilion and dwellers of the Tabernacle of Glory.'[43]

Certainly we should not infer from this that humanity will never again be tested, since one of the fundamental Bahá'í principles regarding human development is that individual or collective progress must inevitably involve some form of struggle or testing, some challenge to strive beyond the bounds of our present capacity. But having gained a fundamental understanding of human unity and purpose, as well as the justice and benignity of the process by which God has assisted human progress throughout history, humankind will never again experience the sort of decline wherein these dual expressions of human purpose are sundered, where governance is separated from moral perspective, science from religion, our femaleness from our maleness. Nor will the Manifestations intended for our resurrection and enlightenment ever again be rejected and persecuted by the followers of the previous Prophet.

Therefore, as we noted in our discussion of the Bahá'í theory of history, we do not infer from this vision of the future that there will never be a need for further guidance. But while we have become accustomed to thinking of the 'new City' as appearing only when the previous edifice has become decadent, we will come to realize that the need for renewal does not require degeneration or retardation of a former condition, any more than individual education requires a declination prior to further advancement. The sort of schism we have traced is indicative of what has happened consistently in the past, but we should not infer that the process is intended to function this way, that religion must necessarily become perverse, dysfunctional and counter-productive before further enlightenment is required.

Certainly succeeding stages of growth in organic life imply a readiness for advancement, not a negative condition, unless the transition to the advanced condition be abated or forestalled. If a seedling is ready to be transplanted from a small pot to a garden, it is not necessarily because the seedling is doing poorly, but rather because it has used well the opportunity to increase its strength under guarded conditions. The former condition becomes negative only when the plant is kept in the constraints of the pot after it has become ready for transplanting and for further development (an expanded identity).

Thus, the perversity that has so often occurred with the advent of a new dispensation is not a matter of course, not the result of divine intent, but the volitional neglecting of that methodology by humanity. As we have also discussed, that impediment results from a variety of sources, such as the attempt on the part of ecclesiastical authority to maintain the status quo and a failure of the generality of followers of the previous Manifestations to recognize the successor to that station.

Each Manifestation cautions His followers that what He has provided, though sufficient for their immediate needs, is not the final instruction that humanity will require. Bahá'u'lláh, like Christ before Him, stated that as vast and significant as would be the progress of human understanding and actions during this dispensation, there was much that He would have liked to share for which humanity was not ready, nor would it become ready during His dispensation. In this vein Shoghi Effendi relates that Bahá'u'lláh instructed His amanuensis Mírzá Áqá Ján to destroy countless verses because they would not be timely during the dispensation of Bahá'u'lláh.* Likewise, Shoghi Effendi explicates one of the more abstruse Hidden Words (no. 77 from the Persian) as alluding to the constraints Bahá'u'lláh had to abide regarding what would be appropriate for this dispensation:

> Does not Bahá'u'lláh Himself allude to the progressiveness of Divine Revelation and to the limitations which an inscrutable Wisdom has chosen to impose upon Him? What else can this passage of the Hidden Words imply, if not that He Who revealed it disclaimed finality for the Revelation entrusted to Him by the Almighty?[44]

Preparing to Partake of the Vintage: Some Requisites for Just Governance

Christ's advice to His own followers about how to recognize the coming of the Son of Man was as subtle as it was useful. To become assured that this turning point in human history had indeed occurred, one would be obliged to examine the fruits of the one professing to be such a Prophet. Or in keeping with our present metaphor, to determine if this be the choice wine, one must sip the vintage. For however much the Bahá'í texts may affirm that the long-awaited reunion of the human family has occurred, and however lucid may be Bahá'u'lláh's explica-

---

* A vast, and indeed the greater, proportion of these writings were, alas, lost irretrievably to posterity. No less an authority that Mírzá Áqá Ján, Bahá'u'lláh's amanuensis, affirms, as reported by Nabíl, that by the express order of Bahá'u'lláh, hundreds of thousands of verses, mostly written by His own hand, were obliterated and cast into the river. 'Finding me reluctant to execute His orders,' Mírzá Áqá Ján has related to Nabíl, 'Bahá'u'lláh would reassure me saying: "None is to be found at this time worthy to hear these melodies' . . . Not once, or twice, but innumerable times, was I commanded to repeat this act' (Shoghi Effendi, *God Passes By*, p. 138).

tion of His advent as the fulfilment of the prophecies and traditions of the world's religions regarding this turning point in human history, the best test of whether or not Bahá'u'lláh has provided both the vision of that reunion and the means for its accomplishment is to examine the artifice He has wrought, both the theoretical paradigm and the embryonic model of that structure that is the present Bahá'í administrative order.

The Problem of Envisioning the Future

Shoghi Effendi cautioned that however complete we may deem our vision of the future to be, it can in no wise adequately portend the actuality of the fully-emerged artifice:

> The Golden Age of the Faith itself that must witness the unification of all the peoples and nations of the world, the establishment of the Most Great Peace, the inauguration of the Kingdom of the Father upon earth, the coming of age of the entire human race and the birth of a world civilization, inspired and directed by the creative energies released by Bahá'u'lláh's World Order, shining in its meridian splendour, is still unborn and its glories unsuspected.[45]

But not only is that ultimate achievement of this transformation 'unsuspected', we are also unable to anticipate the process by which it will be attained:

> To attempt to visualize, even in its barest outline, the glory that must envelop these institutions, to essay even a tentative and partial description of their character or the manner of their operation, or to trace however inadequately the course of events leading to their rise and eventual establishment is far beyond my own capacity and power.[46]

No doubt part of our inability to know exactly how this

edifice will emerge results from the fact that so much of the pace of human progress towards that inherent goal is contingent on the rapidity with which humanity recognizes the integrity, accuracy and efficacy of the social principles and governmental paradigm set forth in the Bahá'í scriptures. This does not mean that meaningful planetary change must await the universal recognition of the Bahá'í revelation as the source of such principles and theories of a global community. But the course of events regarding the immediate future clearly depends on the capacity of world governments to recognize the necessity of forming a federation of governments to ensure world security, protection of the environment, management of world resources and the devising of systems for conducting the business of a world contracted into one social organism.

Of course, we can already witness almost on a daily basis the ever more expansive recognition of the viability, indeed, the absolute necessity of those principles, and we may well infer from the unfolding of world political and economic change that the progress towards what the Bahá'í writings designate as the 'Lesser Peace' is proceeding apace. Certainly the vast change in recent world political conditions, so long polarized into rigid camps of simplistic epithets and easy ideological slogans, would seem to confirm such inferences. But it is abundantly clear in the Bahá'í texts that the construction of a world commonwealth is not a one-step procedure whereby humanity leaps from its current precarious state of fragmentation into a fully harmonious, spiritually based, and justly devised system of world governance.

Nevertheless, while cautioning against speculating about the precise steps or events which must needs herald the advent of this process, the Bahá'í writings verify that the process towards that destiny is already well underway.

They further outline in some detail three stages that will occur in the progress toward the establishment of a world commonwealth: a period of the 'Lesser Peace', an era of 'fulfilment', and a 'Golden Age' in which the Bahá'í world commonwealth becomes established.

Problems of Orientation towards Governance

Before we attempt to examine in some detail how these three stages will occur, we would first benefit from examining briefly an implicit principle underlying the Bahá'í perspective about governance, because at whatever stage in the process we find ourselves, we must inevitably respond to one critical concern – in such a vast system, what will be the relationship between the individual and the state? Put more directly, how is it possible to prevent a utopian vision of a world community from becoming an impersonal, monolithic dystopia oblivious to the needs and concerns of the individuals that comprise that body politic?

The relevance of this issue becomes readily apparent when we consider that regardless at what stage of societal evolution we view human history, we can observe in the administration of human affairs a precarious balance between what is good for governmental institutions and what is good for the individual. We might presume that so long as a governmental administrative body has as its animating principle the sustenance of the individuals in its care, human justice would be relatively secure. And yet there is an almost inevitable and pernicious tension between the security, well-being and prosperity of the collective body politic and the happiness, independence and well-being of the individual. In healthier societies, particularly in certain tribal societies which emerged from the exigencies of natural law, the two forces might not become antithetical; but in most complex synthetic systems of governance, there is a constant tension between what is just for the individual and what is just for the state.

Traditionally, states respond to this dilemma by implementing the principle enunciated in 1720 by Francis Hutcherson: 'That action is best which procures the greatest happiness for the greatest numbers.'[47] In effect, because the formulation of theory into practice is dictated by those who wield power, individual justice is sacrificed to the larger good.

Naturally the question then arises as to what is ultimately 'good' for people, and who is to decide such a thing. If we apply the principles of a pure democracy, then the desires of the majority dictate policy and interpret morality, a process which diminishes the morality of society to the lowest common denominator, something the character of Dr Stockman in Ibsen's *An Enemy of the People* decries as absurd. After suffering humiliation and indignities at the hands of the citizens because he has tried to inform the townsfolk that their water source is contaminated, the good doctor is told by another character that the 'majority always has right on its side'. The doctor responds, 'The majority *never* has right on its side.'[48] He goes on to denounce the doctrine that

> . . . the public, the crowd, the masses, are the essential part of the population – that they constitute the People – that the common folk, the ignorant and incomplete element in the community, have the same right to pronounce judgement and to approve, to direct and to govern, as the isolated, intellectually superior personalities in it.[49]

In light of the very problem Ibsen's character enunciates, most governance recognizes the need for rule by a relatively small body of so-called learned and knowledgeable individuals, not only because the masses do not have the

time or means to become sufficiently informed to participate in a plebiscite for every decision, but also because
there is a commonly accepted premise that governance is
an art which is best practised by those who are trained at
it. The problem then becomes, as history verifies, that
when government becomes vested in the hands of smaller
groups, there is the inevitable temptation to decide affairs
according to what is beneficial to the professional rulers
rather than what is 'good' for people as a whole.

Even when those in government sincerely desire to
provide guidance for those in their charge, decisions must
be made on a daily basis about to what extent government
should be allowed to insinuate itself into the lives of the
people. How do those administering human affairs determine the point of balance between the inalienable rights of
the individual and the health and integrity of society as a
whole?

Of course, implicit in most such debates is an antithesis
between these concerns – that justice for one may not be,
or most often will not be, synonymous with justice for the
other. Therefore, most debates about governance focus on
how to determine at what point it is necessary or best to
sacrifice some individual rights in order to foster, sustain
or secure the collective good. Traditionally this debate is
tightly focused on the struggle between the so-called
'liberal' and 'conservative' points of view. In fact, we can
construct a useful matrix to demonstrate the tension
between these perspectives (see overleaf).

On the 'conservative' side we can place those who
believe that the rights of the individual must be subordi-
nated to the common good and that order and well-being
for the body politic is best achieved when governance
imposes from above its laws and strictly regulates the life
of society. On the 'liberal' side are those who believe in the
natural goodness of the common man, that the rights of

The Tension in Perspective on Human Governance

Area	Liberal View	Conservative View
tradition	Romantic	Neo-Classical
artistic	genius, prophetic soul	master craftsman, student of tradition
governance	few restrictions, concern for masses	law and order, regard for authority
architecture	organic	symmetry
attitude	intensity and passion	sobriety and control
human capacity	celebration of feeling and emotion	celebration of knowledge and logic
attitude	idealistic	realistic
artistic	self-expression ('lamp')	imitation of 'nature' ('mirror')
personality traits	passive or female aspect of self	active, aggressive or male aspect of self
theology	more humanistic emphasis on deeds	other-worldly orientation; irrelevance of deeds
cosmology	humanity part of creation	humanity as centre of universe

the individual are paramount, and that social order and well-being is best achieved when power is placed in the hands of the populace. Obviously these distinctions often become blurred or reversed, but they are useful antitheses that we most commonly associate with 'left-wing' and 'right-wing' political movements.

Underlying these antithetical political perspectives is a

deeper and more pervasive sort of polarization of attitude, a philosophical/theological perspective. For example, in theories of education we find those who believe that the child is best trained when left alone to allow natural genius to flourish, as opposed to those who affirm that the foundation of a child's learning is best nurtured in a highly structured environment. In the arts, a liberal (or 'Romantic') orientation would connote someone who feels that art is best prompted by extricating the artist from traditional models and forms, whereas a conservative (or 'Neo-Classical') perspective might tend to revere training in past traditions.

As the chart indicates, there are endless areas to which we can apply this dichotomy, but for our purposes it is important first to note that this polarization of attitudes parallels our earlier discussion about so-called female and male aspects of human existence. The 'liberal' or 'romantic' orientation parallels the female aspect of ourselves (our primary imagination), whereas the 'conservative' or 'neo-Classical' orientation parallels the male aspect of ourselves (our secondary imagination).

Also implicit in this antithesis is an even more funda-mental assumption about human nature. If we believe that human beings are inherently corrupt, bestial, sinful, though capable of progress through training, then we will naturally presume that only the imposition of strict guidance, rules and restraint will fashion this inherently sinful being into something noble. In short, to view human beings as 'born in sin' and without divine instinct is to assume that without external influence, we would become worse than the animals. On the other hand, to view human beings as innately divine, as naturally good, is to incline towards removing rigorous order, rules and restraints because these tend to restrict the natural capacities and virtues that are inherently human. While the chart hints at the further parallel we have discussed between the attitudes about the relevancy of deeds to salvation in the schism evolving out of Christian theology, this distinction is hardly confined to concerns about theological doctrine. Put simply, this distinction indicates whether we think people are essentially good or essentially bad.

Relevant to this distinction is another generalization we can infer from this matrix: human social history tends to proceed in a pendulum-like action from one extreme to the other. Furthermore, this motion seems to derive from the historical process by which existential fact and empirical evidence sequentially vindicate first one perspective then the other. For example, we can trace in larger movements of Western European history the extreme conservatism of the mediaeval period followed by the more liberal humanism of the Renaissance, followed by the conservative regard for order and tradition in the Neo-Classical period, followed by the liberal revolutionary tenor of the Romantic period.

However, this paradigm is not solely the result of action and reaction. To some extent the humanism of the Renaissance is a reaction against the philosophy of *contemptu mundi* of the mediaeval Christianity, just as the Romanticism of the early nineteenth century results in part from a reaction against the staunch orderliness of the Neo-Classical period. But a more obvious and crucial source of causality in this pendulum swing of social attitude is socio-economic stability as it relates to the collective sense of self. For example, a period of relative peace and economic prosperity is more likely to bring about innovation, individuality, a rebellion against staid regulation; whereas a period of chaos, of plague or war (especially civil war), economic hardship or the breakdown in systems of belief will most often lead to a 'conservative' or 'right-wing' response in an attempt to impose order and stability on an otherwise unstable world.

We can discern this pattern of response in the succession of political philosophies within the history of a given country or even in the succession of events in our own individual lives. Reared in a stable and secure family, or following periods of stasis, security and orderliness, we might tend to be daring, innovative and free to break away from our parents' traditional responses. If we have been through times of hardship and uncertainty, or if we have been abused or neglected as children or feel threatened or insecure or in emotional disarray, we might more likely latch onto some source of order, restraint, even compulsion.

It has been unfortunately the case that governments and the people who run them tend to perceive these two attitudes as mutually exclusive. One result of such a debate, therefore, is that the focus of governmental action, like the schism we discussed in the previous chapter, is the struggle between these opposing forces to gain or retain power while the well-being of the state and the welfare of the body politic is largely ignored or forgotten.

Bahá'í Orientation as Synthesis

The perspective unique to the Bahá'í view of human nature as well as to the Bahá'í sense of the interplay between the individual and the body politic in constructing a just and effective system of human governance is, once again, the idea of reunion. Yet this concept is not an imposed synthesis nor precisely a balance between these extremes. Rather, the Bahá'í perspective is that in a justly devised system there is complementarity, and the health of the whole is inseparable from and integral with the health of the parts. In effect, when governance is correctly devised, it fosters in the individual those qualities that ensure justice for the body politic as well.

In general, this consonance is achieved by some flexible form of governance wherein social policy can change to befit the an ever-evolving human social context. But as with the healthy tribal community, such unanimity of purpose and synthesis of goal with structure can only occur when the collective body has consensus about its identity, its goals and how those goals are best achieved.

To a certain extent, just governance does not depend on the form it should take nor the delineation of some careful balance between the rights of the individual versus the rights of the state. We can imagine justice being administered through a variety of governmental types – we might even presume that governmental form should befit the exigencies of locale and population. Similarly, in a healthy state, the objectives of the populace as a whole and those of the individual are sufficiently in accord that the well-being of one is synonymous with the well-being of the other. Of course, at the heart of just governance is the definition of justice itself. For while we might infer from Hutcheson's dictum that 'happiness' implies more than the freedom or licence to respond to one's appetitive nature and sensual desires, we need to define to what extent governance is concerned with a concept of human justice as designating some form of wellness beyond fulfilling certain physical requirements.

It is understandable that peoples worldwide, so long deprived of the freedom to make independent moral choices or to have political autonomy, would be wary of political systems in general, but particularly of those which hint of any rigid or narrow moral or political perspective. Indeed, most theocracies, dictatorships and totalitarian regimes had their roots in a utopian vision. But true to the fictional dystopias depicted in works like

Orwell's *1984* and Huxley's *Brave New World*, most utopian dreams ultimately degenerate into inflexible and oppressive nightmares that prey upon the very populace they were devised to liberate and assist.

Consequently, governance, like religion, has for perhaps a majority of the world's population become stigmatized as being at odds with individual human well-being. As a result, governments have become in the eyes of the generality of people little more than delivery systems for the bare necessities of life: water, power and domestic security. But without a moral basis for decisions, governmental authority has no sound or consistent method for achieving even the most mundane sorts of management.

At the same time, we have as a species reached an age which, as world leaders are rapidly coming to enunciate, daily demonstrates an increasingly greater need for regulation, structure, more inclusive systems of organization simply to sustain human survival. We also witness on almost a daily basis the devastating results of managing without foresight, of responding haphazardly to one crisis after another: the depletion of the ozone layer, global warming, the contamination of air and water, devastating famines, the explosive growth in impoverishment and alienation, the rampant spread of disease, the exponential growth in virtually every world urban community of random violence, drug usage and other similar signs of desperation, resignation, hopeless despair and in-humanity.

Because these and other global crises are not isolated pathologies but part of systemic dysfunction, they cry out for a solution which reflects the reunion we have described – a synthesis of a coherent moral perspective with an inclusive political mechanism. The question then becomes how to devise governance which is moral without being oppressive and chauvinistic, which is capable of coordinating the earth's resources and responding to the needs of the entire global community, without simultaneously becoming monolithic, impersonal and dehumanizing.

The short-term answer is obvious – to abandon archaic notions of nationalism and self-interest and embrace the newly-emerged reality that 'The earth is but one country, and mankind its citizens'.[50] The long-term answer is to couple that understanding with appropriate action – the creation of a governmental system that ministers to and is reflective of that reality, a system capable of evolving with the evolutionary growth of that union (or reunion) of a world society. The evolving of a world commonwealth as depicted in the Bahá'í writings would seem to portray precisely such a process.

7

From the Lesser Peace to a Golden Age

Stages in the Evolution of a World Commonwealth

> World unity is the goal towards which a harassed humanity is striving. Nation-building has come to an end. The anarchy inherent in state sovereignty is moving towards a climax. A world, growing to maturity, must abandon this fetish, recognize the oneness and wholeness of human relationships, and establish once for all the machinery that can best incarnate this fundamental principle of its life.[1]
>
> *Shoghi Effendi*

A familiar story is told about a traveller who became thoroughly lost on a remote rural road. He approached a solitary farmer at the edge of a field to ask directions to the city. The farmer scratched his head, made several halting attempts to describe a proper route, pointing first one direction, then the other. Finally he looked blankly at the expectant traveller and said, 'I guess you just can't get there from here.'

While Bahá'u'lláh's pronouncement that the world has become one country is a statement of fact, not a pious hope, He clearly demonstrates that the process of constructing a system to befit that newly-emerged identity – the end result of countless ages of human physical and social evolution – can result only from the coordinated, collaborative and wilful agreement among world leaders.

Therefore, while the Bahá'í writings outline in some detail the process by which a federation of governments can be established and even discuss the fundamental components that must constitute such a system, we might understandably question how it will be possible to get there from here in light of the ostensibly entrenched political interests which currently inhibit the initiation of such a federation. For while the generality of humankind may readily acknowledge their desire to abolish warfare, to protect the environment and to create a sane and just administration of human affairs, the power to bring about a reformation in human governance resides largely in the hands of a small cadre of thoroughly entrenched political leaders, most of whom seem perfectly willing to sacrifice the public good to secure their own self-interest. And while some of these leaders may die off or be replaced, the ones who take their place seem little different.

Since it is equally clear that a federation of world governments must come about through the wilful conjoining of national governments, we might well question what will cause a change of heart in these leaders. Or even more to the point, what might effect such a change to occur simultaneously among a sufficient number of world leaders in time to avert global disaster.

The Bahá'í writings portray a relatively clear sequence of events that will usher in global peace and a world federation of governments. In the broadest of terms, there are two stages in this process. The first is the Lesser Peace, a world peace brought about through a global treaty and an alliance or federation of national governments. The second is the Most Great Peace, a global community united under one religion with all peoples working in close harmony to establish a world civilization. There are, however, other components to this evolutionary process, an understanding of which is absolutely essential if one is to comprehend how such a propitious outcome to our present consternation can be effected.

The Birth of a Global Identity

Universal Recognition of Organic Unity

As we discussed in the previous chapter, just governance depends to a great extent on a condition wherein the essential objectives for the society as a whole are synonymous with or in concert with individual objectives. Or stated another way, in a healthy society there is some shared perspective rather than a precarious balance between the health of the individual and the health of the state.

If we apply this same principle to a healthy global community wherein the constituent members are national or territorial governments, then we can infer that to perceive the national interests as independent of or superior to the rights and health of a global community is likewise unhealthy or unjust. Therefore, we can conclude that the first requisite for the initiation of a world system of social management is the increasing awareness on the part of constituent governments that when the world is contracted into one integral organism, it is impossible to pursue the narrow interests or well-being of member states apart from the health and well-being of the global community as a whole.

Because Bahá'u'lláh observes that the world has already emerged as one country, Shoghi Effendi criticizes the American government for adamantly refusing to consider subordinating its national interests to the interests of the health of the world community. He predicts that America will suffer dire consequences as a result of this 'obsolescent doctrine' because the nation is violating a fundamental requisite for its own sustenance:

> The woes and tribulations which threaten [America] are partly avoidable but mostly inevitable and God-sent, for by reason of them a government and people clinging tenaciously to the obsolescent doctrine of absolute sovereignty and upholding a political system, manifestly at variance with the needs of a world already contracted into a neighbourhood and crying out for unity, will find itself purged of its anachronistic conceptions . . .[2]

This condemnation does not imply that all forms of national, regional or ethnic pride are erroneous or unwise. Shoghi Effendi observes that

> . . . this declaration, this clarion-call of Bahá'u'lláh . . . should not, indeed it cannot, be construed as a repudiation, or regarded in the light of a censure, pronounced against a sane and intelligent patriotism, nor does it seek to undermine the allegiance and loyalty of any individual to his country, nor does it conflict with the legitimate aspirations, rights, and duties of any individual state or nation. All it does imply and proclaim is the insufficiency of patriotism, in view of the fundamental changes effected in the economic life of society and the interdependence of the nations, and as the consequence of the contraction of the world . . .[3]

We have inferred that any healthy system of governance cannot be imposed; it must be based on a universally upheld authority. In the same way, a world commonwealth cannot result from a synthetic order imposed on a disunited body, any more than individual health can be imposed by a doctor pronouncing a cure rather than guiding the patient to a remedial course of a healthy regimen.

Consequently, the Bahá'í writings state that another requisite for world unity is the abolition of other forms of prejudice, since such prejudices are based on the assumption that some part of the world body politic is superior to or distinct from the collective organism that is humanity:

> World order can be founded only on an unshakeable consciousness of the oneness of mankind, a spiritual truth which all the human sciences confirm. Anthropology, physiology, psychology, recognize only one human species, albeit infinitely varied in the secondary aspects of life. Recognition of this truth requires abandonment of prejudice – prejudice of every kind – race, class, colour, creed, nation, sex, degree of material civilization, everything which enables people to consider themselves superior to others.[4]

In this vein, Shoghi Effendi assures us that the concept of a world federation of governments as an initial stage in the establishment of a world commonwealth does not seek the 'subversion of the existing foundations of society' but rather seeks to 'remould its institutions in a manner consonant with the needs of an ever-changing world', not

> to stifle the flame of a sane and intelligent patriotism in men's hearts, nor to abolish the system of national autonomy so essential if the evils of excessive centralization are to be avoided. It does not ignore, nor does it attempt to suppress, the diversity of ethnic origins, of climate, of history, of language and tradition, of thought and habit, that differentiate the peoples and nations of the world. It calls for a wider loyalty, for a larger aspiration than any that has animated the human race. It insists upon the subordination of national impulses and interests to the imperative claims of a unified world. It repudiates excessive centralization on one hand, and disclaims all attempts at uniformity on the other. Its watchword is unity in diversity . . .[5]

Therefore, recalling yet again our previous analogy of the cell, we might imagine that a group of cells could take understandable pride in their collective enterprise of being a part of a healthy spleen. There would be no harm in this so long as these cells did not begin to think of the growth

and well-being of the spleen as independent of or having
precedence over the health of the body as a whole. Indeed,
such self-interest, such unmanageable growth of cells out
of sync with the development of the host organism would
be tantamount to a definition of cancer. Similarly, in the
context of a world contracted into a global organism, any
nation which attempts to assert its own interest at the
expense of or to the exclusion of the interest of the
planetary community as a whole is by definition working
against the health of the planetary organism of which it is
an organic part and, therefore, against its own health as
well. According to Shoghi Effendi, those states that
cannot recognize the inescapable logic of this relationship
will be forced to discover its veracity empirically:

> World unity is the goal towards which a harassed humanity is
> striving. Nation-building has come to an end. The anarchy
> inherent in state sovereignty is moving towards a climax. A
> world, growing to maturity, must abandon this fetish,
> recognize the oneness and wholeness of human relationships,
> and establish once for all the machinery that can best
> incarnate this fundamental principle of its life.[6]

It is not hard to see in the exponentially increasing rate of
worldwide social, political and economic change the birth
of a universally held consciousness of the planet as a single
organic enterprise, though at present our attention may be
focused on the destabilizing breakdown of archaic or
outmoded systems. Furthermore, we can also witness the
rapid emergence of collaborative efforts at establishing
some of the fundamental components of world governance
– coordinated economic agreements, attempts at comprehensive peace initiatives to settle long-standing disputes
among nations, negotiations to dismantle the world's
nuclear armaments, international efforts at protecting
the environment, controlling disease, managing world
resources and securing individual rights and freedoms.

At the same time, we can also detect various points of closure for human progress on this planet should global solutions not be devised in due time. It is apparent, in other words, that simply knowing the gravity of world problems and the absolute necessity of establishing some coordinated global solution is not a sufficient impetus to counteract the vested interests of those who hold the reigns of power or for the generality of the world's populace to express their desires effectively through the channels available to them in present political systems. We must conclude, therefore, that if a sane management of human affairs is to occur on our planet before irreparable damage is incurred, some critical event or series of events must so galvanize the will of world leaders that all personal interests will suddenly become fused with the interests of the body politic as a whole and all excuses for delay will be suddenly cast aside and dismissed.

The Fire of Ordeal as Transitional Labour

The forecast in the Bahá'í writings for the emergence of a world government, therefore, while wholeheartedly optimistic about the future of humanity, also includes in the formula for the birth of that new identity a painful labour which the world has yet to experience. Bahá'u'lláh observes that the 'whole earth is now in a state of pregnancy'[7] and the identity of that newborn organism will be world peace and a global community as inaugurated by a federation of world governments. But even presently, while the swift transformation of world politics presage the imminence of such a birth, we have yet to experience the final pangs of the transitional labour that must necessarily precede the fully-emerged organism.*

---

* 'Transitional' labour is the last and most severe part of the first stage of labour, the second stage being birth itself and the third being the expulsion

It is in this context that the Bahá'í writings describe a convulsive ordeal that will accompany the final part of this birthing process. The Bahá'í writings note that the agony of this birth might have been averted had the world leaders responded appropriately in the late 1800s to the admonitions of Bahá'u'lláh to establish the foundation for world federalism. Consequently, while praising the advent of this turning point in human social evolution, Bahá'u'lláh also laments the unfortunate choices by world leaders which have made this transition more difficult than it need have been. Bahá'u'lláh sometimes alludes to this ordeal as a chastisement resulting from the failure of humanity to accede to divine guidance:

> The promised day is come, the day when tormenting trials will have surged above your heads, and beneath your feet, saying: 'Taste ye what your hands have wrought!'[8]

Yet it is clear in this and in other statements that this 'chastisement' will have a redemptive and beneficial result because it will illustrate with unmistakable clarity the logical necessity of the systems revealed by Bahá'u'lláh as the appropriate remedial recourse for healing the disjointed body of the global community.

In this context, Shoghi Effendi discusses this ordeal not as a single event but as a sequence of events set in motion as far back as the First World War, which he alludes to as 'the first stage in a titanic convulsion long predicted by Bahá'u'lláh'[9] culminating in some as yet unforeseen but world-embracing convulsion. Shoghi Effendi noted that despite the painful lessons learned from that war, by the time it had ended humanity still had not recognized the

---

of the placenta. The cervix is almost completely dilated (eight to ten centimeters). Contractions are long and painful, birth is imminent, but the mother must resist the temptation to push until full dilatation is achieved.

necessity of establishing a world federal system. Furthermore, in a treatise penned in 1931, Shoghi Effendi stated that humanity had already passed the point where collective awareness of the universal need for planetary unity and organization could avert a catastrophe:

> That the forces of a world catastrophe can alone precipitate such a new phase of human thought is, alas, becoming increasingly apparent. That nothing short of the fire of a severe ordeal, unparalleled in its intensity, can fuse and weld the discordant entities that constitute the elements of present-day civilization, into the integral components of the world commonwealth of the future, is a truth which future events will increasingly demonstrate.
>
> The prophetic voice of Bahá'u'lláh warning, in the concluding passages of the Hidden Words, 'the peoples of the world' that 'an unforeseen calamity is following them and that grievous retribution awaiteth them' throws indeed a lurid light upon the immediate fortunes of sorrowing humanity. Nothing but a fiery ordeal, out of which humanity will emerge, chastened and prepared, can succeed in implanting that sense of responsibility which the leaders of a new-born age must arise to shoulder.[10]

In another treatise, written in 1941, Shoghi Effendi discussed how the dual forces of this process were already having a worldwide effect. On the one hand, world-embracing changes are portrayed as a 'tempest' that is 'unprecedented in its violence'. At the same time, he portrays this as a 'cleansing force' that is 'unimaginably glorious in its ultimate consequence':

> A tempest, unprecedented in its violence, unpredictable in its course, catastrophic in its immediate effects, unimaginably glorious in its ultimate consequences, is at present sweeping the face of the earth. Its driving power is remorselessly gaining in range and momentum. Its cleansing force, however much undetected, is increasing with every passing

day. Humanity, gripped in the clutches of its devastating power, is smitten by the evidences of its resistless fury. It can neither perceive its origin, nor probe its significance, nor discern its outcome. Bewildered, agonized and helpless, it watches this great and mighty wind of God invading the remotest and fairest regions of the earth, rocking its foundations, deranging its equilibrium, sundering its nations, disrupting the homes of its peoples, wasting its cities, driving into exile its kings, pulling down its bulwarks, uprooting its institutions, dimming its light, and harrowing up the souls of its inhabitants.[11]

Understandably, the horrendous consequences of the Second World War might have been interpreted to constitute the calamity in the plentitude of its fullness, the very force which Bahá'u'lláh had predicted and which Shoghi Effendi described as an unavoidable result of the negligence on the part of humanity to institute the solutions prescribed by Bahá'u'lláh:

. . . it seems apparent that the great failure to respond to Bahá'u'lláh's instructions, appeals and warnings issued in the 19th Century, has now sent the world along a path, and released forces, which must culminate in a still more violent upheaval and agony. The thing is out of hand, so to speak, and it is too late to avert catastrophic trials.[12]

However, in 1954, in alluding to this same ordeal that humanity has brought on itself, Shoghi Effendi described the Second World War as but a 'foretaste' of the 'fiery tribulations' that must needs occur in order to effect that reorientation of priorities and global consciousness which, he asserted, the world desperately needs if it is to achieve its destiny. In particular, Shoghi Effendi alluded to the forthcoming ordeal or sequence of catastrophic events as relating directly to what he calls 'cancerous materialism':

It is this same cancerous materialism, born originally in

Europe, carried to excess in the North American continent, contaminating the Asiatic peoples and nations, spreading its ominous tentacles to the borders of Africa, and now invading its very heart, which Bahá'u'lláh in unequivocal and emphatic language denounced in His Writings, comparing it to a devouring flame and regarding it as the chief factor in precipitating the dire ordeals and world-shaking crises that must necessarily involve the burning of cities and the spread of terror and consternation in the hearts of men.[13]

He further states that, because the American nation is destined to 'play a preponderating role . . . in the hoisting of the standard of the Lesser Peace, in the unification of mankind, and in the establishment of a world federal government on this planet',[14] America would be particularly affected by the forthcoming ordeals:

These same fiery tribulations will not only firmly weld the American nation to its sister nations in both hemispheres, but will through their cleansing effect, purge it thoroughly of the accumulated dross which ingrained racial prejudice, rampant materialism, widespread ungodliness and moral laxity have combined, in the course of successive generations, to produce, and which have prevented her thus far from assuming the role of world spiritual leadership forecast by 'Abdu'l-Bahá's unerring pen – a role which she is bound to fulfil through travail and sorrow.[15]

What the Ordeal must Accomplish

However reassuring were Shoghi Effendi's words in 1941 that this ordeal would be 'unimaginably glorious in its ultimate consequences', we might find it difficult to see in these dire predictions why such an event is absolutely necessary or why it would be implied to be connected with a positive or divine process, the birth of a global community.

The first response to this we have already mentioned, that only through some clear demonstration of the erroneous foundation on which most governments and peoples in power presently manage the earth and its resources can humanity become universally purged of the insidious desire for material prosperity at the expense of every sort of moral or spiritual value or without regard for the well-being of the body politic as a whole. It is clear that such an event must be 'sudden' so that all peoples and leaders will achieve recognition simultaneously and thereby uniformly resolve to take immediate action without the least concern for self-interest. This ordeal must be worldwide because a solution to world crises cannot be accomplished piece-meal. In short, some event or series of events must suddenly make all self-interest synonymous with planetary survival:

> Adversity, prolonged, worldwide, afflictive, allied to chaos and universal destruction, must needs convulse the nations, stir the conscience of the world, disillusion the masses, precipitate a radical change in the very conception of society, and coalesce ultimately the disjointed, the bleeding limbs of mankind into one body, single, organically united, and indivisible.[16]

Because this event will ultimately have a salutary effect, Shoghi Effendi equates this ordeal with a medical procedure, sometimes comparing it to the excising of a cancer and elsewhere comparing it to a purgative. Recalling Bahá'u'lláh's allusion to the Manifestation as a 'divine physician' and to humanity (whose body is the planet) as the patient, Shoghi Effendi states,

> In the spiritual development of man a stage of purgation is indispensable, for it is while passing through it that the over-rated material needs are made to appear in their proper light . . . The present calamities are parts of this process of

purgation, through them alone will man learn his lesson. They are to teach the nations, that they have to view things internationally, they are to make the individual attribute more importance to his moral, than his material welfare.[17]

Of course the patient, especially while in the throes of disease and confusion, can hardly assess the efficacy of the remedy. What might seem desirable and beneficial to the patient might prove fatal. In this sense, the calamity as purgation and remedy is tantamount to a painful but nonetheless essential medical procedure for an advanced disease, a disease which, because the patient earlier refused more palatable remedies, has advanced to a critical stage in which the patient's life is at risk.

In this same context, Shoghi Effendi cautions that as an integral part of this sick organism of the body politic, Bahá'ís themselves cannot hope to be immune to the pain of this treatment:

> In such a process of purgation, when all humanity is in the throes of dire suffering, the Bahá'ís should not hope to remain unaffected. Should we consider the beam that is in our own eye, we would immediately find that these sufferings are also meant for ourselves, who claim to have attained. Such world crisis is necessary to waken us to the importance of our duty and the carrying on of our task . . .[18]

He likewise notes in terms of the medical analogy the moral imperative explicit in the obligation of Bahá'ís to convey the healing teachings of Bahá'u'lláh to a suffering humanity, stating that the fervour with which this is accomplished will to some degree determine the severity of such an ordeal:

> We have no indication of exactly what nature the apocalyptic upheaval will be: it might be another war . . . but as students of our Bahá'í writings it is clear that the longer the 'Divine Physician' (i.e. Bahá'u'lláh) is withheld from healing the ills

of the world, the more severe will be the crisis, and the more terrible the sufferings of the patient.[19]

In sum, then, we can assume that whatever form such an ordeal will take, it will be unexpected, sudden, convulsive, universally experienced, completely disruptive and demonstrative of human recalcitrance and selfishness. Likewise, we can infer that the lessons it will impart will be unmistakably apparent: that unbridled materialism is a perverse motive for human governance, that material well-being is an insufficient criterion by which to judge human success or justice, and that a planetary system of governance in all its manifestations is not merely feasible but the only option available for human survival.

Speculation about the Ordeal

Since the Bahá'í writings affirm that this ordeal will usher in the Lesser Peace, we might assume that Bahá'ís would view this event in a positive light. Yet, even for Bahá'ís, confirmed about the propitious implications of this impending birth and joyously preparing an environment appropriate for the newborn infant, the anticipation of this convulsive event necessarily fills many with trepidation. As a result, there are unpublished and published speculations by Bahá'ís about the time and nature of that birth.

For example, some 'pilgrims' notes'* describe in exact detail the destruction of entire cities, portrayals which might seem to confirm biblical allusions to Armageddon[20] or to the 'time of the end' as heralding the cessation of human life on the planet. Other observations have been published. For example, in her book *The Guardian of the*

---

* Recollections of conversations with 'Abdu'l-Bahá and Shoghi Effendi (and occasionally others) written down by those Bahá'ís who attained an audience with one of them.

Bahá'í Faith, Rúḥíyyih Rabbani, widow of Shoghi Effendi, recounts a conversation with the Guardian about the possibility of such a calamity taking the form of a nuclear holocaust:

> In March 1948 he went still further in a conversation I recorded in my diary: 'Tonight Shoghi Effendi told me some very interesting things: roughly, he said that to say that there was not going to be another war, in the light of present conditions, was foolish, and to say that if there was another war the Atom Bomb would not be used was also foolish.[21]

She infers from this conversation that 'we must believe there probably will be a war and it will be used and there will be terrific destruction'.[22] Of course, an equally valid inference might be that while we cannot presume there will not be such a war, neither can we presume that there will.

J. Tyson in his work *World Peace and World Government* provides a more general assessment about what form such an ordeal might take, speculating that any number of events might have the same result so long as it is 'an unparalleled calamity':

> Although war, particularly nuclear war, seems to fit the description in several ways, other forms of calamity are not ruled out: environmental collapse, chemical or biological warfare, falling asteroids from outer space, or some other calamity that is totally unforeseen.[23]

Yet a 'natural disaster', such as an asteroid, while capable of causing us to rethink our priorities, would not seem to convey the very clear message that we are responsible for our own sordid condition nor would it cause us to see in this event the logical necessity of rethinking our identity or reorganizing our governmental structures to guard against any such calamity ever recurring.

In numerous statements both Shoghi Effendi and the Universal House of Justice confirm that even though the fundamental causes and results can be known, it is impossible for anyone to predict the exact nature of this event, when it will occur, or how long it will endure:

> . . . although there is every reason to expect that the world will experience travails and testing as never before, we do not know what form these upheavals will take, when exactly they will come, how severe they will be, nor how long they will last.[24]

Indeed, Shoghi Effendi and the Universal House of Justice repeatedly caution that not only are the particulars of this ordeal unknowable, but that it is also counterproductive and unwise to expend much energy thinking about it:

> In letters to other believers who have asked questions similar to yours, the House of Justice has emphasized that the friends [Bahá'ís] should not waste their time and energies in fruitless speculations on this question.[25]

Instead, the letter goes on to state, the Bahá'ís should 'concentrate every ounce of energy' on achieving the goals of establishing a worldwide administrative order, 'confident in the knowledge that whatever may happen in the world, however calamitous it may outwardly appear, will promote God's unalterable purpose for the unification of mankind'.[26]

In a similar statement, Shoghi Effendi said that we 'do not know what form the immediate future will take, anywhere'.[27] What we can know, he goes on to say, is that 'it is too late to avert catastrophic trials',[28] and that the more widely-spread and firmly-established are the Bahá'í institutions worldwide, the more chance that the Bahá'ís themselves can effect 'some mitigation to the suffering of the peoples of the world'.[29] In fact, in another letter Shoghi Effendi stated the converse, that if Bahá'ís fail in their 'sacred obligation' to 'deliver the message to their fellowmen at once, and on as large a scale as possible', then they themselves 'are really partly responsible for prolonging the agony of humanity'.[30]

Thus, while we cannot know 'what form these upheavals will take', we do know that they will be an essential and perhaps final part of the birthing process by which the Lesser Peace is born. In fact, Shoghi Effendi uses this imagery when he states: 'It is becoming evident that the world is not yet through with its labour, the New Age not yet fully born, real Peace not yet right around the corner.'[31] In another place he states, 'we know humanity can and must be welded into some form of political unity – such as a World Federal State – through suffering as it seems only intense suffering is capable of rousing men to the spiritual efforts required.'[32]

The Lesser Peace

In the same way that we can observe in the unfolding of world events of this entire century the process of ordeal that will culminate in the birth of a federated governance, so we can observe the gradual evolution of the fundamental components that will constitute that federation. In fact, we might rightly conclude that the initial stages of the Lesser Peace have been under way for some time. Certainly in the formation of the League of Nations and the United Nations we can witness foundational attempts to establish a world body capable of resolving international disputes and administering justice on a global scale. But according to the Bahá'í definition of what the term 'Lesser Peace' signifies, the clearest signal that such a peace has been securely established will be the implementation by world leaders of a binding pact or treaty that establishes the authority of a federation of national governments over all its constituent members. As we further noted, such a peace, though essentially secular in nature, will not be a static condition, but a process of refining concepts of world unity and of initiating and refining systems to support a world federation of governments. After examining the fundamental ingredients in such a pact, we can examine what the Bahá'í writings describe as the likely components of the structure that will comprise the federated system of governance in the Lesser Peace.

Establishing a Permanent Accord

We have already observed as an eternal verity what history confirms and what common sense assumes, that meaningful or substantive human advancement cannot be imposed. The dictum implicit in this observation regarding world governance is that, however starkly apparent the need for planetary systems may be in even the most remote reaches of our planet and to the most lowly of its inhabitants, no such organization can come about until those in power willingly assemble to create such a structure. Furthermore, it is likewise apparent that the initial business of such a convocation must be the wilful formation of a treaty, a pact, a permanent binding agreement to which all governments freely give their allegiance and subordinate their sovereignty.

The convoking of such assemblage is hardly a new idea. In the *Lawḥ-i-Maqṣúd*, penned between 1873 and 1892, Bahá'u'lláh announced the immediate need for such a convocation:

> The time must come when the imperative necessity for the holding of a vast, an all-embracing assemblage of men will be universally realized. The rulers and kings of the earth must needs attend it, and, participating in its deliberations, must consider such ways and means as will lay the foundations

of the world's Great Peace amongst men. Such a peace demandeth that the Great Powers should resolve, for the sake of the tranquillity of the peoples of the earth, to be fully reconciled among themselves. Should any king take up arms against another, all should unitedly arise and prevent him. If this be done, the nations of the world will no longer require any armaments, except for the purpose of preserving the security of their realms and of maintaining internal order within their territories. This will ensure the peace and composure of every people, government and nation. We fain would hope that the kings and rulers of the earth, the mirrors of the gracious and almighty name of God, may attain unto this station, and shield mankind from the onslaught of tyranny.[33]

From this general exhortation for remedial action, which was but reiterating similar admonitions given in earlier Tablets sent by Bahá'u'lláh to the kings and rulers of the world, we infer several ingredients constituting this pact. First, the assemblage must be universal in scope and attended by all the world's political leaders. Second, at the heart of such a pact should be what becomes termed in the Bahá'í writings 'Bahá'u'lláh's principle of collective security',[34] an agreement wherein any ruler or nation violating this peace will be deterred by a force comprised of the collective participation of all member nations. Third is a general disarmament wherein 'nations of the world will have willingly ceded every claim to make war . . . and all rights to maintain armaments, except for purposes of maintaining internal order within their respective dominions'.[35]

'Abdu'l-Bahá elucidates further the nature of such a convocation and the contents of such a pact in *The Secret of Divine Civilization*,* a treatise He wrote in 1875:

---

* First published in English in London in 1910 as *The Mysterious Forces of Civilization*.

In this all-embracing Pact the limits and frontiers of each and every nation should be clearly fixed, the principles underlying the relations of governments towards one another definitely laid down, and all international agreements and obligations ascertained. In like manner, the size of the armaments of every government should be strictly limited, for if the preparations for war and the military forces of any nation should be allowed to increase, they will arouse the suspicion of others.[36]

We see in this statement the fundamental goals which the agenda for such an assemblage would necessarily address before the components of this pact could be devised: 1) the establishment of territorial boundaries; 2) the devising of principles of international relations; 3) the establishment of international agreements and obligations; and 4) the securing of arms limitations.

In this same essay, 'Abdu'l-Bahá also places great emphasis on the principle of collective security as the essential deterrent to and remedy for the breach of such a pact by an aggressor nation or territory:

The fundamental principle underlying this solemn Pact should be so fixed that if any government later violate any one of its provisions, all the governments on earth should arise to reduce it to utter submission, nay the human race as a whole should resolve, with every power at its disposal, to destroy that government. Should this greatest of all remedies be applied to the sick body of the world, it will assuredly recover from its ills and will remain eternally safe and secure.[37]

Some Features of this Agreement

While extensive speculation about how these matters will be resolved is pointless, it is worthwhile to note some obvious issues that would become relevant to the convoking of this global assemblage. First, with the break-up of the Soviet Union and other political states formed out of the exigencies of war and power politics, we are witnessing the disintegration of what might be called artificial territorial boundaries. This is not to say that territorial governance is unnecessary – it can be valuable and effective in administering human affairs, especially when some natural source of unity exists among a people, either as the result of geographical configuration or as the result of some ethnic or cultural identity. Therefore, we might assume that the devising of such a pact would entail a comprehensive re-evaluation of territorial divisions, giving primary consideration to natural cohesion, to redressing historical injustices, and to contriving the most effective and efficient administration of human affairs.

While we presently witness the difficulty of attempting to resolve longstanding quarrels among peoples and nations regarding sovereignty and boundaries, we can imagine that, having passed through an excruciating ordeal of global proportions, the perspective on these issues would have become significantly changed. We can assume that the motive for such decisions would have ceased to be the securing of narrow interests and would instead have become the establishment of sane, logically based and manageable subsidiary governmental entities that would best accomplish the goal of a world federated system. Further, because another purpose of this pact will be to lay the foundations for a just and responsive world legislative body, we can presume that boundaries would continue to be altered as conditions and relationships themselves evolve.

Another component of this pact that might be deemed equally troublesome is the concept of disarmament and arms limitation. We can, from our present perspective, hardly conceive of nations or territories willingly disarming at the same time that an international force is being created. Here, too, several considerations would seem to ameliorate such concerns. First, we presume that most probably the earth-shaking ordeal that results directly from a failure to construct or accede to the components of this pact would have demonstrated with undeniable clarity – whether through some catastrophic accident, through an economic crisis as a result of expenditures on arms, or through actual warfare – the unwisdom of amassing arms. In this connection, for example, 'Abdu'l-Bahá observed that

> the burden of military maintenance is taxing the various countries beyond the point of endurance. Armies and navies devour the substance and possessions of the people; the toiling poor, the innocent and helpless are forced by taxation to provide munitions and armament for governments bent upon conquest of territory and defence against powerful rival nations.[38]

He goes on to state,

> There is no greater or more woeful ordeal in the world of humanity today than impending war. Therefore, international peace is a crucial necessity. An arbitral court of justice shall be established by which international disputes are to be settled.[39]

However, the most powerful inducement to feel secure in such a disarmament would be the constructing of an intelligently devised international peace-keeping force which, because it is constituted by components from all nations and territories, would have no narrow self-interest, no goal of any sort except the securing of international peace.

Shoghi Effendi indicated in a number of statements the vital relationship between the success of the peace pact and the establishment of an international peace-keeping force. For example, in 1936 he observed that the main focus of the League of Nations had been the production of a pact such as that suggested by Bahá'u'lláh and 'Abdu'l-Bahá: 'A general Pact on security has been the central purpose towards which these efforts have, ever since the League was born, tended to converge.'[40] Then, after praising a number of its efforts at world unity, he particularly praised the League's deliberations about and subsequent condemnation of Italy's invasion of Ethiopia, and he also lauded its further efforts to impose sanctions against the aggressor nation. In fact, he describes this event, ineffective as it might appear to have been to the student of world politics, as being

> without parallel in human history. For the first time in the history of humanity the system of collective security, foreshadowed by Bahá'u'lláh and explained by 'Abdu'l-Bahá, has been seriously envisaged, discussed and tested.[41]*

In his analysis of this milestone in the emergence of world governance and the Lesser Peace he also cites the particular features that distinguished the actions of this body:

> For the first time in history it has been officially recognized

---

* It is worth noting here that the daughter of Woodrow Wilson, founder of the League of Nations, may have been a Bahá'í. In praise of Wilson, Shoghi Effendi said, 'To her [America's] President, the immortal Woodrow Wilson, must be ascribed the unique honour, among the statesmen of any nation, whether of the East or of the West, of having voiced sentiments so akin to the principles animating the Cause of Bahá'u'lláh, and of having more than any other world leader, contributed to the creation of the League of Nations – achievements which the pen of the Centre of God's Covenant acclaimed as signalizing the dawn of the Most Great Peace, whose sun, according to that same pen, must needs arise as the direct consequence of the enforcement of the laws of the Dispensation of Bahá'u'lláh' (Shoghi Effendi, *Citadel of Faith*, p. 36).

and publicly stated that for this system of collective security to be effectively established strength and elasticity are both essential – strength involving the use of an adequate force to ensure the efficacy of the proposed system, and elasticity to enable the machinery that has been devised to meet the legitimate needs and aspirations of its aggrieved upholders. For the first time in human history tentative efforts have been exerted by the nations of the world to assume collective responsibility, and to supplement their verbal pledges by actual preparation for collective action. And again, for the first time in history, a movement of public opinion has manifested itself in support of the verdict which the leaders and representatives of nations have pronounced, and for securing collective action in pursuance of such a decision.[42]

It is in this same context and with this same regard for the historical unfolding of the wisdom inherent in the Revelation of Bahá'u'lláh that the Universal House of Justice in its 1991 Riḍván message to the Bahá'ís of the world praised the collective effort on the part of United Nations member states to rebuke the aggression against Kuwait in 1990 by President Saddam Hussein of Iraq:

> The forces which united the remedial reactions of so many nations to the sudden crisis in this region demonstrated beyond any doubt the necessity of the principle of collective security prescribed by Bahá'u'lláh more than a century ago as a means of resolving conflict. While the international arrangement envisioned by Him for the full application of this principle is far from having been adopted by the rulers of mankind, a long step towards the behaviour outlined for the nations by the Lord of the Age has thus been taken.[43]

The letter goes on to note how hope is generated by the 'call for a new world order', even though the leaders who employ such a phrase may be 'incapable of defining their own meaning'. In particular, the letter praises the leadership in both arenas taken by the president of the

United States inasmuch as 'Abdu'l-Bahá affirmed that America would be 'the first nation to establish the foundation of international agreement' and to 'lead all nations spiritually'.[44]

But of course, the efficacy of such a force and such a pact of collective security in sustaining a just and lasting peace is ultimately dependent on the federated system of governance which commands such a force. That is, Bahá'í speculation about a possible paradigm for the initial establishment of a world federated system of governance envisions a mandate wherein such a force would have as its sole function the enforcing of the decisions arrived at by a world legislative body. To assess the viability of such a plan we need to examine more specifically the Bahá'í vision of the fundamental components of the federated system that would be charged with carrying out some of the other requisites for this pact: establishing the principles of international relations and establishing international agreements and obligations.

Unity in Diversity

We can assume that the initial federation of governments will assemble a variety of cultures and peoples, nations and territories all in different stages of development, each with assorted traditions of governmental organization, each with its peculiar needs, each with special contributions to make. Therefore, we can hardly estimate what course of evolution will describe the progress of individual nations from the inception of this federated system to the emergence in time of a world commonwealth: '. . . the Guardian indicated that the development of mankind from its present chaotic condition to the stage of the Bahá'í World Commonwealth would be a long and gradual one.'[45]

In the initial stages of such a federation, we can envision

great variety of governmental structures among the constituent nations and territories. We cannot expect that such
a federation or even some dire ordeal that might serve as
the galvanizing impetus for the formation of such an
alliance would instantly alter the essential character or
personalities of peoples, nor would such homogeneity
necessarily be desirable. On the contrary, as we have seen*
the Bahá'í writings praise such diversity as valid and
healthy, affirming that justice in its most fundamental
sense is not dependent on some exclusive structure.

> Let there be no misgivings as to the animating purpose of the
> world-wide Law of Bahá'u'lláh. Far from aiming at the
> subversion of the existing foundations of society, it seeks to
> broaden its basis, to remould its institutions in a manner
> consonant with the needs of an ever-changing world. It can
> conflict with no legitimate allegiances, nor can it undermine
> essential loyalties.[46]

While in one sense the formation of such a federation will
be a wider loyalty, an expanded identity, it is also clear
that the gravitation towards such further unity will not be
a casual or haphazard inclination. The enthusiastic and
volitional welding of diverse states into one unified system
will be achieved in large part because of the recognition of
the necessity of such an edifice, a wisdom gained from
passing through the fire of worldwide ordeals. In this
context, Shoghi Effendi compares the formation of this
federation to the unity forged in the American nation as a
result of the American Civil War:

> How confident were the assertions made in the days preced-
> ing the unification of the states of the North American
> continent regarding the insuperable barriers that stood in the
> way of their ultimate federation! Was it not widely and
> emphatically declared that the conflicting interests, the

* See page 239.

mutual distrust, the differences of government and habit that divided the states were such as no force, whether spiritual or temporal, could ever hope to harmonize or control? . . .

Who knows that for so exalted a conception to take shape a suffering more intense than any it has yet experienced will have to be inflicted upon humanity? Could anything less than the fire of a civil war with all its violence and vicissitudes – a war that nearly rent the great American Republic – have welded the states, not only into a Union of independent units, but into a Nation, in spite of all the ethnic differences that characterized its component parts? That so fundamental a revolution, involving such far-reaching changes in the structure of society, can be achieved through the ordinary processes of diplomacy and education seems highly improbable. We have but to turn our gaze to humanity's blood-stained history to realize that nothing short of intense mental as well as physical agony has been able to precipitate those epoch-making changes that constitute the greatest landmarks in the history of human civilization.[47]

We can presume, consequently, that the structure of the federation will evolve to befit rapidly changing conditions of the global community. Initial stages of concern might focus on fundamental tasks – providing electric power, food, clothing, medical assistance and shelter for the masses of humanity. Simultaneous with responding to these exigencies will be the establishment of worldwide systems of transportation, communication and commerce, the provision of equitable means of distributing resources, the determination of matters of taxation, expenditure of funds, and a myriad other concerns that will become evident only when this federation is attempting to administer the affairs of a planetary community. No doubt at that time the wisdom of many of the systems ordained by Bahá'u'lláh in the Kitáb-i-Aqdas will become immediately apparent: a world script, a universal auxiliary language, a universal system of weights and measures, a world currency. In short, as the narrower provincial perspectives are supplanted by the vision of a 'new World Order, destined to rise upon the ruins of a tottering civilization',[48] the practical imperatives for such systems will be apparent long before their spiritual impetus and underlying meaning is fully appreciated.

Speculation about the Structure of a Federated Government

Before these obvious and rudimentary steps can be taken, the government itself must be envisioned and formed. And while this process will also be gradual and will no doubt have various possible configurations, the Bahá'í writings hint at some of the possible ingredients in such a structure.

In discussing the formation of the federation which will occur in the initial stages of the Lesser Peace, Shoghi Effendi states that the primary components of a 'world super-State',[49] at least 'as far as we can visualize it',[50] will consist of an 'international executive', a 'world parliament', and a 'supreme tribunal'.[51] Elsewhere he employs slightly different terms to designate these same components: a 'world legislature', a 'world executive, backed by an international Force', and a 'world tribunal'. He includes in this paradigm an 'international Force', not as a fourth component of the government, but as a multinational force employed to enforce decisions of 'this world legislature'.[52]

Other appellations for these same components are also used. The 'supreme tribunal' is sometimes alluded to as the 'International Tribunal'[53] and elsewhere as the 'Universal Court of Arbitration'.[54] Stated more simply, this paradigm implies a world parliament, an executive body, a world court, and an international military force to assist governments and enforce the decisions of the court.

While the initial encounter with these terms might seem confusing, we can assemble these parts into a relatively simple paradigm of government. The chart overleaf illustrates two of the most complete discussions of this paradigm, together with Shoghi Effendi's brief comment on their essential functions.

WORLD LEGISLATURE

Clearly the focal point of a federated government will be the world legislature, since it will assess the ills and prescribe the remedies for assembling the edifice of world governance. Therefore, if it is to uphold and be upheld with the unquestioned loyalty and allegiance of member national and territorial governments, it must justly represent the body politic it presumes to serve. In this context, the Bahá'í writings suggest that such a body should be 'elected by the people in their respective countries', and that these elections should be 'confirmed by their respective governments'.[55] By this dual process of confirmation, the representatives are expressive of the trust of both the generality of people and the government itself.

The question of apportionment then becomes a pivotal issue, as it has been in the United Nations. In fact, J. Tyson notes that one of the major fears about a federation of governments has to do with the possible usurpation of power by 'minor' states:

> The 'tyranny of minor states' is one of the most frequently heard objections to the UN's General Assembly, and any other such world body that is based on the one-nation-one-vote system. Certainly, 51% of the nations can represent much less than 51% of the world's people.[56]

He then quotes 'Abdu'l-Bahá for the 'Bahá'í response' to this potential problem – having these representatives 'be in proportion to the number of inhabitants of that country'.[57]

Body	**Function**

Paradigm 1 – *World Order of Bahá'u'lláh*, pp. 40–1

Body	Function
World Parliament	'members shall be elected by the people in their respective countries and whose election shall be confirmed by their respective governments'
International Executive	'. . . enforce supreme and unchallengeable authority on every recalcitrant member of the commonwealth'
Supreme Tribunal	'judgement will have binding effect even in such cases where the parties concerned did not voluntarily agree to submit their case to its consideration'

Paradigm 2 – *World Order of Bahá'u'lláh*, p. 203

Body	Function
world legislature	'members will, as the trustees of the whole of mankind, ultimately control the entire resources of all the component nations, and will enact such laws as shall be required to regulate the life, satisfy the needs and adjust the relationships of all races and peoples'
world executive	'carry out the decisions arrived at, and apply the laws enacted by, this world legislature, and will safeguard the organic unity of the whole commonwealth'
world tribunal	'adjudicate and deliver its compulsory and final verdict in all and any disputes that may arise between the various elements constituting this universal system'
international Force	will assist world executive in carrying out the decisions of the world legislature

It should be noted, however, that 'Abdu'l-Bahá is here not talking about the world parliament, but the 'Supreme Tribunal' or world court which will render rulings 'on any international question'.[58] In fact, there does not seem to be any precise guidance in the Bahá'í writings about how the members of this world legislative body will be apportioned; therefore, we must assume that such a crucial matter would be determined when representatives of governments assemble to create the initial pact establishing the foundation of such a government.

The function of this body would be to legislate on all matters pertaining to the federated state. Of course, as discussed above, initially the objective of this body would be to spell out the pact of federation by confirming national boundaries, proscribing armaments, establishing systems of communication, transportation, distribution of resources, a world economy, and a 'single code of international law'.[39] In short, the function of this body would be to gradually mould the commonwealth itself, building a federated government (a 'new world order') from the foundation up, responding with as much foresight as possible to the organic and inherent needs of such an entity, but retaining sufficient flexibility and mechanism for growth that its decisions and methodology could change with what would be a rapidly evolving political reality.

WORLD EXECUTIVE

We might assume that the executive body for this world legislature would be chosen or elected from among the members of the world legislature itself, since its primary function would be to implement the decisions of that body. Having at its command an 'international Force', this world executive authority would 'carry out the decisions arrived at, and apply the laws enacted by, this world legislature, and will safeguard the organic unity of the whole commonwealth'.[60]

The executive authority would not make law, interpret law or determine the best course of action for the commonwealth, but would determine the most effective means of implementing policy. In attempting to clarify this function, Shoghi Effendi notes that this body would correspond 'to the executive head or board in present-day national governments'.[61] Tyson attempts to clarify its function by alluding to a parallel body in his discussion of the 1958 document by Clark and Sohn entitled *World Peace through World Law*. With a variation on the present United Nations charter, this federated government would replace the UN Security Council with an 'Executive Council' that would have no veto power and would be subordinate to the General Assembly.[62]*

WORLD TRIBUNAL

The election and function of the third major component of such a federation, the world tribunal, is delineated in the greatest detail. 'Abdu'l-Bahá employs the term 'Supreme Tribunal' in alluding to this body, and He describes its function as follows:

> When the Supreme Tribunal gives ruling on any international question, either unanimously or by majority rule, there will no longer be any pretext for the plaintiff or ground of objection for the defendant.[63]

Obviously, the mandate for this body as delineated by 'Abdu'l-Bahá is the function ascribed by Shoghi Effendi to the world court ('world tribunal' or 'supreme tribunal') – 'to adjudicate and deliver its compulsory and final

---

* Tyson does not discuss the executive body as a constituent part of the Bahá'í paradigm for a world commonwealth.

verdict in all and any disputes that may arise between the various elements constituting this universal system'.[64]

As we have already mentioned, the procedures for electing such a body are also spelled out in some detail by 'Abdu'l-Bahá because, He explains, there should not remain in the minds and hearts of member states any doubt as to the justly derived status of any verdict issued by this court:

> . . . the national assemblies of each country and nation – that is to say parliaments – should elect two or three persons who are the choicest men of that nation, and are well informed concerning international laws and the relations between governments and aware of the essential needs of the world of humanity in this day. The number of these representatives should be in proportion to the number of inhabitants of that country. The election of these souls who are chosen by the national assembly, that is, the parliament, must be confirmed by the upper house, the congress and the cabinet and also by the president or monarch so these persons may be the elected ones of all the nation and the government. From among these people the members of the Supreme Tribunal will be elected, and all mankind will thus have a share therein, for every one of these delegates is fully representative of his nation.[65]

In short, because these members represent both the peoples and the governments of the world, the decisions of the Tribunal will have universal support, or at least, if any party does not agree with the decisions of this body, it will have no cause for portraying the actions of this body as being unjustly derived.

The Bahá'í texts amplify the function of this world court in at least two other ways. Shoghi Effendi states that the court will not only have the authority to render a final verdict on all disputes brought before it by involved parties, it will further have the authority to render a binding judgement 'even in such cases where the parties concerned did not voluntarily agree to submit their case to its consideration'.[66] Secondly, 'Abdu'l-Bahá notes that the same principle of collective security which applies to aggressor nations would also apply to those states that reject the decision of this world court:

> In case any of the governments or nations, in the execution of the irrefutable decision of the Supreme Tribunal, be negligent or dilatory, the rest of the nations will rise up against it, because all the governments and nations of the world are the supporters of this Supreme Tribunal.[67]

WORLD FORCE

The term 'world force' might initially conjure visions of a massive military establishment akin to tyrannical armies of the past or to those fictional nightmare visions of Orwell's *1984*. The concept of a multinational force that functions at the behest of the world court or the world executive body does not elicit such a response, principally because we have seen the salutary results of international peace-keeping forces in recent history.* That is, when a military force is multinational and operates at the behest of and following the considered judgements of an international body, it has no vested interest other than the maintenance of the collective well-being of the planetary body politic. Or stated another way, when the standing army of a single state may fight for national interests against an inveterate foe, there is a necessary process of mentally conjoining the violent struggle with notions of national or racial superiority or interest, or, conversely, with the perception of the

---

* Tyson ably notes in his discussion 'To the Fearful' the legitimate fears people might have of such an ostensibly monolithic structure. He points out, however, that in the Bahá'í concept the essential autonomy of constituent member states, as well as the diversity of governmental forms and cultural heritage, will be sustained and protected.

enemy as inhuman, alien, inferior, immoral. Its successful operation and essential identity must necessarily be fused with simplistic ideals and emotionally-based rather than rationally-based considerations. But a properly devised multinational force functioning as a keeper of world peace is not the representative of a passionate cause or narrow interests. Neither does it need to question whether its mandate is justly derived. It sole aim is the protection of the security of the federation as a whole, the enforcement of the considered laws of the world parliament and the specific decisions of the tribunal, and the subsequent implementation of those decisions by the world executive.

It might well be that the composition of such a force would also be more or less in proportion to national populations. Obviously it would not be dominated by any single nation, and it would view its task in exactly the same light as does a well-trained civil police force – to protect and serve the body politic. Furthermore, since all the nations will have strictly limited armaments, the size and weaponry of this international force would not require extraordinary expenditures on the part of the federated government.

The Stage of Establishment

It is clear that the 'Lesser Peace' will not come about as the direct result of the Bahá'í Faith nor will the essential ingredients of this revised perspective be directly associated with Bahá'í teachings. Shoghi Effendi confirms that the 'lesser peace will come about through political efforts of the states and nations of the world, and independently of any direct Bahá'í plan or effort'.[68] Yet we must presume that, once the Lesser Peace is under way, the evolving of secular governance in consonance with the increasing

influence of the Bahá'í Faith will bring about a gradually
more associative relationship between the two processes.
As the constituent members of this world community
adopt those principles enunciated in the Bahá'í teachings regarding the unity of humankind and the essential
oneness of religion, there will come what Shoghi Effend
calls 'the stage of establishment'. During this stage
of the Lesser Peace, 'the Faith of Bahá'u'lláh will be
recognized by the civil authorities as the state religion,
similar to that which Christianity entered in the years
following the death of the Emperor Constantine, a stage
which must later be followed by the emergence of the
Bahá'í state'.[69]

The Special Qualifications of the Bahá'í Faith for this Status

The advent of the Lesser Peace as an essentially secular
process does not imply that the influence of the teachings
of Bahá'u'lláh or the efforts of the Bahá'ís will not have a
profound effect on the progress of humanity towards it.
This influence can already be demonstrated, and we can
certainly presume that such influence will be graduated as
the Bahá'í teachings become more universally known,
understood and accepted, and as the Bahá'í administrative
institutions further evolve in the plentitude of their
powers. But more important for our purposes, as the
secular federation of governments evolves, so will the
collective consciousness of peoples and government
leaders about the obvious parallels between the institutions
being established by secular authority and the insightful
discussions in the Bahá'í writings regarding these same
edifices. Even more significantly, we can presume that
along with the evolving integration of secular governance
and humanitarian principles will likewise emerge a rapidly
expanding awareness of the inextricable relationship

between spiritual or moral perspectives and the practical management of a planetary community.

From a theological perspective alone, it seems clear that while various religions might seem capable of fostering an integration of the physical with the spiritual, only the Bahá'í Faith has as its most essential theological tenet the belief in the validity of all the world's religions. Therefore, in the same way that Constantine seized upon Christianity as a force to unify the disparate elements in his empire under the aegis of a single allegiance and identity, so we can imagine that a secular federation of governments would similarly find a single system of belief capable of unifying all the peoples without denigrating any existing systems.

The Continuity of the Bahá'í Faith upheld by the Lesser Covenant

This does not imply that other religious systems do not also share a view of religion as an historical process, but most also have some past history of antipathy towards other systems so that none can offer both a sustaining philosophical or theological perspective without simultaneously implying the supplanting of another perspective. Furthermore, where Constantine found to his dismay that the very religion he adopted as a source of unity was itself divided, the Bahá'í Faith has an administrative order sufficiently well-guarded against such schism that the assumption of the Faith as a state religion would not invite a similar division.

The reason for this cohesion is the historical emphasis in the Bahá'í Faith on the integrity of the Covenant as an unbroken chain of authority. That is, from the beginning of the Revelation of the Báb in 1844 to the completion of the Bahá'í administrative order with the election of the

Universal House of Justice in 1963, there were a number of crucial transitions, points where authority was transferred from one figure to another. These were crucial because it is precisely at such points that religion becomes vulnerable to those who would usurp for themselves what they perceive as the prestige of authority. Indeed, as we have noted, it is at such points that most religious institutions become severed from the spirit of the teachings of the Manifestation.

In fact, it was precisely at these points of transition that there were conscious attempts to destroy the orderly process of implementing the edifice designed by Bahá'u'lláh. However, for each point of transition there was intact both an explicit document to refute such claims and a body of informed and faithful believers to implement the binding accords of these documents:

> The essence of the Covenant is the continuation of divine guidance after the Ascension of the Prophet through the presence in this world of an institution to which all the friends turn and which can indisputably state what is the Will of God.[70]

Each point of transition between the advent of the Manifestation and the establishment of the institutions He Himself designed becomes a link in a chain connecting the individual believer to the divine source, a connection Bahá'u'lláh often compares to a 'firm cord':

> Extolled by the writer of the Apocalypse as 'the Ark of His (God) Testament'; associated with the gathering beneath the 'Tree of Anísá' (Tree of Life) mentioned by Bahá'u'lláh in the Hidden Words; glorified by Him, in other passages of His writings, as the 'Ark of Salvation' and as 'the Cord stretched betwixt the earth and the Abhá Kingdom', this Covenant has been bequeathed to posterity in a Will and Testament which, together with the Kitáb-i-Aqdas and several Tablets, in which the rank and station of 'Abdu'l-Bahá are unequivocally

disclosed, constitute the chief buttresses designed by the Lord of the Covenant Himself to shield and support, after His ascension, the appointed Centre of His Faith and the Delineator of its future institutions.[71]

This doctrine of authority for the Bahá'ís thus resides in the concept of the 'Most Great Infallibility' as enunciated in the Kitáb-i-Aqdas and as explicated by 'Abdu'l-Bahá in *Some Answered Questions*. In discussing this principle, 'Abdu'l-Bahá describes two kinds of infallible authority – the 'essential infallibility' that is an inherent attribute 'peculiar to the supreme Manifestation' in His station as God's mouthpiece, and the 'acquired' infallibility conferred by the Manifestation on individuals and institutions.[72] Therefore, this 'cord' or the links in this chain are vital to an appreciation of the integrity of Bahá'í history. In particular, such understanding depends on Bahá'u'lláh's designation of 'Abdu'l-Bahá as 'Centre of My Covenant' in the Kitáb-i-Aqdas and in the *Kitáb-i-'Ahd* (Book of the Covenant), 'Abdu'l-Bahá's appointment in His *Will and Testament* of Shoghi Effendi as Guardian of the Bahá'í Faith, the safeguarding of the transition from the Guardianship to the election of the Universal House of Justice as delineated in the statements by the Hands of the Cause in 'Proclamation of the Hands of the Cause to the Bahá'ís of East and West',[73] and the parameters of the authority of the Universal House of Justice enunciated by Bahá'u'lláh, clarified by 'Abdu'l-Bahá and the Guardian, and formulated in the Constitution of the Universal House of Justice.

The Evolution of the Faith in Relation to the Stages of Its Establishment

The essential administrative components of the Bahá'í Faith are already established, and according to the *Encyclo-*

paedia Britannica, the Bahá'í Faith is the second most widespread religion in the world. Yet, as the influence of the Faith spreads and it attracts increasingly larger numbers of adherents, the role and function of the institutions will also progress and evolve. For example, in *Citadel of Faith* Shoghi Effendi distinguishes between the main features of the evolution of the Bahá'í Faith in the Formative Age of the Lesser Peace and in the Golden Age of the Most Great Peace. The Formative Age, he asserts, will be characterized by seven major accomplishments, some of them within the Bahá'í Faith, some of them outside it:

> During this Formative Age of the Faith, and in the course of present and succeeding epochs, [1] the last and crowning stage in the erection of the framework of the Administrative Order of the Faith of Bahá'u'lláh – the election of the Universal House of Justice – will have been completed, [2] the Kitáb-i-Aqdas, the Mother-Book of His Revelation, will have been codified and its laws promulgated, [3] the Lesser Peace will have been established, [4] the unity of mankind will have been achieved and its maturity attained, [5] the plan conceived by 'Abdu'l-Bahá will have been executed, [6] the emancipation of the Faith from the fetters of religious orthodoxy will have been effected, and [7] its independent religious status will have been universally recognized . . .'[74]

Some of these accomplishments are clearly-defined events, and a few have already occurred. The Universal House of Justice was elected in 1963. The codification of the Kitáb-i-Aqdas was accomplished in 1973, and its translation into English completed in 1992. Some of the other features of the Formative Age, however, are processes, the completion of which will be less easy to detect. For example, from the previous chapter we can infer that an important degree of world unity will have been achieved by the end of this century, and yet we cannot be sure that such a unity also implies the 'maturity' of that collaboration or the complete arrival of the Lesser Peace. Commenting on 'Abdu'l-Bahá's allusion to the advent of the Lesser Peace as occurring before the end of the twentieth century, the Universal House of Justice says that ' 'Abdu'l-Bahá anticipated that the Lesser Peace *could** be established before the end of the twentieth century'.[75]

But regardless of the precise time frame, it is clear that the emergence of the Lesser Peace will not be an instantaneous transformation, but a sequence of events. Furthermore, the last two indices ('the emancipation of the Faith from the fetters of religious orthodoxy' and its 'independent religious status' 'universally recognized') are likely to be well under way, if not accomplished, before humanity is very far along into the Lesser Peace. In short, these two features clearly imply the beginning of a direct influence of the Bahá'í Faith on the social and political forces forging a world government. For while the initial fashioning of a world peace and world unity will take place outside the province of the Bahá'í community, no doubt over the course of time the Faith will become increasingly recognized both as a repository of information about the very system humanity is attempting to construct and, more importantly, as a model of how such principles can be incorporated into a social and administrative edifice.

Therefore, when Shoghi Effendi speaks of the establishment of the Faith in the eyes of the world, he would seem to be alluding to a process that will occur in large part after the political peace and unity are established. Similarly, when he speaks of the conditions of the present stage of the evolution of the Faith as consisting 'of obscurity, of repression, of emancipation and of recognition',[76] he may well be alluding to a continuation of conditions which, he

---

* Italics are mine.

affirms, are already occurring in varying degrees in diverse parts of the world.

Therefore, the stage of 'establishment' will occur by degrees as the Bahá'í Faith achieves an incrementally greater influence on the thinking and structure of the global community. But however gradual the spread of the Faith worldwide might be, it is clear that the affirmative influence of the Faith on the gradual unfolding of a world government does not await a future time. The Universal House of Justice has stated that while the Lesser Peace will 'initially be a political unity arrived at by the decision of the governments of various nations', the Bahá'ís have a crucial part to play in bringing this about:

> This does not mean, however, that the Bahá'ís are standing aside and waiting for the Lesser Peace to come before they do something about the peace of mankind. Indeed, by promoting the principles of the Faith, which are indispensable to the maintenance of peace, and by fashioning the instruments of the Bahá'í Administrative Order, which we are told by the beloved Guardian is the pattern for future society, the Bahá'ís are constantly engaged in laying the groundwork for a permanent peace, the Most Great Peace being their ultimate goal.[77]

In another instance, the Universal House of Justice stated that while the mechanism for the Lesser Peace is being established, the Faith will exert an important influence on this process:

> Undoubtedly, as these developments are taking place, the counsel the institutions of the Faith can give to governments, the pattern of world administration offered by the Bahá'í community and the great humanitarian projects which will be launched under the aegis of the Universal House of Justice, will exercise a great influence on the course of progress.[78]

8

The Kingdom Come

A Model of the Bahá'í Commonwealth

The unity of the human race, as envisaged by Bahá'u'lláh,
implies the establishment of a world commonwealth in
which all nations, races, creeds and classes are closely and
permanently united, and in which the autonomy of its state
members and the personal freedom and initiative of the
individuals that compose them are definitely and completely
safeguarded.[1]

Shoghi Effendi

The Emergence of the Most Great Peace

Adam and Eve Reconcile

The author of the book of Revelation states that in his
vision he 'saw the holy city, new Jerusalem, coming down
out of heaven from God, prepared as a bride adorned for
her husband; and I heard a great voice from the throne
saying, "Behold, the dwelling of God is with men."'[2]
While this mystic vision of the heavenly city has attracted
a variety of literal and figurative interpretations, 'Abdu'l-
Bahá states that the 'New Jerusalem' in these biblical
passages is, in the broadest sense, 'none other than divine
civilization, and it is now ready. It is to be and shall be
organized, and the oneness of humankind will be a visible
fact.'[3] He goes on in this same discussion to portray how

this expression of divine principles in an earthly artifice will occur:

> Humanity will then be brought together as one. The various religions will be united, and different races will be known as one kind. The Orient and Occident will be conjoined, and the banner of international peace will be unfurled. The world shall at last find peace, and the equalities and rights of men shall be established. The capacity of humankind will be tested, and a degree shall be attained where equality is a reality.[4]

'Abdu'l-Bahá then sets forth some of the fundamental attributes that will typify the equality and justice of that society:

> All the peoples of the world will enjoy like interests, and the poor shall possess a portion of the comforts of life. Just as the rich are surrounded by their luxuries in palaces, the poor will have at least their comfortable and pleasant places of abode; and just as the wealthy enjoy a variety of food, the needy shall have their necessities and no longer live in poverty. In short, a readjustment of the economic order will come about, the divine Sonship will attract, the Sun of Reality will shine forth, and all phenomenal being will attain a portion.[5]

In *Some Answered Questions* 'Abdu'l-Bahá elucidates further the implications of the imagery regarding the new Jerusalem in the book of Revelation. He notes that what is most frequently intended by 'the Holy City, the Jerusalem of God', is the 'Law of God', whereas the further allusions to the 'new heaven' and 'new earth' and the disappearance of the 'sea' relate to the advent of just world governance:

> Notice how clear and evident it is that the first heaven and earth signify the former Law. For it is said that the first heaven and earth have passed away and there is no more sea – that is to say, that the earth is the place of judgement, and on

this earth of judgement there is no sea, meaning that the teachings and the Law of God will entirely spread over the earth, and all men will enter the Cause of God, and the earth will be completely inhabited by believers; therefore, there will be no more sea, for the dwelling place and abode of man is the dry land. In other words, at that epoch the field of that Law will become the pleasure-ground of man. Such earth is solid; the feet do not slip upon it.[6]*

No doubt future scholars will discover and unravel many other useful and lucid interpretations of the prophecies and traditions from the world's religions as they corroborate the divine process of progressive revelation in general and as they allude to the emergence of this global civilization in particular; but we would do well to note one image that is especially relevant to our previous discussions regarding the twin duties of human purpose and the schism between those powers that we traced. 'Abdu'l-Bahá states that the description in Revelation of the 'new Jerusalem' as a 'bride adorned for her husband' is a symbolic representation of the union (or reunion) of earth (or human society on earth) with spiritual principles, the final stage of social progress and the consummation of human social evolution:

> The holy City, new Jerusalem, hath come down from on high in the form of a maid of heaven, veiled, beauteous, and unique, and prepared for reunion with her lovers on earth.[7]

---

* 'Abdu'l-Bahá then focuses on passages in Revelation that allude to those events concerned with the advent of Muḥammad. The 'sun' and the 'moon' allude to the Persian and Ottoman kingdoms which were under the power of the 'Law of God'. The crown of twelve stars upon the 'woman clothed with the sun, and the moon under her feet' represents the twelve Imáms 'who were the promoters of the Law of Muḥammad and the educators of the people, shining like stars in the heaven of guidance'. Other passages, He goes on to explain, symbolize the further history of Islam and the fulfilment of Islamic prophecy with the appearance of the Báb.

Not only does this interpretation amplify our previous insights about the essential relationship between these twin duties as symbolized by the conjoining (or re-marriage) of human female and male attributes (the Evian self with the Adamic self), but it also relates importantly to the whole idea of the twin aspects of divine revelation as correlating to these twin duties or capacities.

A further explication of this same image would seem to vindicate such an inference. For every Manifestation there is a figure or image through which the voice of God emanates. For Moses it was a burning bush, for the Buddha a bodhi tree, for Christ a dove, for Muḥammad the angel Gabriel, for the Báb a vision of the martyred Imám Ḥusayn, and for Bahá'u'lláh a veiled maiden. Symbolically, it seems likely that this 'veiled maiden' functioning for Bahá'u'lláh as the voice of God is this bride, the new Jerusalem, 'that Law which is the guarantor of human happiness and the effulgence of the world of God',[8] ready for the wedding or reunion with social form and structure through the ordinances revealed by Bahá'u'lláh (the female Eve as spiritual inspiration re-united with the male Adam as the physical form of that insight). Even more particularly, therefore, the new Jerusalem might be seen as an allusion to the Kitáb-i-Aqdas,

> . . . the principal repository of that Law which the Prophet Isaiah had anticipated, and which the writer of the Apoca-lypse had described as the 'new heaven' and the 'new earth', as 'the Tabernacle of God', as the 'Holy City', as the 'Bride', the 'New Jerusalem coming down from God', this 'Most Holy Book', whose provisions must remain inviolate for no less than a thousand years, and whose system will embrace the entire planet, may well be regarded as the brightest emanation of the mind of Bahá'u'lláh, as the Mother Book

of His Dispensation, and the Charter of His New World Order.[9]

Convergence of the Secular with the Sacred

As we have been careful to note, the advent of this wedding, this reunion, this descent of the new Jerusalem, will not be an instantaneous event. This process, already in motion, will consist of a series of steps or stages of evolutionary implementation of a global identity or consciousness into social and governmental structures. We have also noted that for an indefinite period at the beginning of this process, the secular and sacred institutions will evolve separately, the Lesser Peace being a political pact of federation, and the further progress of the Bahá'í institutions occurring with the continued expansion and growth of the Bahá'í community.

This does not mean that there will be no influence exerted by the Bahá'í Faith or its teachings on the secular processes; as we have observed, this influence is already evident. Furthermore, the advent of a Manifestation transforms human society regardless of whether or not the peoples of the world are aware of the source of such revolutionary change. But as we observed in the previous chapter, while the secular federation of governments struggles to manage the affairs of a planetary community, there will come a stage in the evolution of these distinct institutions when the world federated government will assume a Bahá'í identity by recognizing the Bahá'í Faith as the 'state religion' of this secular body.

The final and complete stage in this process will occur when, through some process we can only imagine, the secular system of federated governance merges with the Bahá'í administrative order. This event will simultaneously signal the arrival of the Most Great Peace, the wedding of the bride with the bridegroom, the new heaven with the new earth, and the emergence of the Bahá'í Commonwealth as the Kingdom of God come on earth in all its plentitude.

Perhaps as piece by piece the secular system comes to appreciate and emulate ever more completely the systems and procedures of the Bahá'í administrative order, the distinction between the two will eventually become so nebulous that it will be seen as unnecessary to maintain two systems. Stated another way, there may come a point in time when the essential dynamic of the secular governance will be in concert with or will have assumed more or less the same structure and motive force as the Bahá'í institution. When a universal appreciation of the authority and integrity of the Bahá'í administrative order is coupled with the acceptance of the Bahá'í ethical and spiritual principles, then it will be an easy step for the two systems to become one.

Yet it is clear in the Bahá'í writings, and logical to our own speculation, that this convergence will not produce a third entity from the two distinct systems, nor will the Bahá'í institutions become subsumed by secular governance. Neither will the Bahá'í Faith usurp the prerogatives of secular governance. Rather we can imagine that it will be seen as needless to maintain two systems doing essentially the same task. Consequently, the secular federation, devoid of the organic integrity and unique synthesis of spiritual and practical ingredients that are inherent in the Bahá'í system, will, we may presume, forego its own perpetuation in favour of the Bahá'í institutions. But regardless of how the process may occur, this point in human history will represent the emergence of human society into full maturity, 'the Day when the kingdoms of this world shall have become the Kingdom of God Himself'.[10]

Reunion in Relation to Social Evolution

Possibly the most weighty insight into what this reunion will signify is portrayed in the statement by Shoghi Effendi that the resulting system would signify the completed evolution of planetary human organization:

> The emergence of a world community, the consciousness of world citizenship, the founding of a world civilization and culture – all of which must synchronize with the initial stages in the unfoldment of the Golden Age of the Bahá'í Era – should, by their very nature, be regarded, as far as this planetary life is concerned, as the furthermost limits in the organization of human society, though man, as an individual, will, nay must indeed as a result of such a consummation, continue indefinitely to progress and develop.[11]

As Shoghi Effendi goes on to note, this accomplishment does not signify the end of human progress any more than the completion of an individual's coming of age at maturity signals the cessation of human advancement. On the contrary, achieving adulthood signalizes the coalescing of powers and the beginning of the most profound sorts of meaningful growth – the advancement in knowledge and the application of that knowledge. In the same way, the completion of the societal or organizational evolution of humankind on this planet is a preparation for radically more advanced sorts of human development, though always operating within this completed organizational structure. We cannot even rule out the probability that a more inclusive and expansive sense of self beyond planetary unity will in time become apparent, as will some more inclusive administrative order to embrace that identity. The point is that never would there be a need for essential change in global organization, only in perfecting the system that is inherently suitable for the administration of human affairs on a planetary level.

Stated differently, one phase of human evolution has been achieved in preparation for another sort of advancement, in the same way that the previous completion of human physical evolution paved the way for fundamental intellectual and social advancement. It is in this context that the advent of the Báb is portrayed in the Bahá'í writings as the symbolic completion of divine revelation. That is, in discussing the historical significance of the appearance of the Báb, Bahá'u'lláh states the following:

> He hath declared Knowledge to consist of twenty and seven letters, and regarded all the Prophets, from Adam even unto the 'Seal', as Expounders of only two letters thereof and of having been sent down with these two letters. He also saith that the Qá'im will reveal all the remaining twenty and five letters.[12]

Obviously this analogy does not imply that there will be no further Manifestations or that no further insights or advancements will be gained. Rather it symbolizes what we previously noted in our discussion of the Bahá'í cyclical view of history – that the essential purposes or objectives of the Adamic cycle will be achieved during the dispensation which the Báb inaugurates, and that the fundamental goals of human social evolution will have been consummated, even though the spiritual quality of human civilization will retain the capacity for infinite development.

This completion is represented by various symbolic expressions. The word 'Váḥid', for example, means 'unity'. Its numerical value is nineteen, a symbol of the unity of God. The Bahá'í or Badí' calendar established by the Báb and approved by Bahá'u'lláh contains nineteen months of nineteen days each. Each month represents symbolically an attribute of God, and the whole symbolizes the completed cycle of a year, or a statement or expression of divinity translated into earthly action. Just as the fulfilment of the Bahá'í administrative order symbolizes the Kingdom of God come on earth by implementing 'the furthermost limits in the organization of human society', so the advent of this dispensation symbolizes the completion or fulfilment or culmination or consummation of the cycle of human development set in motion with the advent of Adam.

Relevant to this symbolic expression of the significance of this point in history is the fact that the Báb had eighteen disciples, the 'Letters of the Living', and considered Himself the nineteenth letter:

> The Persian for 'The Letters of the Living' is Hurúf-i-Ḥay'; there were 18 of these first disciples of the Báb and the numerical value of the word 'Ḥay' is 18. These 18 letters together, with the Báb Himself, constitute the first 'Váḥid' of the Revolution [sic – Revelation]. The word 'Váḥid' has a numerical value of 19, and means 'Unity'. It symbolizes the unity of God, and thus the number 19 itself symbolizes the unity of God, and it was used by the Báb as the basis for His Calendar. One may also note the reference in 'The Synopsis and Codification of the Kitáb-i-Aqdas' to 19 or 95 Mithqáls of gold or silver in connection with the laws of marriage and of Ḥuqúqu'lláh.[13]

Referring back to the statement of Bahá'u'lláh regarding the revelation of the Báb as revealing the remaining twenty-five letters of the twenty-seven letters that constitute human knowledge, we can see an obvious symbolic relationship. On the one hand, Bahá'u'lláh is simply alluding to the relative impact of the Báb's revelation compared to what had gone before:

> Regarding the passage beginning with the words: 'Knowledge consists of twenty-seven letters': this should not be

interpreted literally. It only indicates the relative greatness and superiority of the new Revelation.[14]

At the same time, Shoghi Effendi cites a statement of 'Abdu'l-Bahá which interprets the allusion in Revelation (4:10 and 5:8) to the twenty-four elders as alluding to these same Letters of the Living:

> Regarding the four and twenty elders: The Master, in a Tablet, stated that they are the Báb, the 18 Letters of the Living and five others who would be known in the future. So far we do not know who these five others are.[15]

The point here is not that the mathematics of prophecy is the surest guide or even a significant index to the importance of the Bahá'í revelation in fulfilling the purposes of a divinely impelled history. Rather, such symbols enhance the sense in this evolution of a completed cycle of development, which, like the cycle of a year, has integrity, wholeness, and, as a symbolic expression of the attributes of God given earthly expression, divine import.

Spiritual Attributes of a Fully-Evolved Global Community

Human society will continue to evolve, to become ever more refined in its ability to manifest in physical form the attributes of spiritual reality and to develop an even more inclusive identity or sense of self. But regardless of how bright the distant prospect for human spiritual development might be, the Bahá'í writings are replete with lofty praise and glorification of human society once this culminating stage of evolution has been achieved. One of the most detailed portrayals of the overall nature of the fully emerged Bahá'í Commonwealth occurs with Shoghi Effendi's conclusion of his analysis of the evolution of the Bahá'í administrative order in *The World Order of Bahá'u'lláh*.

His most general assessment of this civilization focuses on the manner in which every aspect of that society will be expressive of the essential unity of creation itself:

> The unity of the human race, as envisaged by Bahá'u'lláh, implies the establishment of a world commonwealth in which all nations, races, creeds and classes are closely and permanently united, and in which the autonomy of its state members and the personal freedom and initiative of the individuals that compose them are definitely and completely safeguarded.[16]

In a somewhat more specific analysis of the overall tenor of such a civilization, he alludes to the same concept of a reunion we have emphasized in our own analysis. For example, he states, 'In such a world society, science and religion, the two most potent forces in human life, will be reconciled, will cooperate, and will harmoniously develop.'[17] In another passage thematically related to our previous discussion of this wedding of spiritual truth with social form, Shoghi Effendi notes that this system will blend and embody 'the ideals of both the East and the West'.[18]

He likewise notes that the advent of such a society will signal the permanent cessation of the prejudices and hostilities that have until now become such a sad characterization of human history in general and of religious history in particular:

> National rivalries, hatred, and intrigues will cease, and racial animosity and prejudice will be replaced by racial amity, understanding and cooperation. The causes of religious strife will be permanently removed, economic barriers and restrictions will be completely abolished, and the inordinate distinction between classes will be obliterated.[19]

This statement echoes a passage of 'Abdu'l-Bahá which Shoghi Effendi cites in this same analysis:

Religious and sectarian antagonism, the hostility of races and peoples, and differences among nations, will be eliminated. All men will adhere to one religion, will have once common faith, will be blended into one race and become a single people. All will dwell in one common fatherland, which is the planet itself.[20]

Shoghi Effendi notes that among the more practical results of such a system will be the elimination of warfare, together with a renovated worldwide economic system that will unleash untold resources for the betterment of the human condition:

Destitution on the one hand, and gross accumulation of ownership on the other, will disappear. The enormous energy dissipated and wasted on war, whether economic or political, will be consecrated to such ends as will extend the range of human inventions and technical development, to the increase of the productivity of mankind, to the extermination of disease, to the extension of scientific research, to the raising of the standard of physical health, to the sharpening and refinement of the human brain, to the exploitation of the unused and unsuspected resources of the planet, to the prolongation of human life, and to the furtherance of any other agency that can stimulate the intellectual, the moral, and spiritual life of the entire human race.[21]

In part, such gains will be accomplished through the intelligent, systematic, coordinated and worldwide management of the earth's resources through a 'world federal system, ruling the whole earth and exercising unchallengeable authority over its unimaginably vast resources':[22]

The economic resources of the world will be organized, its sources of raw materials will be tapped and fully utilized, its markets will be coordinated and developed, and the distribution of its products will be equitably regulated.[23]

More specifically, Shoghi Effendi notes some of the

systems that will produce these amazing results, systems which Bahá'u'lláh has in His own writings elucidated in some detail:

> A mechanism of world inter-communication will be devised, embracing the whole planet, freed from national hindrances and restrictions, and functioning with marvellous swiftness and perfect regularity. A world metropolis will act as the nerve centre of a world civilization, the focus towards which the unifying forces of life will converge and from which its energizing influences will radiate. A world language will either be invented or chosen from among the existing languages and will be taught in the schools of all the federated nations as an auxiliary to their mother tongue. A world script, a world literature, a uniform and universal system of currency, of weights and measures, will simplify and facilitate intercourse and understanding among the nations and races of mankind.[24]

Shoghi Effendi concludes this general assessment of the World Commonwealth by describing the emergence of this Most Great Peace as the explicit fulfilment of the vision in Revelation of the 'new Jerusalem' regarding God dwelling on earth:

> 'And I heard a great voice out of heaven saying, "Behold, the tabernacle of God is with men, and he will dwell with them, and they shall be his people, and God himself shall be with them, and be their God. And God shall wipe away all tears from their eyes; and there shall be no more death, neither sorrow, nor crying, neither shall there be any more pain: for the former things are passed away." '[25]

Such a world federal commonwealth will be capable of rendering these results, he concludes, because it will be a system 'in which Force is made the servant of Justice, whose life is sustained by its universal recognition of one God and by its allegiance to one common Revelation'. He is careful to note, however, that 'the goal towards which humanity . . . is moving' will not be achieved by force or by imposition; it will be 'impelled by the unifying forces of life'.[26]

The Structure of the Bahá'í Commonwealth

As we have repeatedly mentioned, we can hardly predict precisely what sequence of events will lead secular authority to adopt the Bahá'í administrative order. Neither can we presume to understand what evolutionary changes the Bahá'í institutions will go through before such an event takes place. We might understandably presume, therefore, that it would be fruitless to speculate about the structure of such a commonwealth. Indeed Shoghi Effendi cautions that we can scarcely imagine what the total effect of such universal change will mean.

Nevertheless, while the complete vision of that future society may be presently concealed, an examination of the present Bahá'í administrative order offers significant insight about that future commonwealth:

> [Bahá'u'lláh] has not merely enunciated certain universal principles, or propounded a particular philosophy, however potent, sound and universal these may be. In addition to these He, as well as 'Abdu'l-Bahá after Him, has, unlike the Dispensations of the past, clearly and specifically laid down a set of Laws, established definite institutions, and provided for the essentials of a Divine Economy. These are destined to be a pattern for future society, a supreme instrument for the establishment of the Most Great Peace, and the one agency for the unification of the world, and the proclamation of the reign of righteousness and justice upon the earth.[27]

Shoghi Effendi likewise notes in his later discussion of the distinguishing features of this administrative design that the present 'vast Administrative Order is the sole framework' of the Bahá'í Commonwealth of the future'.[28]

Thus, we know that much will change in the functioning of the Bahá'í administrative order, especially as its institutions must deal with the affairs of increasingly vaster numbers of adherents and must become increasingly more involved in assisting with socio-economic conditions and other secular affairs of this community. Nevertheless, the present model implies some fundamental principles of operation and structure that will not change. Therefore, the best insights we can gain about how that ultimate expression of divine principles in social forms will be structured is to study the present structure and mode of operations of the Bahá'í administrative order, especially those parts of that structure that are permanently established and whose *modus operandi* will remain largely intact.

Channels of Authority in the Present Model

Shoghi Effendi observes how the administrative order revealed by Bahá'u'lláh is 'in theory and practice, not only unique in the entire history of political institutions, but can find no parallel in the annals of any of the world's recognized religious systems'.[29] A brief study of how lines of authority are established and maintained demonstrates the validity of his observation, as well as how we might study those lines of authority in relation to our discussion about the inextricable relationship between the twin duties of knowing and doing.

The first thing we should observe about the essential structure of the Bahá'í administrative order is that however much the application of this system expands, the

Paradigm of Present Bahá'í Administrative Order

'Twin Manifestations'
The Báb ('the Primal Point')
Bahá'u'lláh ('Him Whom God will make manifest')

Eternal Spiritual Verities	New Laws and Institutions
The Kitáb-i-Íqán	*The Kitáb-i-Aqdas*
(The New Heaven)	(The New Earth)

'Abdu'l-Bahá
(Centre of Covenant)

Interpreter	*Exemplar*
sources of knowledge	*sources of applied knowledge*
(appointed)	(elected)

'Twin Institutions'

Guardian	Universal House of Justice
	elucidation of Word
interpreter of Word	*legislation and implementation*

Hands of the Cause

International Teaching Centre

Continental Counsellors	National Spiritual Assemblies

Auxiliary Boards

Assistants to Boards	Local Spiritual Assemblies

Individual Bahá'ís

essential structure as depicted in this chart will remain the same. For example, the National Spiritual Assemblies will become Secondary Houses of Justice and the Local Spiritual Assemblies will become Local Houses of Justice, but the paradigm of three tiers of elected administrative institutions will remain essentially as it is. Similarly, the authority of the writings of the central figures of the Faith will remain inviolate, and the conferred authority of the Universal House of Justice permanently fixed as set forth in existing texts and documents.

A second important observation about this paradigm is that after the figures of the Manifestations (the Báb and Bahá'u'lláh), Bahá'u'lláh's appointed successor 'Abdu'l-Bahá, and the Guardian, there are in this system no individuals or individual positions of legislative or judicial authority. Even the authority of 'Abdu'l-Bahá and of the Guardian is precisely defined. There are some individual positions in the system (Hands of the Cause, Counsellors and Auxiliary Board members), but as their appellations imply, these positions are advisory and function to assist and aid the elected institutions. Furthermore, even in this office, they do not have complete autonomy, but serve at the behest and pleasure of the Universal House of Justice, itself an elected institution.

This is an extremely important feature in the system, that after the guidance of Bahá'u'lláh, 'Abdu'l-Bahá and the Guardian, all authority is vested in administrative bodies which are elected through universal suffrage and in which all members have an equal voice. Appointed positions have no authority to legislate over or control the elected institutions.

Absolutely crucial to this process, therefore, is the election process itself, a system carefully designed to prevent individuals from being to able to seek such positions on administrative bodies.* Furthermore, having achieved a position on an administrative body, an individual is, through the mechanism of Bahá'í consultative procedures, effectively deterred from being able to exercise individual sway.†

Lines of Authority in Relation to the Twin Duties of Human Purpose

The overall structure of this order embodies and combines metaphorically the dual purpose of human existence – the knowing and the doing. For the first two levels of authority, both of these aspects of purpose are vested in one individual. The Báb and Bahá'u'lláh reveal eternal spiritual verities (knowledge, the new wine), and also the law, the institutions, the means whereby that knowledge can be expressed in social form (action, the wineskin). Bahá'u'lláh conferred upon 'Abdu'l-Bahá the station of being the infallible interpreter of Bahá'u'lláh's word (knowledge) and also vested Him with the title of Centre of the Covenant (authority, action). He also attributed to Him the special mantle of Exemplar (knowledge in action).‡ Thus, 'Abdu'l-Bahá functions as an infallible source of insight as well as an infallible example of that insight translated into human action.

---

* This system, which is the same for all Bahá'í elections, prescribes a secret ballot, plurality vote, and proscribes nominations, electioneering, political parties or any attempt to influence the vote of another. See Appendix A for further elucidation.

† See Appendix A for a discussion of the Bahá'í consultative process.

‡ In previous revelations, there may have been shining examples of religious virtue, but the Manifestation Himself was the only perfect example of the virtues appropriate to that dispensation. Unique in the annals of religious history, 'Abdu'l-Bahá, though a human being, is designated as the exemplar, the perfect Bahá'í. While Bahá'u'lláh is

After these individuals, these dual purposes are variously divided. The Guardian and the Universal House of Justice function as 'twin institutions' in that, while both 'have certain duties and functions in common, each also operates within a separate and distinct sphere'.[30] The 'Guardian of the Faith has been made the Interpreter of the Word' and the Universal House of Justice 'has been invested with the function of legislating on matters not expressly revealed in the teachings,'[31] of elucidating the sacred texts and implementing the laws.

Thus, while it was intended that the Guardian be a permanent member of and preside over the Universal House of Justice, it was never intended that he be able to 'assume the right of exclusive legislation' or to 'override the decision of the majority of his fellow-members'.[32] Because the Guardian's interpretation of the sacred texts remains an infallible source of guidance, the dual nature of that relationship remains intact and inviolable and will ever remain unbroken even though there will be no future Guardians. Therefore it is an integral part of the consultative process of the Universal House of Justice that in its legislation it observe 'the greatest care in studying the Sacred Texts and the interpretations of the Guardian as well as considering views of all the members'.[33]

Stated more fully, because it was never intended that the Guardian have legislative powers over or separate from the Universal House of Justice, these two institutions are still able completely to fulfil their distinct functions:

> During the whole thirty-six years of his Guardianship Shoghi Effendi functioned without the Universal House of Justice.

---

likewise considered to have been the perfect embodiment of Bahá'í virtue, He was toward the end of His ministry more or less remote from public eye, and ascribed to 'Abdu'l-Bahá the function of meeting with officials and the public.

Now the Universal House of Justice must function without the Guardian, but the principle of inseparability remains. The Guardianship does not lose its significance nor position in the Order of Bahá'u'lláh merely because there is no living Guardian.[34]*

Below these levels of administration, the twin aspects of human purpose are divided between appointed and elected institutions. In Bahá'í parlance, the distinction between these branches of administration is designated by the terms the 'learned' and the 'rulers', appellations originally employed by Bahá'u'lláh in the *Kitáb-i-Ahd* when He stated, 'Blessed are the rulers and the learned among the people of Bahá'.[35] In addition to sustaining and continuing this dual aspect of human governance, this critical distinction also relates to the previously noted Bahá'í belief that true learning cannot be imposed (i.e. the institution of the learned has no legislative authority nor can it impose its will on the institution of the rulers). However, each branch is essential to the strength and integrity of the entire edifice:

> This Administrative Order consists, on the one hand, of a series of elected councils, universal, secondary and local, in which are vested legislative, executive and judicial powers over the Bahá'í community and, on the other, of eminent and devoted believers appointed for the specific purposes of protecting and propagating the Faith of Bahá'u'lláh under the guidance of the Head of that Faith.[36]

---

* Since the first Guardian, Shoghi Effendi, appointed no successor and there is no way for a successor to be appointed, the institution of the Guardianship is confined to the writings and actions of Shoghi Effendi. For full discussion of this, see 'Proclamation by the Hands of the Cause to the Bahá'ís of East and West', *Bahá'í World*, vol. XIII, pp. 341–5.

This is not a breach in the efficacy or integrity of the administrative order as devised by Bahá'u'lláh and elucidated and explicated by 'Abdu'l-Bahá. Indeed, the feasibility of such an occurrence was anticipated by Bahá'u'lláh Himself in the Kitáb-i-Aqdas.

The three levels of elected institutions ('the rulers') derive their existence from universal suffrage among the body of believers, whereas the 'learned' are appointed by the elected Universal House of Justice, except for the Hands of the Cause who were appointed by the Guardian. Ultimately, in other words, the entire structure derives from and is supported by universal suffrage. Also worth noting in this structure is that while the three levels of elected institutions have a great deal of autonomy, the various levels of appointment within the institution of the learned, though hierarchical in order, function more or less as one administrative entity:

> The Hands of the Cause of God, the Counsellors, and the members of the Auxiliary Boards [and their Assistants] fall within the definition of the 'learned' given by the beloved Guardian. Thus they are all intimately interrelated and it is not incorrect to refer to the three ranks collectively as one institution.[37]

Since the sole purpose of this institution of the 'learned' is to assist the elected institutions, the chart indicates how the various levels of the 'learned' are ancillary to particular levels of elected bodies. Counsellors primarily assist National Assemblies, whereas Auxiliary Board members and their assistants are primarily concerned with Local Assemblies. Therefore, besides rendering direct assistance to these bodies in administrative matters, this structure provides an auxiliary and sometimes more direct channel of communication up and down the structure without violating or vitiating lines of authority. In this sense, the institution of the learned helps protect the entire edifice by functioning like nerve endings out in the body of the elected institutions, connecting the entire body of the administrative order (which by definition includes every single Bahá'í) with the head or nerve centre of the edifice, the Universal

House of Justice. Yet, while this paradigm contains a centralized nerve centre, it is not a markedly centralized system. Instead, it recognizes the essential autonomy of subsidiary governing bodies and remains so flexible in its procedures that it is capable of being implemented and successfully employed by any culture. Furthermore, the essential components of this system are adaptable to any level of education or sophistication.

The 'Arc' as Metaphor for the Administrative Order

Perhaps the most useful insight into the prospect for the future evolution of the Bahá'í administrative order as a paradigm for future governance is in the literal and metaphorical arrangements of the edifices designed to constitute the Bahá'í World Centre. That is, because the design of this centre is established around principles set forth in the writings of Bahá'u'lláh which anticipate the future status and function of the Bahá'í administrative order, the centre is being designed not to accommodate present exigencies but to meet the needs of future conditions wherein the Bahá'í World Centre will serve as the 'nerve centre of a world civilization'.[38]

In this context, the arrangement of buildings, the use of materials, the symbolic relationship of these edifices anticipate that future and function as a grand metaphor of the emerging status of the administrative order.

Literal Components

As both the architect's model and the picture of the present progress in the construction of the Bahá'í World Centre indicate, the overall design of the Centre is a 'far-flung arc, around which the edifices constituting the Seat of the

A 'Far-Flung Arc'

World Bahá'í Administrative Order are to be built'.[39] The institutions situated on this arc are the International Library, the Seat of the International Teaching Centre, the Seat of the Universal House of Justice, the Centre for the Study of the Sacred Texts, and the International Archives Building.* The relationship among these institutions, therefore, is tightly focused on the study and understanding of the sacred texts of the Bahá'í revelation, and the legislation and administration of the relevant laws and ordinances. Whatever other edifices might in the future be constructed to supplement the expanded role of the Bahá'í Commonwealth, these primary institutions will always be at the heart of the administrative order.

'Ark' as Metaphor

The arc design itself can be seen to have a variety of symbolic and metaphorical meanings. One obvious significance is the arc as a symbol of hope and salvation similar to the use of that same symbol in the treatment of the story of Noah in the Old Testament and in the Qur'án: 'I set my bow in the cloud, and it shall be for a sign of the covenant between me and the earth.'[40] Another related symbol also alludes to the dispensation of Noah, the allusion in the writings of the Báb and Bahá'u'lláh to a boat or ark as a vehicle for human salvation. More specifically, the Ark comes to symbolize the law of God revealed to humanity, and the sailing of that vessel represents the establishment of the Universal House of Justice with Bahá'u'lláh the captain or 'Holy Mariner' of that vessel:

---

* At this writing, the Seat of the Universal House of Justice and the International Archives buildings are completed and work on the other structures is in progress.

In the Bahá'í Writings the term 'Ark' is often used to signify the Cause of God, or the Covenant, and Bahá'u'lláh, the Holy Mariner. For example, the Báb in the *Qayyumu'l-Asmá* has lauded the community of the Most Great Name, the Bahá'ís, as the companions of the Crimson-coloured Ark.[41]

In the Tablet of Carmel Bahá'u'lláh declares, 'Ere long will God sail His Ark upon thee, and will manifest the people of Bahá who have been mentioned in the Book of Names'.[42] In this context, Shoghi Effendi has said that the Ark refers to 'the establishment of the Universal House of Justice, the supreme legislative body of the Faith from which the law of God will flow to all mankind'.[43]

Symbolic Relation to the Shrine of the Báb

Another significant metaphor used in conjunction with the arrangement of these institutions is the nearby edifice of the Shrine of the Báb, which, though not the focal point of the arc, symbolizes both the point of beginning for the Bahá'í revelation, as well as the spiritual centre of the planet. For example, one appellation the Báb assumed to designate His function in inaugurating the cycle of fulfil- ment was the 'Primal Point', an appellation which derives from His statement that He was 'the Primal Point from which have been generated all created things'.[44] The metaphor 'Primal Point' derives in one sense from the fact that in 'Persian mysticism, all writing is said to originate from a "nuqṭih", a point or dot'.[45] As we can infer from our previous discussion of the Bahá'í perspective on history, the meaning of this metaphor also relates to the advent of the Báb as the beginning point of the stage in planetary history that will usher in the consummation of human social evolution. But in discussing the metaphori- cal meaning in the overall design for the Arc and the surrounding gardens which incorporate the Shrine or mausoleum of the Báb,* Shoghi Effendi explains how this concept of the 'Primal Point' relates to the advent of a world administrative order:

> For, just as in the realm of the spirit, the reality of the Báb has been hailed by the Author of the Bahá'í Revelation as 'The Point round Whom the realities of the Prophets and Messengers revolve', so, on this visible plane, His sacred remains constitute the heart and centre of what may be regarded as nine concentric circles, paralleling thereby, and adding further emphasis to the central position accorded by the Founder of our Faith to One 'from Whom God hath caused to proceed the knowledge of all that was and shall be', 'the Primal Point from which have been generated all created things'.[46]

More specifically, Shoghi Effendi describes nine concentric circles which radiate from the Báb's sarcophagus and encompass the entire planet, thereby paralleling in structure the orbiting planets around the sun.† Shoghi

---

* This is also the burial place of 'Abdu'l-Bahá.

† [9] The outermost circle in this vast system, the visible counterpart of the pivotal position conferred on the Herald of our Faith, is none other than the entire planet. [8] Within the heart of this planet lies the 'Most Holy Land', acclaimed by 'Abdu'l-Bahá as 'the Nest of the Prophets' and which must be regarded as the centre of the world and the Qiblih of the nations. [7] Within this Most Holy Land rises the Mountain of God of immemorial sanctity, the Vineyard of the Lord, the Retreat of Elijah, Whose return the Báb Himself symbolizes. [6] Reposing on the breast of this holy mountain are the extensive properties permanently dedicated to, and constituting the sacred precincts of, the Báb's holy Sepulcher. [5] In the midst of these properties, recognized as the international endowments of the Faith, is situated the most holy court, an enclosure comprising gardens and terraces which at once embellish, and lend a peculiar charm to, these sacred precincts. [4] Embosomed in these lovely and verdant surroundings stands in all its exquisite beauty the mausoleum of the Báb, the shell designed to preserve and adorn the original structure raised by 'Abdu'l-Bahá as the tomb of the Martyr-Herald of our Faith. [3] Within this shell is enshrined that Pearl of Great Price, the holy of holies, those chambers which constitute the tomb itself, and which were constructed by 'Abdu'l-Bahá.

Effendi goes on to extol this sacred dust as having the generating power of the sun:

> So precious is this dust that the very earth surrounding the edifice enshrining this dust has been extolled by the Centre of Bahá'u'lláh's Covenant, in one of His Tablets in which He named the five doors belonging to the six chambers which He originally erected after five of the believers associated with the construction of the Shrine, as being endowed with such potency as to have inspired Him in bestowing these names, whilst the tomb itself housing this dust He acclaimed as the spot round which the Concourse on high circle in adoration.[47]

It is because of the inestimable prestige and historical importance that this place assumes from a Bahá'í perspective that meticulous care and foresight has been taken in the design and construction of this property and these buildings. In this artistic sense, the Bahá'í Faith is not awaiting some future time to build the edifice that will serve as the ark of human salvation; it is already attempting to translate into both metaphorical and literal form the foundation for the 'furthermost limits in the organization of human society'.[48]

The Prospect for the Future

It is not our purpose here to delineate in detail all the duties and procedures presently employed in the Bahá'í administrative order.* No doubt many of these will change and

---

[2] Within the heart of this holy of holies is the tabernacle, the vault wherein reposes the most holy casket. [1] Within this vault rests the alabaster sarcophagus in which is deposited that inestimable jewel, the Báb's holy dust (Shoghi Effendi, *The Citadel of Faith*, pp. 95–6).

* There are numerous manuals and authoritative documents which do provide such detailed information. *Principles of Bahá'í Administration: A Compilation* and *Developing Distinctive Bahá'í Communities: Guidelines of*

evolve to befit the needs of what will increasingly become
the secular affairs of a community evolved from a religious
institution into a literal community in need of governance
in all its most mundane aspects. But we do know a few
important noteworthy certainties.

General Attributes

First, we know that the 'elected councils' of the Bahá'í
administrative order ('universal, secondary and local') will
continue to have 'legislative, executive, and judicial
powers over the Bahá'í community'.[49] Thus, the powers
which on the world level will during the Lesser Peace
become vested in the world parliament, the world executive, and the world tribunal will become merged in the
context of the Bahá'í Commonwealth.

Shoghi Effendi confirms this by observing that when
'the Bahá'í state will be established', the international
tribunal (sometimes alluded to as the 'Universal Court of
Arbitration') will be 'merged in the Universal House of
Justice'.[50] Similarly, Shoghi Effendi states that only when
in the emergence of the Most Great Peace the truth of the
Bahá'í revelation is embraced by the peoples of the world,
'will the Universal House of Justice attain the plentitude of
its power, and exercise, as the supreme organ of the
Bahá'í Commonwealth, all the rights, the duties, and
responsibilities incumbent upon the world's future super-
state'.[51]

From this we must infer not only that the Universal

Spiritual Assemblies offer good discussions of Bahá'í administration. *The
Will and Testament of 'Abdu'l-Bahá*, the various works of Shoghi Effendi,
together with the *Constitution of the Universal House of Justice* and the *Articles
of Association* for the National Assemblies are among the more helpful
documents outlining the operation of the present Bahá'í administrative
order.

House of Justice will function as the 'supreme organ' of that future commonwealth, but also that the powers of the Universal House of Justice, as well as those of the other elected councils, will increase, not decrease. Therefore, when 'Abdu'l-Bahá states that 'the House of Justice, whether National or Universal, has only legislative power and not executive power',[52] He is not delimiting the powers of those bodies. As the Universal House of Justice notes, 'While ultimately the major function of the Universal House of Justice will be that of legislation, it has continuing responsibility for executive and judicial functions of the institution.'[53]

In effect, what 'Abdu'l-Bahá seems to be indicating in this statement is the general distinction between the twin duties of knowing and doing. The Universal House of Justice by right of authority vested in it functions like the head in relation to the rest of the body: it may determine the best course of action, but the execution of that task must be carried out by the body politic as a whole, a condition which already obtains. The purpose of administration is to direct the flow of energy and activity within the worldwide community, but the generation of activity itself is largely in the hands of the councils and individuals who comprise the Bahá'í community.

Since the Local and National Spiritual Assemblies will function in a fashion parallel to that of the Universal House of Justice, we might well presume that these same inferences would be applicable to the future responsibilities of these institutions. Shoghi Effendi seems to confirm this inference when he says, 'Not only will the present-day Spiritual Assemblies be styled differently in future, but they will be enabled also to add to their present functions those powers, duties, and prerogatives necessitated by the recognition of the Faith of Bahá'u'lláh . . .'[54]

It is in this context that we come to appreciate more

fully the collaborative effort implicit and explicit in the hierarchical relationship among the three levels of administrative institutions, as well as between these institutions and the generality of adherents whose affairs and interests they serve:

> Let us also bear in mind that the keynote of the Cause of God is not dictatorial authority but humble fellowship, not arbitrary power, but the spirit of frank and loving consultation.[55]

A Unique Form of Governance

Though it might seem that the system of the world commonwealth implied in the Bahá'í model of governance is fundamentally hierarchical in structure, in reality each administrative body is designed to have a maximum of autonomy and to operate as an organic entity. Here again the analogy of a planetary system is useful.

At the centre of these institutions functioning as the nucleus are the twin aspects of the revelation – the spiritual guidance and the law. Circling around that centre are the nine members of the institution. By themselves, the members have no individual authority, administrative powers or special status, but functioning together, they create organic vitality. Each system is organically related to successively more encompassing organisms, and these are organized in the same fashion, much as in the Newtonian paradigm of cosmological order: moons orbit planets which in turn orbit the sun, and the solar system in turn swirls about in the arms that extend out from the nucleus of our galaxy. Indeed, we can imagine that in the future evolution of human society, the intimate awareness of the earth as one system would become expanded to incorporate a more inclusive sense of ourselves as part of an infinitely expandable expression of divine will.

The point is that even with the hazy glimpse of our immediate future which the present Bahá'í model of governance provides, we can begin to discover the traits that distinguish the system revealed by Bahá'u'lláh from other systems with which we may be familiar. In a general assessment of such a comparison, Shoghi Effendi states:

> This new-born Administrative Order incorporates within its structure certain elements which are to be found in each of the three recognized forms of secular government, without being in any sense a mere replica of any one of them, and without introducing within its machinery any of the objectionable features which they inherently possess. It blends and harmonizes, as no government fashioned by mortal hands has as yet accomplished, the salutary truths which each of these systems undoubtedly contains without vitiating the integrity of those God-given verities on which it is ultimately founded.[56]

To demonstrate the truth of this assertion, Shoghi Effendi discusses some of the apparent similarities between the Bahá'í model and the other major paradigms of governance. For example, he explains that while Bahá'í representatives are democratically elected, they do not get 'their mandate from the people' nor are they 'responsible to those whom they represent'.[57] He compares the hereditary principle as regards the institution of the Guardianship to other systems of inherited authority, such as constitutional monarchies, explaining that in the Bahá'í model, the Guardian has no legislative authority, but is 'the interpreter of the words of its Author'. As such, the Guardian 'ceases consequently, by virtue of the actual authority vested in him, to be the figurehead'.[58]

Perhaps most relevant to our previous observations about how ecclesiastical authority so often becomes aberrated once it is vested with secular power, Shoghi Effendi observes that while Bahá'í governance is theocratic in its alignment of spiritual principles and theological belief with the secular affairs of governance, this system is neither a 'rigid system of unmitigated autocracy' nor is it an 'idle imitation of any form of absolutistic ecclesiastical government'. He vindicates this assertion by noting that the sole right of 'legislating on matters not expressly revealed in the Bahá'í writings' belongs to the 'international elected representatives' who constitute the Universal House of Justice.[59] He further notes that this system is not a form of 'purely aristocratic government' because it incorporates the hereditary principles as regards the Guardianship and provides for 'free and direct election' of the 'highest legislative organ'.[60]

Shoghi Effendi concludes this comparison by observing that by 'rigidly and permanently' excluding the 'admitted evils inherent in each of these systems', the Bahá'í administrative order 'cannot ever degenerate into any form of despotism, of oligarchy, or of demagogy'.[61]

Of course, however soundly Shoghi Effendi may vindicate the Bahá'í theory of governance, our primary objective in this analysis has not been to render a complete analysis of Bahá'í administration. Rather our goal here is to examine the logical basis of the theoretical paradigm on which the Bahá'í administrative order is established so that we can relate that structure to the entire Bahá'í paradigm of history as a justly devised and spiritually guided process. Yet, however justly devised and logically consistent such a utopian vision may be, it matters little to us if our own individual lives are not changed.

It is only appropriate, then, that we complete our theoretical examination of the Bahá'í administrative order by returning to where we began – to the individual and the daily struggle to translate a vision of the family of man into a regimen of fellowship and action.

9

The Heart of the Commonwealth

The Local Community as Tribal Ethos

The Bahá'í community life provides you with an indispensable laboratory, where you can translate into living and constructive action the principles which you imbibe from the Teachings. By becoming a real part of that living organism you can catch the real spirit which runs throughout the Bahá'í Teachings. To study the principles, and to try to live according to them, are, therefore, the two essential mediums through which you can ensure the development and progress of your inner spiritual life and of your outer existence as well . . .

Letter written on behalf of Shoghi Effendi

Relationship between the 'Super-State' and the Local Community

It matters little how well devised world governance may be if the life of the individual is not a just and felicitous experience. For however propitious the Bahá'í paradigm of a world commonwealth might portend to be, it is in the local community that the individual interfaces with this worldwide edifice, and it is here that one must discover on a daily basis the integrity, the spiritual significance, the benignity and divine justice of this paradigm.

So it is that in many ways the single most noteworthy

distinction of the commonwealth for which the Bahá'í community serves as model is the focus on and primacy of family and community life as the essential building materials out of which this edifice is structured. Indeed, it would not be wrong to compare the emphasis on and intimacy of family and community in the Bahá'í model with the healthier aspects of a tribal community. For while the federation of subsidiary levels of national or territorial governance into a world commonwealth may be 'the furthermost limits in the organization of human society',[2] family life and community life as updated and secured in the Bahá'í paradigm are the 'furthermost limits' of organization for these smaller expressions of organic unity.

We have thus come full circle. We began our discussion by demonstrating that individual spiritual ascent necessarily involves a social imperative, an expression or exercise of potential virtue through social relationships. We further inferred that the goal or destiny of this ascent was an ever-expanding identity, a more inclusive sense of self. Now we conclude that these more expansive expressions of self must needs derive their power, their very existence from the integrity of these smaller organic expressions of self. Or stated more concretely, we can hardly appreciate selflessness in the context of a planetary unity if we have not first learned to appreciate and exercise this same quality of expanded identity in the context of family and community life.

But the importance of the family and the community in which the family thrives is more than a training ground for something else. These organic structures ever remain vital and essential institutions, nurturing and being nurtured by the successively more encompassing organic structures of the Secondary Houses of Justice and the Universal House of Justice. Shoghi Effendi thus observed that the strength of the Bahá'í Faith as a whole depends on the strength and autonomy of the local communities: 'the best way to insure and consolidate the organic unity of the Faith is to strengthen the authority of the Local Assemblies and to bring them within the full orbit of the National Assembly's jurisdiction. The National Assembly is the head, and the Local Assemblies are the various organs of the body of the Cause.'[3]

Emulating this organic relationship between the local and secondary levels of governance is the relationship between the family and the local community, since the organic unity of family is itself a kind of community:

> A family, however, is a very special kind of 'community' . . .
> The members of a family all have duties and responsibilities towards one another and to the family as a whole, and these duties and responsibilities vary from member to member because of their natural relationships.[4]

In short, the family and the local community are not only essential organisms for the health of the entire commonwealth; it is in these institutions that we are trained, grow and develop, and it is from these institutions that we first acquire the more expansive visions of ourselves and daily learn to express that world vision.

The Local Community and the Tribal Model

Because the family and community life are thus at the heart of any meaningful human change, we could discuss at great length the specific methods by which Bahá'u'lláh has strengthened and reshaped these institutions, both to foster the sense of humanity as citizens of one world community and to forge these presently battered and abused institutions into autonomous and worthy fortresses for human well being. To the extent that Bahá'u'lláh has spelled out in detail laws regarding engagement, marriage, the rearing of children, chastity, cleanliness, filial piety, education and the myriad other details of daily life, He has thoroughly recreated the institution of the family. But our very limited purpose here is to demonstrate the relationship between the primary level of the administrated organism, the local community, and the efficacy of the Bahá'í model of a world commonwealth:

> The divinely ordained institution of the Local Spiritual Assembly operates at the first levels of human society and is the basic administrative unit of Bahá'u'lláh's World Order. It is concerned with individuals and families whom it must constantly encourage to unite in a distinctive Bahá'í society, vitalized and guarded by the laws, ordinances and principles of Bahá'u'lláh's Revelation. It protects the Cause of God; it acts as the loving shepherd of the Bahá'í flock.[5]

To appreciate even in a most general way how this primary level of administration helps sustain the individuals and the families that it serves, therefore, we might find it useful to note certain parallels between the structure and operation of the Bahá'í model of the local community and the integrity of some tribal models of community life. For while tribal organization as a satisfactory or sufficient stage of human social organization has long since been surpassed by the exigencies of more encompassing structures, we find certain vital and unifying mechanisms at work in a tribal community that are sorely lacking in most contemporary societies, systems of positive socialization that are reintroduced in the Bahá'í model.*

Before we note these parallels, however, we should be careful not to presume that tribalism in and of itself is inherently pure or incorruptible. In those countries where

---

* In this sense, tribalism is not so much a stage in world history as it is a stage in the evolution of any culture. For this reason, we still find cultures that are in this stage of development.

tribalism still obtains as an important social force, tribal loyalty can become an impediment to larger expressions of human unity (the expanded sense of self) and to positive social change. In fact, in the context of the present Bahá'í community, the Universal House of Justice has responded to this problem by noting that the recognition of a more inclusive identity and loyalty does not require the loss of regard for one's more narrow sense of self:

> The second issue which causes difficulties for the African friends in these days is the matter of tribalism. As Bahá'ís they are convinced that mankind is one and must be viewed as one entity, yet, as members of their respective tribes, they find themselves expected by their non-Bahá'í brothers to give their first loyalty to, and even aggressively pursue the interests of their tribe. They live, moreover, in an atmosphere which is only too often one of mistrust, fear and even hatred against the members of other tribes.[6]

What distinguishes the Bahá'í sense of tribal or other sorts of narrower organic unity, then, is that identity as a world citizen does not impinge on or conflict with one's narrower loyalties and identities, but neither does the community identity detract from the expanded sense of identity. Each enhances the other: 'As Bahá'ís we are attached to our tribes and clans, just as we are to our families and, on a larger scale, to our nations, but we do not allow this attachment to conflict with our wider loyalty to humanity.'[7] Just as our earlier analogy between the body and the world commonwealth portrayed the precise interdependence between a healthy body and its constituent cells and organs, so the Bahá'í administrative order does not require a choice between loyalties, since the system itself is integral. The Bahá'í community thus incorporates the benefits of a kind of community or tribal intimacy with the more expansive loyalties of territorial and global identities.

The Local House of Justice as Tribal Council

At the heart of tribal life is some form of council which conducts the affairs of that community within the context of tribal laws and traditions. In the ancient Achaean Greece of Homeric epics (*c.* 1200 BC), the assembly (the *agora*) was a veritable emblem of a civilized society:

> An assembly is no simple institution. As a precondition it requires a relatively settled, stable community made up of many households and kinship groups; in other words, the imposition upon kinship of some territorial superstructure. That means that the several households and larger family groups had substituted for physical coexistence at arm's length a measure of common existence, a community, and hence a partial surrender of their own autonomy.[8]

Similarly, in the Anglo-Saxon or Germanic heroic tribal society (*c.* 400 AD) there was the *witan* (*witangemot*), a council of elders 'who represented the opinion of the tribe',[9] and whose consultation provided guidance for the entire community.

Although freely elected, the Local Spiritual Assembly functions in much the same way as did these ancient institutions and as do tribal councils in tribal communities throughout the world. Consulting on the programmes, goals and general administration of community affairs, the Local Spiritual Assembly is likewise concerned with personal matters: 'It is incumbent upon them to take counsel together and to have regard for the interests of the servants of God, for His sake, even as they regard their own interests . . .'[10]

Even in its present state of infancy, this council has a wide range of obligations and duties, both sacred and secular. Among those listed by Shoghi Effendi are 1) protection of the community; 2) promotion of 'amity and concord'; 3) assistance to the 'poor, the sick, the disabled, the orphan, the widow, irrespective of colour, caste and creed'; 4) promotion of the education of children and youth; and 5) arrangement of regular gatherings of the community.[11]

In addition to the essential similarity in status and function of the Local Spiritual Assembly with the tribal council, there is a second similarity evident in the methods by which this council wields its authority – the Bahá'í process of consultation, perhaps the most essential tool of Bahá'í governance, finds some parallels to similar practices in tribal governance.* In the Bahá'í model, therefore, certain uniform guidelines characterize the methodology of the council. For example, as we have seen, decisions are made not by 'dictatorial authority but humble fellowship, not arbitrary power, but the spirit of frank and loving consultation'.[12] Therefore, where in a tribal model members of a council might well be considered to have achieved rank or status because of their election or appointment to such a body, in the Bahá'í model it is the institution itself that is revered as having divine authority, not the individuals who serve on it:

> Let us recall His explicit and often-repeated assurances that every Assembly elected in that rarefied atmosphere of self-lessness and detachment is, in truth, appointed of God, that its verdict is truly inspired, that one and all should submit to its decision unreservedly and with cheerfulness.[13]

Instead of being perceived as individually superior to or remote from the rank and file members of the community, the elected representatives who serve on these councils work in a spirit of collaboration with the community as a whole:

---

* See Appendix A for a discussion of the distinctive features of Bahá'í consultation.

The duties of those whom the friends have freely and conscientiously elected as their representatives are no less vital and binding than the obligations of those who have chosen them. Their function is not to dictate, but to consult, and consult not only among themselves, but as much as possible with the friends whom they represent. They must regard themselves in no other light but that of chosen instruments for a more efficient and dignified presentation of the Cause of God. They should never be led to suppose that they are the central ornaments of the body of the Cause, intrinsically superior to others in capacity or merit, and sole promoters of its teachings and principles. They should approach their task with extreme humility, and endeavour, by their open-mindedness, their high sense of justice and duty, their candour, their modesty, their entire devotion to the welfare and interests of the friends, the Cause, and humanity, to win, not only the confidence and the genuine support and respect of those whom they serve, but also their esteem and real affection. They must, at all times, avoid the spirit of exclusiveness, the atmosphere of secrecy, free themselves from a domineering attitude, and banish all forms of prejudice and passion from their deliberations. They should, within the limits of wise discretion, take the friends into their confidence, acquaint them with their plans, share with them their problems and anxieties, and seek their advice and counsel.[14]

As we have noted, the scope of responsibilities for this institution will in the future change dramatically as in time it assumes the responsibilities for administering the secular affairs of the community.* But the essential tenor of the relationship between this council and the community it serves will not change. Furthermore, inasmuch as the Local Spiritual Assembly in its present form already

---

* This has already occurred in some Bahá'í communities in Central and South America, in Africa and in India.

conducts marriages, counsels families, establishes schools and oversees various other socio-economic functions, we can find in this model valuable insights about the unique properties of this system of community governance.

The Mashriqu'l-Adhkár as Megaron

Another useful and revealing parallel between the local community in the Bahá'í commonwealth and the tribal model is the importance of a central building which functions as both a literal and symbolic nucleus around which all other activity revolves.* In tribal communities, such an edifice has a vast range of functions, depending, of course, on the particular culture. The Achaeans had a Megaron; the Anglo-Saxon tribes, a mead hall; the Pueblo Indians of North America, a kiva. But regardless of what such an edifice may be called, it may serve variously as 1) the residence for the chieftain, 2) the meeting place for the council, 3) the place of worship, 4) the place to perform religious ceremonies and rites, 5) a place of celebration and feasting, 6) a storehouse and 7) a fortress. Most important of all, however, the edifice functions as symbol of the community itself and, for the individuals in that community, as an integrating force, as a symbol of one's personal relationship to the community and the community's relationship to the cosmos as a whole.

In the Bahá'í community the Mashriqu'l-Adhkár (Dawning-place of the mention of God) has many of these same functions, though in a general sense, it can be seen to relate very pertinently to our previous discussions regarding the dual aspects of human endeavour. As it relates to spiritual understanding (knowledge of God or 'primary

---

* Here again both atomic structure and planetary systems function as physical parallels.

imagination'), the Ma<u>sh</u>riqu'l-A<u>dh</u>kár serves as a place of prayer and meditation. For inasmuch as humanity has passed beyond the need for individuals as symbols of divine authority, the building is the residence of no one, but in its structure symbolizes access to God. Architecturally, for example, it is 'a nine-sided building surmounted by a dome',[15] a configuration which symbolizes that all revealed religions are but different paths to the same Deity and, therefore, to the same essential source of life and guidance.

At the same time, because worship and knowledge of God in the context of the Bahá'í teaching are, as we have taken pains to demonstrate, a thoroughly personal experience, neither worship nor belief can be coerced or imposed. In this sense, the purpose of the Ma<u>sh</u>riqu'l-A<u>dh</u>kár is sublimely simple. In the Kitáb-i-Aqdas Bahá'u'lláh states,

> Blessed is he who, at the hour of dawn, centring his thoughts on God, occupied with His remembrance, and supplicating His forgiveness, directeth his steps to the Ma<u>sh</u>riqu'l-A<u>dh</u>kár and, entering therein, seatheth himself in silence to listen to the verses of God, the Sovereign, the Mighty, the All-Praised.[16]

In connection with this function, therefore, Bahá'u'lláh has revealed a number of ordinances safeguarding how worship takes place in the Ma<u>sh</u>riqu'l-A<u>dh</u>kár. For example, 'sermons are prohibited and only the words of Holy Scripture may be read'.[17] In keeping with the purity of this purpose and process, Bahá'u'lláh has 'forbidden the display of pictures or statues within its walls and the use of musical instruments. Only the human voice may be used to sing, chant or read the Word of God . . .'[18]

Furthermore, also in keeping with the Bahá'í concept of worship as a volitional and individual act is the prohibition against homilies or discourse. For in the same way that congregational prayer is proscribed by Bahá'u'lláh, so one's right and obligation to investigate religion independently without even the hint of coercion is safeguarded, even in a place of worship: 'It is striking how private and personal the most fundamental spiritual exercises of prayer and meditation are in the Faith.'[19]

While this bounty is available to all alike, worship is also set forth as a prescribed part of the daily routine of the elected and appointed administrators headquartered in the vicinity of the House of Worship. Interestingly, Bahá'u'lláh explicitly describes this exercise as a process of deriving 'necessary inspiration' for tackling the practical affairs of governance, a paradigm precisely parallel to our earlier discussion of the artistic process:

> From the Mashriqu'l-Adhkár . . . the representatives of Bahá'í communities, both local and national, together with the members of their respective committees, will, as they gather daily within its walls at the hour of dawn, derive the necessary inspiration that will enable them to discharge . . . their duties and responsibilities . . .[20]

In addition to functioning as 'the spiritual heart'[21] and the 'spiritual centre of every Bahá'í community',[22] the building also serves symbolically the second aspect of human purpose, the translation of insight into action. The edifice thus has specific social and practical purposes, much as the central building does in tribal societies:

> The oneness of mankind, which is at once the operating principle and ultimate goal of His Revelation, implies the achievement of a dynamic coherence between the spiritual and practical requirements of life on earth. The indispensability of this coherence is unmistakably illustrated in His [Bahá'u'lláh's] ordination of the Mashriqu'l-Adhkár, the spiritual centre of every Bahá'í community round which

must flourish dependencies dedicated to the social, humanitarian, educational and scientific advancement of mankind.[23]

In this sense, the Mashriqu'l-Adhkár is not merely one edifice but an institution which incorporates within its purview the related edifices that channel the flow of divine inspiration into various expressions of social action. Therefore, while the 'first part to be built is the central edifice which is the spiritual heart of the community', gradually are added the various dependencies, those 'institutions of social service as shall afford relief to the suffering, sustenance to the poor, shelter to the wayfarer, solace to the bereaved, and education to the ignorant'.[24]*

The erection of the Mashriqu'l-Adhkár as a formal edifice is, for most Bahá'í communities, a future consideration,† but the House of Justice goes on to note that the erecting of this focal point of the community is really a process that begins at the earliest stages of a community's development:

> This process begins in an embryonic way long before a Bahá'í community reaches the stage of building its own Mashriqu'l-Adhkár, for even the first local centre that a Bahá'í community erects can begin to serve not only as the spiritual and administrative centre and gathering place of the community, but also as the site of a tutorial school and the heart of other aspects of the community life.[25]

---

* 'Abdu'l-Bahá assigns at least five dependencies of the Mashriqu'l-Adhkár: a hospital, a drug dispensary, a travellers' hospice, a school for orphans and a university for advanced studies ('Abdu'l-Bahá, *Selections*, p. 100).

† There are presently seven Mashriqu'l-Adhkárs: Wilmette, Illinois; Sidney, Australia; Kampala, Uganda; Frankfurt, Germany; Panama City, Panama; Western Samoa; and Bahapur, India. The first Mashriqu'l-Adhkár to be erected was in Ishqábad, but it was seized by the Soviet government in 1928 and, following an earthquake which damaged its structure, demolished by government order in 1963.

Whether in physical form or in conceptual use, the Mashriqu'l-Adhkár thus functions as the centre or heart of the community, particularly as it symbolizes the convergence of the dual aspects of the process of human ascent by which spiritual inspiration and individual motivation are translated into social structures. Consequently, the Mashriqu'l-Adhkár is the 'nerve centre' of the community it serves, comparable to the 'Ark' of the World Centre on a planetary level.

The Individual and the Tribal Perspective

In the same way that Shoghi Effendi observes that the Bahá'í Commonwealth of the Most Great Peace will represent the 'furthermost limits' of organization on the planet, we might conclude that the family and tribal models are in a general sense also optimum organizational structures for the lesser expression of collective identity and governance. That is, however vast and inclusive human social order becomes, even if beyond the confines of a planetary or global society, we will never outgrow the need for these subsidiary constituent parts of that structure. In fact, as we have repeatedly observed, the health of the larger expressions of social structure depends entirely on the health and integrity of these smaller organic components of family and community.

Consequently, after the training and socialization which takes place in the family, which we can infer will ever remain the heart and soul of all human growth and development, we discover the most important trait of community life is its capacity to integrate the life of the individual into the more encompassing expressions of self. This process of socialization is critical not only because it provides community members with a vital sense of the collective self, but also because it is capable of providing

an effective relationship between one's individual activities
and the goals and ideals of the society as a whole without
requiring mindless fanaticism or abasement. Here too
Bahá'í community life calls to mind the tribal model or
ethos.

The Importance of History and Heroes

One of the most powerful means by which the individual
life is connected to the society as a whole in a tribal
environment is through shared identity achieved through
a celebration of a common history. Indeed, at the heart of
most tribal life is the narration of stories, genealogies, the
recollected lives of ancestral heroes who exemplify the
cultural or spiritual ideals of the people. Among most
tribal communities, for example, there usually emerges a
tradition or profession of the tribal poet or historian, one
who can recall the genealogies of the people and rehearse
in exacting detail the superhuman exploits of tribal heroes.
In such fashion, individuals are reminded of their heritage,
their common identity, their shared aspirations, and are
exhorted to emulate these heroic deeds so that one day
their own lives might be recollected around the hearth.

Since the Bahá'í community of the future will consider
itself as having an identity that encompasses the entire
family of man, people living in that inclusive environment
will no doubt celebrate the lives of all those throughout
human history who have helped foster the successive
stages in the progress of that process by which humanity
has achieved fruition. No doubt the historians of such a
culture will discover heroes and heroines whose selfless
deeds have never before been recounted. Of particular
interest will be those figures in Bahá'í history who made
heroic sacrifices that were crucial in bringing about our
transition to a planetary identity.

In this connection, it is worth noting that the appellation used to designate the earliest stage of the unfolding of the Bahá'í revelation, a stage which necessarily required untold acts of heroism and sacrifice, is the 'Heroic Age' (1844–1921). During this period, from 1844 to 1853, over twenty thousand believers in Persia courageously endured torture and martyrdom rather than betray their faith by recanting their beliefs.* Given the appellation 'Dawn-breakers' as a symbol of their recognition of the first rays of the dawning of a new dispensation in the person of the Báb, these historical figures are revered by Bahá'ís as the first heroes and heroines of Bahá'í history.

In exhorting the American Bahá'í community to respond to the lofty position it has been designated to assume in facilitating the transformation of world society, Shoghi Effendi often employed the epithet 'spiritual descendants of the dawn-breakers':

> The community of the organized promoters of the Faith of Bahá'u'lláh in the American continent – the spiritual descendants of the dawn-breakers of an heroic Age, who by their death proclaimed the birth of that Faith – must, in turn, usher in, not by their death but through living sacrifice, that promised World Order, the shell ordained to enshrine that priceless jewel, the world civilization, of which the Faith itself is the sole begetter.[26]

In numerous places, the Bahá'í community is exhorted to study the lives of these figures, and perhaps most relevant to our analysis of the community life, local communities are constantly urged by Bahá'í administrative institutions to initiate and maintain archival records of the history of the development of the Bahá'í Faith in their own communities. The clear implication in this is that, while

---

* For detailed accounts of these events, see Nabíl, *The Dawn-Breakers*; and Shoghi Effendi, *God Passes By*.

presently unimportant to the world at large, such accounts will serve in the future to demonstrate how little-noticed or noted acts of unselfish devotion by ordinary individuals laid the foundation for a worldwide enterprise.

We can presume that as the underlying and unifying purpose of human history becomes more clearly understood, so the perspective about human history will likewise become revised. As a primary result of such a revised analysis of human progress towards fulfilment of spiritual destiny, we can imagine that figures who might presently be deemed to have little importance will assume a stature, a place of honour and reverence, as would astound present-day historians and would have amazed the contemporaries of those individuals who could hardly have suspected the veiled nobility that they witnessed. As our collective perspective about history changes as we come to understand more clearly the interplay between the advent of religion and the advance of humankind, so will our inferences about the figures who comprise our history become appreciably altered.

For these reasons, as well as for the practical need to maintain continuity of administration, the institution of Bahá'í archives functions not only as a integral part of the central edifices of the World Centre, but also as an essential institution for the local community as well:

> Future generations of believers will be surely in a better position than we are to truly and adequately appreciate the many advantages and facilities which the institution of the Archives offers to individual believers and also to the community at large.[27]

The Calendar as Symbol of Shared Perspective

Another source and expression of tribal health and coherence centres around shared rites, rituals, commemorations, a calendar of events which inevitably maps out in symbolic observances the cycle of life implicit in seasons of the year, just as the cycle of the year symbolizes the increasingly more expansive cycles of human development we discussed earlier.

Because tribal cultures often live close to nature, whether they be an agrarian people or nomadic hunters, the calendar of tribal activities will traditionally focus on commemorating those events associated with seasonal changes as they relate to community life (planting, harvest, etc.), with significant endeavours (preparation for hunts, warfare, etc.), or with historical personages and events (particularly those associated with the common heritage and shared ideal that bonds the community together and is expressive of their collective identity). In these and other ways, the calendar functions as a central means of organizing the lives of the people. It is doubtless for this reason that there is so much archaeological evidence demonstrating the ingenious devices ancient peoples created for maintaining absolute accuracy about the cycle of the year.*

Obviously we can only guess at all the implications such precision had for tribal peoples. Certainly it betokened an external order to the otherwise apparently random nature of life. And doubtless such order in turn confirmed belief in an abiding justice that could override the ostensible mutability and the seemingly capricious forces that could so dramatically disorder daily life. A calendar of predictable events implied an orderliness to nature, a regularity, a dependability, a predictability in the macrocosm and a

---

* The discoveries of how Stonehenge and other similar structures in tribal societies were devised to indicate the summer solstice, eclipses and other important events on the calendar has broadened our understanding of how critical the calendar was to a tribal community.

hope that the orderliness in the world at large might make the reign of justice possible in their own microcosmic existence.

Related to such assurance from a Bahá'í perspective is the observation that with the advent of each Manifestation there is a new calendar. In effect, this critical symbol connotes that meaningful life begins with the advent of this guidance. In addition to renewal, the new calendar symbolizes the eternality, the unremitting persistence of God's grace. Symbolically this reorientation to the passage of time thus relates importantly to the next stage in the progress of human society. With the renewed influx of creative energy, time begins again – it is a new day. In addition, with the new calendar will be a revised organization of the life of the people, a new regimen and routine to comply with revised laws and ordinances.

For the Bahá'í community there is likewise a new calendar, the Bahá'í or Badí' calendar, established by the Báb and approved by Bahá'u'lláh. Using 1844 (AH 1260) as the beginning year of this new cycle (the beginning of the Bahá'í Era), the Bahá'í calendar is based on the solar year of 365 days. Of particular importance to the administration of the Bahá'í community, however, the calendar divides the year into nineteen months of nineteen days each, with four 'intercalary days' (five in leap year). *

All community affairs are organized around this arrangement. The first day in each new month is a 'feast' day, and each of the nineteen feast days is named after a divine attribute. On the feast day Bahá'í communities worldwide hold a tri-partite meeting consisting of 1) prayers and meditative readings from the sacred texts,

---

* As we have mentioned earlier, the number 19 symbolizes a unity or a completion of a cycle, and a Váhid or 19-year cycle is used in relation to some Bahá'í laws.

2) consultation between the elected council and the community at large, and 3) fellowship of whatever sort is appropriate to the culture.

Bahá'í Months

1	Bahá	Splendour	21 March – 8 April
2	Jalál	Glory	9 March – 27 April
3	Jamál	Beauty	28 April – 16 May
4	'Azamat	Grandeur	17 May – 4 June
5	Núr	Light	5 June – 23 June
6	Rahmat	Mercy	24 June – 12 July
7	Kalimát	Words	13 July – 31 July
8	Kamál	Perfection	1 August – 19 August
9	Asmá'	Names	20 August – 7 September
10	'Izzat	Might	8 September – 26 September
11	Mashíyyat	Will	27 September – 15 October
12	'Ilm	Knowledged	16 October – 3 November
13	Qudrat	Power	4 November – 22 November
14	Qawl	Speech	23 November – 11 December
15	Masá'il	Questions	12 December – 30 December
16	Sharaf	Honour	31 December – 18 January
17	Sultán	Sovereignty	19 January – 6 February
18	Mulk	Dominion	7 February – 25 February
19	'Alá'	Loftiness	2 March – 20 March

The day begins at sunset, and the days of the week are also named after divine attributes: Saturday is Jalál (Glory), Sunday is Jamál (Beauty), Monday is Kamál (Perfection), Tuesday is Fidál (Grace); Wednesday is 'Idál (Justice), Thursday is Istijlál (Majesty) and Friday is Istiqlál (Independence).

The Bahá'í year begins on 21 March with the spring equinox. The calendar contains nine holy days on which work is to be suspended, each associated with an event from Bahá'í history. In addition, the last month of the year, 'Alá, is a period of fasting for adult Bahá'ís (2 March through 21 March), and the fast is preceded by the Intercalary Days, the Ayyám-i-Há,* a period of gift-giving and preparation for the fast.† Perhaps the most crucial period on the calendar insofar as Bahá'í administration is concerned is the twelve-day commemor-ation of the Feast or Festival of Riḍván (21 April through 2 May), a period which commemorates Bahá'u'lláh's declaration to His followers in 1863 that He was the Manifestation foretold by the Báb. Local and national Bahá'í councils are elected annually during this period, and the Universal House of Justice is also elected during Riḍván every five years.

There is much more essential information relevant to the Bahá'í calendar, but for our purposes it is sufficient to observe that, like a tribal calendar, individual and community life takes its overall organization from the intimate association of the community with this organiz-ing device.

Rites and Rituals associated with the Cycle of Life

Unlike tribal cultures, the Bahá'í community is largely devoid of ritual. Bahá'u'lláh has specifically and permanently abrogated virtually all forms of ritualistic worship, and most observances are also devoid of prescribed ceremony, though many have explicitly prescribed procedures and

---

* 'Literally, Days of Há (i.e. the letter Há, which in the abjad system has the numerical value of 5). Intercalary Days. The four days (five in leap year) before the last month of the Bahá'í year' (Momen, *A Basic Bahá'í Dictionary*, p. 27).

† Bahá'ís abstain from eating and drinking from sunrise to sunset as a symbolic reminder of 'abstinence from selfish and carnal desires' (Letter written on behalf of Shoghi Effondi, quoted in *Lights of Guidance*, no. 775, p. 233).

guidelines. However, rather than repressing cultural identity or integrity as regards the community involvement with these observances, Bahá'u'lláh has instead liberated humanity from a particular cultural bias. For inasmuch as the laws and ordinances of Bahá'u'lláh are to endure throughout this dispensation, they must accommodate all peoples and all cultural orientations.

Therefore, while there is rarely a prescribed ceremony, there are in the Bahá'í community significant events in the life of an individual for which the community has some recognized procedure. For example, one of the most significant events in the life of an individual in a tribal culture is some form of rite of passage to symbolize the attainment of adulthood. Such ceremonies or observances may involve a severe test or some elaborate ritual to represent the casting away of one identity and the assumption of an adult role with its attendant responsibilities.

Bahá'u'lláh has designated fifteen as the age of maturity for the Bahá'í. Administratively the age of maturity signifies the individual's responsibility to abide by Bahá'í law, as well as the earliest age at which individuals may marry. Yet the community may celebrate this milestone in whatever way it deems appropriate to acknowledge this transition.

Engagement and marriage, though equally devoid of prescribed ritual and ceremony, are regulated through a set of required procedures. For example, the engagement is not to exceed ninety-five days and cannot occur before the age of fifteen. Marriage itself is conditioned on the couple's consent and the permission of both of their parents. A minimal dowry is paid by the husband to the wife as a symbol of her autonomy as an individual.* The

* The Research Department of the Universal House of Justice notes the following: 'Seen in the context of the fundamental Bahá'í principle of

marriage ceremony itself varies from culture to culture, from family to family, requiring only one simple action: the bride and groom must individually recite the following vow in the presence of at least two witnesses acceptable to the Local Spiritual Assembly: 'We will all, verily, abide by the Will of God.'[28]

Bahá'í burial has this same sort of distinction – regulation regarding procedures, but an almost complete lack of prescribed ritual or ceremony. The body is to be cleansed and wrapped in a shroud. It should not be embalmed and should be placed in a casket. The body should not be cremated or removed more than an hour's journey from the place of death. An inscribed burial ring should be placed on the finger of the deceased,* and the 'Prayer for the Dead', the only obligatory Bahá'í communal prayer, should be recited before interment. The commemorative services and other arrangements are, however, entirely at the discretion of the family and community.

Here again, as an index to the flexibility of the Bahá'í paradigm, are laws and procedures revealed by Bahá'u'lláh regarding the individual and community life ingeniously devised to foster unity, order and justice while remaining adaptable to any culture. This is a tremendously important distinction in demonstrating how a single paradigm of a world commonwealth could foster concord and unity among the diverse cultures and personalities of a planetary community without simultaneously repressing creativity

---

the equality of men and women, this can be understood as a symbol of the bride's right to her own independent property; of the bridegroom's responsibility to support his family; and also as an action sealing the marriage bond' (Letter to John Hatcher, 25 December 1990).

* The inscription reads, 'I came forth from God, and return unto Him, detached from all save Him, holding fast to His Name, the Merciful, the Compassionate' (Bahá'u'lláh, *The Kitáb-i-Aqdas*, no. 129).

and ethnic diversity and without requiring or imposing homogeneity or cultural bias.

Law Enforcement and the Community

Since our intention here is not to provide a complete portrait of all aspects of Bahá'í law and administration but rather to understand its strategic relationship to the body politic as a whole, we might find useful one further comparison between tribal society and the Bahá'í model – a similar attitude towards enforcement of law that these communities foster.

Socialization and Law Enforcement

If we have satisfactorily established that socialization is an essential ingredient in defining and training human nature, we have also inferred that this same force can be wielded equally effectively in repressing human development or in enforcing injustice. But as we noted earlier, most contemporary societies worldwide have divorced morality from socialization. As a result, parents must presently struggle to foster some semblance of a just society in the microcosmic confines of the home or else among a handful of similarly minded friends. In this sense, the same essential force whose function it is to support and nurture this most difficult, subtle and critical of all human endeavours is either absent or perniciously countermanding the parent's noble efforts.

A tribal society functions to define and foster the wellbeing of its families and thereby to ensure the perpetuity of the society itself. Thus, the Bahá'í society, as reflected in the present model of the Bahá'í life and as further implied in the as yet unimplemented laws of Bahá'u'lláh, assists the family at every stage to reinforce the noble ideals of human spiritual ascent. As an affirmative force, this socialization provides a shared moral vision channelled into a myriad forms of education to reward growth. As a retributive force, the Bahá'í society, like the tribal community, provides a strong deterrent to anti-social behaviour upheld by a system of enforceable law.

It is important to note here, however, that the Bahá'í model of social ordinance does not contain an elaborate code or canon which can so often become a lifeless body of mindless dogma. In fact, Bahá'í law contains few pre-scribed punishments and provides instead an infinitely flexible system of response that depends not so much on precedence as it does on the capacity of elected councils to respond to the exigencies of each individual situation. In other words, it is an essential goal of the Bahá'í commun-ity to foster a society that, like a tribal community, enforces the ideals and virtues primarily by means of fostering a positive socialization, a milieu in which the fear of being morally negligent will itself be the most weighty deterrent to immoral behaviour:

> Divine civilization, however, so traineth every member of society that no one, with the exception of a negligible few, will undertake to commit a crime. There is thus a great difference between the prevention of crime through measures that are violent and retaliatory, and so training the people, and enlightening them, and spiritualizing them, that without any fear of punishment or vengeance to come, they will shun all criminal acts. They will, indeed, look upon the very commission of a crime as a great disgrace and in itself the harshest of punishments. They will become enamoured of human perfections, and will consecrate their lives to what-ever will bring light to the world and will further those qualities which are acceptable at the Holy Threshold of God.[29]

Clearly correlative to this process, then, will be the weight of social repute and the opinion of friends. For example, it is in the context of a closely-knit military milieu portrayed in Shakespeare's *Othello* that the malignant Iago attempts to reassure the fallen Cassio that 'Reputation is an idle and most false imposition'.[30]

But to a professional soldier like Cassio, the opinion of his close companions is precious beyond measure:

> Reputation, reputation, reputation! O, I have lost my reputation! I have lost the immortal part of myself, and what remains is bestial.[31]

In such a closely-knit community where the most powerful force of socialization is the desire on the part of the individual to be esteemed or well-regarded by one's larger self (the community as a whole), the most grievous punishment one can suffer is not imprisonment, torture or death, but exile or banishment.

In contemporary society where there is little sense of a social self, of a social bond or of belonging, the criminal looks to escape from his community as a propitious means of avoiding prosecution. In the society of the Bahá'í commonwealth, however, we infer a return to the tribal model. For example, theft is one of the few crimes for which Bahá'u'lláh took it upon Himself to prescribe punishment.* In the Kitáb-i-Aqdas, Bahá'u'lláh ordains 'banishment and confinement for the first two offences; for the third offence a mark must be placed on the thief's forehead . . . so that people will be warned of his pro-

---

* For the most part, it will be left to the judgement of the Universal House of Justice to establish a penal code, and we can presume that will change to befit the changing conditions in society. According to the Universal House of Justice, the 'profound quality of divine law' will be in 'fostering the spiritual development of individuals and mankind as a whole, in addition to the general functions of restricting socially unacceptable behaviour, keeping order and promoting unity in society' (Letter 2 November 1986).

clivities'.[32] Both the severity and efficacy of this enforcement is obviously dependent on a society in which the opinion and acceptance of others is extremely important to one's sense of worth and well-being, where such a mark would be deemed the worst of punishments rather than a sign of defiance and indifference, as it would be in many contemporary urban communities.

Retribution and Justice

Another noteworthy parallel between tribal communities and the Bahá'í community regarding violation of law concerns retribution. On the one hand, the Bahá'í writings make it clear that it is the purpose of governance to maintain justice and that the punishing of criminals is part of this process:

> O people of God! That which traineth the world is Justice, for it is upheld by two pillars, reward and punishment. These two pillars are the sources of life to the world.[33]

However, it is also clear that the purpose of the punishment of crime is the training of humankind; punishment should never degenerate into personal retaliation. In discussing the distinction between the individual's obligation to forgive and the community's obligation to protect itself, 'Abdu'l-Bahá provides the following observations:

> For example, if someone oppresses, injures and wrongs another, and the wronged man retaliates, this is vengeance and is censurable . . .
>
> But the community has the right of defence and of self-protection; moreover, the community has no hatred nor animosity for the murderer: it imprisons or punishes him merely for the protection and security of others. It is not for the purpose of taking vengeance upon the murderer, but for the purpose of inflicting a punishment by which the

community will be protected. If the community and the inheritors of the murdered one were to forgive and return good for evil, the cruel would be continually ill-treating others, and assassinations would continually occur.[34]

As 'Abdu'l-Bahá goes on to describe, the community is thus obliged to punish the malefactor through retributive action, but this does not imply that the community acts out of vengeance or retaliation:

The community has no ill-will and rancour in the infliction of punishment, and it does not desire to appease the anger of the heart; its purpose is by punishment to protect others so that no atrocious actions may be committed.[35]

'Abdu'l-Bahá also concludes that it was never Christ's intent in teaching His followers to turn the other cheek that society should not punish criminals or that people should not protect themselves, but rather that men ought not 'to take personal revenge'.[36] Thus, where forgiveness is an admirable individual trait, so also is justice: 'The tent of existence is upheld upon the pillar of justice and not upon forgiveness. The continuance of mankind depends upon justice and not upon forgiveness.'[37]

Therefore, we cannot in this context judge tribal justice as it might be demonstrated in the Mosaic law of 'an eye for an eye' as archaic or superseded, except as one might apply such a law to personal response or emotional attitude. Consequently, at the heart of Bahá'í concepts of penology is the tribal ideal of making the perpetrator feel the weight of his or her crime. As a result, there are in the laws of Bahá'u'lláh allowance for capital punishment:

Wilful murder is to be punished either by capital punishment or life imprisonment. Such matters as degrees of offence and whether any extenuating circumstances are to be taken into account . . . Bahá'u'lláh prescribes that a person who burns a house intentionally is to be burned or imprisoned for life, but again, the application of these punishments and the fixing of degrees of offence are left to the Universal House of Justice.[38]*

The response of the administrative body to a crime will thus depend on 'extenuating circumstances' and 'the prevailing conditions when the law is in operation'. Here again the ingenuity of the system is apparent. Bahá'u'lláh has prescribed relatively few specific punishments, and even those seem to function primarily as models of response to various levels of injustice. In short, while justice and law and order are of paramount importance, the Bahá'í commonwealth ordains not a canon of fixed law, but an infinitely flexible system capable of ministering to the exigencies of whatever conditions may arise.

An Abiding Image of a World Commonwealth

There are other valid similarities between the foundational principles operant in a tribal community and those designed to operate in the context of a global society. But the overall sense of the comparison is clear enough: the important transformation of individual life occurs at the

---

* The notes to the Kitáb-i-Aqdas state: 'The details of the Bahá'í law of punishment for murder and arson, a law designed for a future state of society, were not specified by Bahá'u'lláh. The various details of the law, such as degrees of offence, whether extenuating circumstances are to be taken into account, and which of the two prescribed punishments is to be the norm are left to the Universal House of Justice to decide in light of prevailing conditions when the law is to be in operation. The manner in which the punishment is to be carried out is also left to the Universal House of Justice to decide.

'In relation to arson, this depends on what "house" is burned. There is obviously a tremendous difference in the degree of offence between the person who burns down an empty warehouse and one who sets fire to a school full of children (Bahá'u'lláh, *Kitab-i-Aqdas*, note 86, p. 204).

most intimate levels of human interaction. Individual identity is first trained and expanded within the context of the family and then within the local community. While that expanding sense of self never really abates, one is in this life always living within both of these contexts. Therefore, one never loses the need to devote daily attention to the creative expression of spiritual principles in social relationships.

Stated another way, however soundly world governance may be devised or administered, no meaningful change in world civilization can take place unless such a vision focuses on fostering justice in the daily lives of the ordinary citizen – justice cannot be infused through osmosis or trickle down from on high. Equally clear is the abiding theme which permeates our attempt to glimpse that future society contained implicitly in the present Bahá'í community and explicitly in the Bahá'í literature: that some ingenious worldwide structure does not alone foster a new 'race of men'.* Families and communities accomplish this by helping to foster individuals whose vision is world embracing, whose sense of themselves is firmly grounded in a moral perspective so pervasive in their lives that they will be empowered to forge a new civilization capable of expressing divine principles in the artifice of the physical world.

A New Race of Men

Perhaps the most important conclusion we have reached, then, is that the largest aspirations for a global common-

---

* 'A race of men,' is His written promise, 'incomparable in character, shall be raised up which, with the feet of detachment, will tread under all who are in heaven and on earth, and will cast the sleeve of holiness over all that hath been created from water and clay' (Bahá'u'lláh, quoted in *The Advent of Divine Justice*, p. 31).

wealth are vested in the health of the smallest organic entity constituting that encompassing structure, the individual human soul. Yet equally clear is the undeniable dependence that each of us has on the larger expressions of ourselves, whether in the family, in the immediate community, or in the extended sense of ourselves as world citizens struggling to fashion on one very small island in space a community whose harmony and justice reflects the same sort of integrity with which the Creator has fashioned the natural environment. And if we have through our modern sciences come to understand much about the spiritual theme that the natural world of correspondences has to teach us, it is an unrelenting saga about the mutuality of our existence.

So it is that merely envisioning a just society cannot by itself bring it into existence. The logic of such a paradigm may foster hope within us that there can exist simultaneously world unity without tyranny or homogeneity; systematic order without oppressive coercion, regulation or loss of those freedoms essential to any worthwhile quality of life; sufficiency and equitable distribution of resources without the loss of individual incentive, initiative and ingenuity; an abiding reverence for humanity as a single organism without the sacrifice of individual identity and genius; an intelligent utilization of the earth's resources simultaneous with an evolving cognizance how our own well-being is inseparable from the health of the spiritually dynamic organism that brought us into being; and, most important, a general recognition of the spiritual basis for human society without the chauvinism, rigidity and oppression that have in the past most often typified theocracies and obliterated the very piety and reverence such systems sought to engender and secure.

It is a vision that calls to mind Robert Hayden's poem 'Words in the Mourning Time'. While lamenting the violence and inhumanity of this 'deathbed childbed age', the speaker exhorts us to 'go on struggling to be human' and to 'Reclaim now, now renew the vision/ of a human world where godliness is possible . . .'[39] It likewise recalls Hayden's earlier poem about the Afro-American orator and scholar Frederick Douglass, a former slave who was able to envision 'a world/ where none is lonely, none hunted, alien . . .'[40]

The vision of the Bahá'í commonwealth we have only cursorily assessed ultimately depends for its actualization upon the progressive accumulation of individual lives transformed one at a time, upon the establishment of a skeletal framework, an emblematic model, a sure foundation for future possibilities. We discover this abiding theme throughout the Bahá'í writings, that the artistic rendering of a world society must ultimately derive from individual choices, by the example of individual lives transformed through wilful application of spiritual laws and principles on a daily basis: 'No amount of administrative procedure or adherence to rules can take the place of this soul-characteristic, this spirituality which is the essence of Man.'[41] Shoghi Effendi makes this verity abundantly clear when he says that the influence of the Bahá'í teachings, however true they may be, will only have their full effect when individuals take it upon themselves to become visibly distinct in their conduct and character:

Not by the force of numbers, not by the mere exposition of a set of new and noble principles, not by an organized campaign of teaching – no matter how worldwide and elaborate in its character – not even by the staunchness of our faith or the exaltation of our enthusiasm, can we ultimately hope to vindicate in the eyes of a critical and sceptical age the supreme claim of the Abhá Revelation. One thing and only one thing will unfailingly and alone secure the undoubted triumph of this sacred Cause, namely, the extent to which our own inner life and private character mirror forth in their manifold aspects the splendour of those eternal principles proclaimed by Bahá'u'lláh.[42]

The Music of the Spheres

In her introduction to *Epistle to the Son of the Wolf*, Marzieh Gail observes that where in the past religion has 'produced the good individual', the goal of the Bahá'í Faith is 'to produce the good society'. She goes on to note that the system established by Bahá'u'lláh will be especially capable of achieving 'the only satisfactory arrangement between individual and community, between free will and authority, equilibrating the prerogatives of each'.[43] She concludes this statement by observing that both organisms will have to relinquish something to sustain such an order:

> When the balance between the person and society finally obtains we shall know that man has begun his maturity. Obviously, both individual and group will have to give up something of what they now have, just as the nations will have to yield some of their present sovereignty in favour of the world commonwealth, but this will prove no more of a hardship than the sacrifice of bait to catch a fish.[44]

As we have previously noted, this idea of sacrificing or relinquishing a portion of national sovereignty to achieve a more inclusive reality is not dissimilar to the process that occurred when the states of the American nation federated.

We have previously discussed how the recognition of and allegiance to a just and abiding authority is a prerequisite to the establishment of a world government. What bears repeating here is that while this sense of sacrificing something for the greater good is, relatively speaking, quantitatively accurate, it is misleading if we infer from such observations a lessening or weakening of freedom, authority or fulfilment, any more than relinquishing our childhood behaviour to become adults requires a diminishing of our powers. Obviously the opposite is the case.

Therefore, to say that the fostering and sustaining of the relationship between the individual and the body politic is a balance could be misleading or misunderstood if we infer that the health of one organism should be sacrificed to sustain the well-being of another. Health results from recognizing the organic mutuality of the entire system.

When such an understanding is reached, there is no longer a question of whose health has primacy in this. As we have repeatedly noted, the health of the whole and the health of the parts is synonymous.

This coordinated effort is very much like the construction of an organ in a great European cathedral. This was an amazingly intricate and tedious undertaking, necessitating a painstaking array of skills, each a profession in itself, each requiring apprenticeship in crafts passed down for countless generations. There was first the design of the organ to fit the physical arrangement and acoustics of the particular building, since each cathedral had its special potentialities. There was the forging of each pipe, hand hammered sheets formed around individual wooden lasts, each one precisely the right circumference and length. There was the fashioning of the linkage from keys to valves, the construction of bellows and a myriad other complex parts.

And when the instrument was at last completed, there were the dexterous hands of a musician whose years of training prepared him to translate through the instrumentality of his fingers the composer's strains into vibrant sound which would resound throughout the house of worship, itself both the recipient of that blessed tone and the sounding board for the music. And the villagers who occupied that instrument-edifice, who one and all had helped fashion the great cathedral, and whose hard-earned wages paid for this confluence of artists, artisans and art, listened, rapt by that euphony as it rehearsed in perceptible sound their patient faith.

So it is that humanity, now as artisans within the unfinished edifice of this our global self, are exhorted to hear the melodies of imminent change, are challenged to complete the divine instrument of a new social order which, for all its unimaginable possibilities, presently seems to lie in such confusion, its parts in disarray.

Yet also before us is the architect's plan, a job for each of us to do, and a working model of the finished edifice. And if we listen carefully, we might hear the faint and distant strains of beauteous music playing upon our handiwork:

> Thou beholdest, O my God, how every bone in my body soundeth like a pipe with the music of Thine inspiration, revealing the signs of Thy oneness and the clear tokens of Thy unity. I entreat Thee, O my God, by Thy Name which irradiateth all things, to raise up such servants as shall incline their ears to the voice of the melodies that hath ascended from the right hand of the throne of Thy glory.[45]

Some Distinctive Features of Operation

Having outlined the fundamental structure of the Bahá'í administrative order, we can appreciate some of the essential features of its operation in order to see why this institution might prove a useful model of the future commonwealth. But of parallel significance in the unique properties of this system, in addition to the fundamental outline of the institutions and the essential relationship among them, are some of the essential tools of this paradigm. What distinguishes the institutions and secures their integrity are the processes by which they come into being, the mode of their operation, and the nature of their relationship to the body politic as a whole. An examination of a few of the more salient of these will illustrate these distinguishing characteristics.

Individual Status and the Administration

While the Bahá'í paradigm recognizes the legitimacy of authority conferred on institutions, as well as a hierarchy of authority among those institutions, the Bahá'í administrative order makes no distinction in rank among individual believers. Instead, there is equality of status, of rights and privileges among all Bahá'ís, even if one is elected or appointed to serve on an institution.

A corollary of this principle is the essential requisite that all prejudice of whatever sort be abolished, since all Bahá'ís possess the same rights. This does not mean that those who have attained achievements and honours or who are deemed to have insight or wisdom are not appropriately regarded by their fellow Bahá'ís. But such accomplishments do not carry with them any attendant authority, rank, privilege. Likewise, since all authority derives from elected institutions, not from individuals, one cannot even aspire to individual status, inasmuch as service on an administrative body does not imply any status or authority outside the chambers of that consultative body.

The Electoral Process

The three levels or layers of administration are elected by essentially the same process, though by distinct electorate. At present, all three administrative bodies have nine members. The Local Spiritual Assemblies are elected annually by all adult Bahá'ís residing within the jurisdiction for which that Assembly is responsible, and only adult Bahá'ís residing in that jurisdiction are eligible.*

The National Spiritual Assemblies are elected indirectly on an annual basis by delegates who represent electoral districts apportioned according to the Bahá'í population. All adult Bahá'ís residing in a district are eligible to be elected as a delegate, unless they are Counsellors. If Auxiliary Board members are elected, they must choose whether to serve as a delegate or remain as an Auxiliary Board member.

The delegates assemble annually to elect the National Spiritual Assembly from among all the adult Bahá'ís

---

* The present age for eligibility is 21.

residing in the nation or territory. The Universal House of Justice is elected every five years by the members of the National Spiritual Assemblies, and all adult male Bahá'ís worldwide are eligible.*

The election procedures themselves are the same for each of these three levels of administration. First, the election consists of a secret ballot and a plurality vote. The electorate write the names of nine adult Bahá'ís on a ballot, and the nine Bahá'ís receiving the most votes are elected. Second, there are no campaigns, no parties, no nominations. Electioneering or even the discussion of personalities is strictly prohibited. One's vote is considered a completely private matter, and no one is allowed to influence the vote of another or to be influenced.

The implications of these restrictions are far reaching and yet subtle. The most obvious ramification of this process is that the qualification for election is not public virtue or personal achievement:

> Hence it is incumbent upon the chosen delegates to consider without the least trace of passion and prejudice, and irrespective of any material consideration, the names of only those who can best combine the necessary qualities of unquestioned loyalty, of selfless devotion, of a well-trained mind, of recognized ability and mature experience.[1]

Since such a process implies both subjectivity and a

---

* The Bahá'í writings assert that the exclusion of women from eligibility to serve on the House of Justice does not relate to any notion of inequality of status or capacity, something confirmed by the eligibility of women for every other administrative body and institution. This is not a temporary condition; it will remain in effect for the duration of this dispensation. 'Abdu'l-Bahá states that the 'wisdom of the Lord God's' regarding this distinction 'will erelong be made manifest as clearly as the sun at high noon' ('Abdu'l-Bahá, *Selections*, p. 80). For a further discussion of this issue, see J. S. Hatcher, 'The Equality of Women: The Bahá'í Principle of Complementarity', *Journal of Bahá'í Studies*, vol. 2, no. 3, pp. 55–66.

virtually infinite variety of possible administrative bodies, several questions immediately arise. What assurance is there that individuals so elected are the best? How is continuity maintained? How does a qualified person become recognized? Does one vote for individuals of publicly acknowledged accomplishment who may, therefore, be 'electable', or only for those about whom the elector has personal confidence and knowledge?

The response to the first of these concerns is that the consultative or decision-making process of these institutions is spelled out in some detail, and in this process the individuals rely primarily on the principles set forth in the authoritative texts. As a result, the institutions are not 'personality' driven. Therefore, the premise in the election of these institutions is that a virtually infinite combination of individuals capable of following the procedures set forth as guidance for these bodies could serve well to administer the affairs of the community. Furthermore, since the qualifications for election are signs of 'unquestioned loyalty, of selfless devotion, of a well-trained mind, of recognized ability and mature experience', it is hardly likely that utterly incompetent individuals would be spontaneously elected. In addition, if one aspired to election and were sufficiently adept at feigning such qualities and managed to become elected, his or her only reward would be to serve in virtual anonymity on a body whose decisions are the result of a collective process.

Of course, since each individual must vote according to his or her conscience, no one can in good faith vote for another unless personally assured of that individual's capacity. Therefore, we must presume that in these elections there might well be a significant number of individuals receiving some votes. In addition, we can presume that in some cases those elected might receive only minimally more votes than others, since only a plurality is required.

But since each elector is privately voting according to his or her conscience without regard for what others might think and without concern for recriminations, we might presume that the majority of such votes would be cast for those who would have some degree of competency and some purity of motive. Furthermore, since this process occurs with increasing refinement, each successive level in this tripartite process would tend to designate an electorate of increasingly greater knowledge, capacity and experience.

At the heart of the Bahá'í electoral process, then, is an expression of confidence in a spiritual process demonstrated by the acceptance of a sanctified system instead of sanctified individuals. In this sense, individuals on the institution may change, but the institution is always in motion, continuous, perpetual.

The Bahá'í Consultative Process

While these bodies operate under the guidance of those bodies above them and within the context of the authoritative laws and ordinances already established, the elected representatives are not responsible to the electorate for their decisions. Of crucial importance in the administration of these institutions, therefore, is the consultative process by which decisions are made. For while the concept of consultation as it is generally understood implies some collaborative effort, the guidelines for Bahá'í consultation imply a very specific procedure.

For example, these bodies elect officers from among their ranks, but all nine members of these councils have equal voice and rank. In addition, a proposal or motion is not ascribed to an individual. Once suggested, an idea or a motion becomes the property of the entire body, thereby preventing personal attachment to the success or efficacy of a proposal. When an idea is proposed or a solution to a problem suggested, open consultation is exhorted:

> Let us also remember that at the very root of the Cause lies the principle of the undoubted right of the individual to self-expression, his freedom to declare his conscience and set forth his views.[2]

> The honoured members must with all freedom express their own thoughts, and it is in no wise permissible for one to belittle the thought of another, nay, he must with moderation set forth the truth, and should differences of opinion arise a majority of voices must prevail, and all must obey and submit to the majority.[3]

After a decision is taken, it becomes the decision of the entire body; there is no minority opinion or minority report. Neither is it permissible for individuals to speak against a decision or to otherwise withhold support.

This does not mean that a decision cannot be appealed, but it means that until an appeal is upheld, all are obliged to abide by the decision. The theory in this is that while the 'shining spark of truth cometh forth only after the clash of differing opinions',[4] once a consensus has been reached or a vote taken, the unity of the consultative body becomes as important as the exactitude or correctness of the decision:

> If they agree upon a subject, even though it be wrong, it is better than to disagree and be in the right, for this difference will produce the demolition of the divine foundation. Though one of the parties may be in the right and they disagree that will be the cause of a thousand wrongs, but if they agree and both parties are in the wrong, as it is in unity the truth will be revealed and the wrong made right.[5]

This attitude does not imply that the quest for truth is irrelevant, but rather that the process of consultation itself should pit idea against idea, not personality against personality. In this sense, motions and opinions before these bodies are not consigned or attached to the one making the observation; all ideas are alike the property of the body as a whole:

> He who expresses an opinion should not voice it as correct and right but set it forth as a contribution to the consensus of opinion, for the light of reality becomes apparent when two opinions coincide . . . Before expressing his own views he should carefully consider the views already advanced by others. If he finds that a previously expressed opinion is more true and worthy, he should accept it immediately and not wilfully hold to an opinion of his own. By this excellent method he endeavours to arrive at unity and truth. Opposition and division are deplorable. It is better then to have the opinion of a wise, sagacious man; otherwise, contradiction and altercation, in which varied and divergent views are presented, will make it necessary for a judicial body to render decision upon the question. Even a majority opinion or consensus may be incorrect. A thousand people may hold to one view and be mistaken, whereas one sagacious person may be right. Therefore, true consultation is spiritual conference in the attitude and atmosphere of love.[6]

As distinct from the usual sort of parliamentary debate wherein an individual or group of individuals attempt to dominate the proceeding or else sway the opinion of others through rhetorical prowess, the Bahá'í consultative process attempts to foster a paradigm wherein the entire administrative body perceives itself as unified in quest of the solution to a dilemma. Metaphorically we might compare this arrangement to planetary structures where there is a careful balance between wilful centrifugality impelling each individual away from others (selfishness or attachment) and the magnetic attraction that pulls everyone towards a common centre (selflessness or detachment).

In such an arrangement, that centre, that source of attraction might be considered the power of the revelation itself, or the attraction or love all feel towards the divine reality (as we discussed that power in Chapter 2). In a spiritual sense, that centre might be considered the unifying power of 'Abdu'l-Bahá as exemplar:

> Every meeting which is organized for the purpose of unity and concord will be conducive to changing strangers into friends, enemies into associates, and 'Abdu'l-Bahá will be present in His heart and soul with that meeting.'

The appeal process itself requires first that one request the decision-making body to reconsider its decision. If an appeal is rejected, then the appeal may be addressed to the higher institution. If the initial appeal is to a Local Spiritual Assembly, for example, the appeal may then be addressed to the National Spiritual Assembly, and, if that fails, to the Universal House of Justice, whose decision is final.*

Metaphorically, then, consultation as the essential method of operation for all Bahá'í administrative institutions is possibly the single most profound expression of the aptness of this structure to the newly-emerged identity we have repeatedly discussed. As a sign of maturity, such a process implies that the body politic is no longer in need of patristic figures of individual authority, that the collective body has taken over its own governance. That such elected representatives are not professional clergy, but representatives of the generality of humanity further confirms this maturity. For in the same way that a parent relinquishes direct intervention in the decisions of its offspring as an indication of achieved maturity and independence, so the Manifestation has bestowed on humanity

---

* See 'By-Laws', *The Constitution of the Universal House of Justice*, pp. 14–15 for a more ample delineation of this procedure.

the reins of authority for governance of the planetary community.

But perhaps more important as an expression of this new identity, consultation puts into symbolic or metaphorical action the reality of the expanded identity, or the abandonment of a selfish sort of individuality. Individual contributions to the process are exhorted, even commanded, but decisions are the property of the collective will.

A Divine Economy

We could expend endless amounts of energy considering the prospects for the future of the Bahá'í commonwealth based on our observations of the present Bahá'í model and on the plentiful elucidation of that model in the authoritative works of the Bahá'í Faith. But we can hardly give even the most cursory treatment of this theme without alluding to the relationship of the success of this model to a visionary economic system. For if the administrative order revealed in the writings of Bahá'u'lláh is a metaphorical expression of the body through which the collective soul of humanity finds expression in this life, then the economic system is the lifeblood of that body.

Nothing we deal with in this life is perhaps more metaphorical than money and finance, since currency only has meaning as it comes to symbolize a system of value. Therefore, monetary systems, like the system of value they metaphorize, have a double function:

> The standards and rules that make up a value system have a double function. They are the norms a person appeals to in validating other (lower) standards and rules, and they guide a person's conduct. When a person adopts a value system, he decides to accept certain standards and rules as the basis for justifying his value judgements. But he also decides to place his conduct under the regulation of all the standards and rules of the value system. He commits himself to trying to fulfil the standards and to acting in accordance with the rules. This in turn involves his attitudes.[1]

Metaphorical Significance of 'Divine Economy'

It is perhaps because economics is both a gauge of a value system as well as a means of instigating and sustaining it that in discussing the evolution of the Bahá'í administrative order into the Bahá'í commonwealth of the Most Great Peace, Shoghi Effendi often employs the term 'Divine Economy':

> For Bahá'u'lláh, we should readily recognize, has not only imbued mankind with a new and regenerating Spirit. He has not merely enunciated certain universal principles, or propounded a particular philosophy, however potent, sound and universal these may be. In addition to these He, as well as 'Abdu'l-Bahá after Him, has, unlike the Dispensations of the past, clearly and specifically laid down a set of Laws, established definite institutions, and provided for the essentials of a Divine Economy.[2]

Related to understanding Shoghi Effendi's use of this term is the fact that in its Greek etymology the word *economy* means literally 'the management of a household', though in a more general sense the term concerns the administration of resources. Inasmuch as the Manifestation has announced that there is now only one household, He has through the revelation of various laws and principles metaphorically opened up the doors to the various rooms in that household that all of the family within that edifice might become acquainted, might nurture and care for one another, might become reunited and thereby better manage family affairs. But as we have so often noted, knowledge of this newly-revealed identity achieved when the doors are flung open is only the first step. What is then required is to act appropriately to facilitate the management of that household, to determine what needs the various members have, what obligations each member has to the others, what is just and equitable for all concerned.

The Critical Importance of Economics

'Abdu'l-Bahá confirms that an equitable economic system is an essential requisite for a coordinated world community and states that to achieve a unified household, 'a readjustment of the economic order will come about . . .'[3] Rather than simply becoming an index to existing inequities or exigencies, a literal economic system will be employed to foster a new spiritual reality and relationship.

He indicates that the methods of achieving this condition will be the 'readjustment and equalization of the economic standards',[4] the legislation of which and the 'principles of guidance' for which are enunciated in the teachings of Bahá'u'lláh. He concludes, 'This readjustment of the social economy is of the greatest importance inasmuch as it ensures the stability of the world of humanity; and until it is effected, happiness and prosperity are impossible.'[5]

Shoghi Effendi cautions that while the Bahá'í writings indicate certain general principles about what should occur in a just world commonwealth, there are no detailed or specific statements in the Bahá'í writings regarding a single economic theory or practice:

> There are practically no technical teachings on economics in the Cause, such as banking, the price system, and others. The Cause is not an economic system, nor can its Founders be considered as having been technical economists. The contribution of the Faith to this subject is essentially indirect, as it consists in the application of spiritual principles to our present-day economic system. Bahá'u'lláh has given us a few basic principles which should guide future Bahá'í econ-

omists in establishing such institutions which will adjust the economic relationships of the world.[6]

More recent statements by the Universal House of Justice confirm this and clarify this caution by stating that a 'fresh look at the problem is required, entailing consultation with experts from a wide spectrum of disciplines, devoid of economic and ideological polemics, and involving the people directly affected in the decisions that must urgently be made'.[7] Furthermore, as with other aspects of the Bahá'í model as it relates to an evolving commonwealth, we can be sure that the application of economic practices to foster and secure a just commonwealth will necessarily change as the world federation evolves and matures. The point is that there is a subtle relationship between human spiritual principles and the metaphorical expression and implementation of that value system; they are inextricably linked, something perhaps more clearly indicated in the various laws of Bahá'u'lláh that relate to the individual's daily life.*

Abolition of Extremes of Poverty and Wealth

While we are quite limited in the specificity of observations we might make about what particular steps should be taken to bring about economic justice in a world commonwealth, we can with a degree of certainty infer several worthwhile considerations about the kinds of change that must occur to bring about a genuine world commonwealth. For example, while nations and territories will retain a practical degree of autonomy, the Bahá'í

---

* Bahá'u'lláh reveals economic laws regarding dowry, the Ḥuqúqu'lláh, inheritance, mendicancy, charitable donations, etc., some of which were discussed in the final chapter.

writings state that a world currency will be established.[8] Furthermore, we know that an abiding principle of that future system will be the abolition of the extremes of poverty and wealth.[9] Therefore, we might correctly presume that in countries where an extremely small percentage of the population controls a vast majority of a nation's wealth, there would be a immediate need for remedial legislation to bring about economic health.

But clearly all particular national or territorial economic problems will be reviewed in terms of the worldwide condition of humanity. For example, it is estimated that even under present circumstances, humanity is currently capable of producing sufficient food to provide for the world's population. What is lacking is a synthesis of collective will and a system of distribution. However such a synthesis comes about, the principle for such an action is clear:

> Is it possible for one member of a family to be subjected to the utmost misery and to abject poverty and for the rest of the family to be comfortable? It is impossible unless those members of the family be senseless, atrophied, inhospitable, unkind.[10]

How a more equitable distribution of wealth will occur will no doubt become an increasingly pertinent and crucial subject of an evolving commonwealth. 'Abdu'l-Bahá enunciates certain principles which, if applied as parts of an overall plan of treatment, would foster economic justice without destroying the incentive to be productive which economic reward can sometimes foster. In this context it is important to note that the abolition of extremes does not imply the abolition of incentive nor that all people should receive the same wage, any more than we can assert that all people are capable of the same productivity and contribution to society:

Difference of capacity in human individuals is fundamental. It is impossible for all to be alike, all to be equal, all to be wise.[11]

The Master has definitely stated that wages should be unequal, simply because that [sic] men are unequal in their ability, and hence should receive wages that would correspond to their varying capacities and resources.[12]

A System of Taxation

Balanced against this concept of remuneration as related to capacity and performance is the concept of extreme disparity which is so characteristic of contemporary society. 'Abdu'l-Bahá enunciates at least two temporary methods of responding to this. One is a just system of graduated taxation. In one example of how such a system might be applied, 'Abdu'l-Bahá describes a community wherein each individual's taxes are adjudged according to the weight of his income against his expenses:

Now, if his income be equal to his expenditures, from such a farmer nothing whatever will be taken. That is, he will not be subjected to taxation of any sort, needing as he does all his income. Another farmer may have expenses running up to one thousand dollars we will say, and his income is two thousand dollars. From such an one a tenth will be required, because he has a surplus.[13]

'Abdu'l-Bahá goes on to describe how the percentage of tax increases as the individual surplus increases, though unlike similar systems of taxation operant in some countries at present, there is no stated ceiling to such increases, though it could well be that in implementing such a system, the world commonwealth would see fit to impose one.

Linked to this concept of graduated taxation is 'Abdu'l-Bahá's description of a kind of welfare system on a community level wherein there is established a common fund, a 'general storehouse which will have a number of revenues'.[14*] From such a public trust or storehouse will derive monies to meet such needs as assisting farmers and, caring for orphans, the disabled, the poor, the elderly. In short, 'no one will remain in need or in want'.[15] Trustees will be elected in villages to oversee the income of the storehouse, and any surplus will be transferred to the national treasury. 'Abdu'l-Bahá notes that such a system in a large city will necessarily be much more complex, but the abiding principle will still be operant.

One other interesting point about this system, itself hinting at another economic principle, is the attention given in 'Abdu'l-Bahá's example to the farmer in this arrangement. This does not seem to be a coincidence. He states that 'the peasant class and the agricultural class exceed other classes in the importance of their service'.[16] Where so many contemporary societies, in the East as well as the West, have come to attribute importance to the acquisition of wealth, the system as implied in these examples reverses this process and gives economic support according to the real service a vocation renders society. In this sense we can envision that part of future economic decisions will be based on pragmatic benefit a vocation renders to the just and healthy function of society, not simply to what the market will allow.

---

* 'The first revenue will be that of the tenth or tithes. The second revenue (will be derived) from the animals. The third revenue, from the minerals, that is to say, every mine prospected or discovered, a third thereof will go to this vast storehouse. The fourth is this: whosoever dies without leaving any heirs all his heritage will go to the general storehouse. Fifth, if any treasures shall be found on the land they should be devoted to this storehouse' ('Abdu'l-Bahá, *Foundations of World Unity*, p. 39).

Other Means of Rectifying Inequities

Besides measures taken to eliminate the extremes of poverty and wealth are other methods to foster economic justice in a world commonwealth. For example, 'Abdu'l-Bahá discusses the value of profit-sharing as one means of deterring the antipathy between labour and management, as well as assisting in a more equitable distribution of wealth, the elimination of strikes, and the increase of the worker's enthusiasm for his or her job, something modern companies are rapidly coming to appreciate.* While this arrangement is hardly a sufficient solution to economic disparity and injustice, the Guardian notes that 'Profit-sharing is recommended as a solution to one form of economic problems'.[17]

Perhaps the greatest single phenomenon in the establishment of this commonwealth to heal the economic woes that currently threaten so much of humanity will be the incalculable increase in available monies when nations agree to disarm. 'Abdu'l-Bahá cites the growing economic burden resulting from governments attempting to maintain standing armies as one decisive factor in bringing about a universal peace accord, and Shoghi Effendi

---

* 'For instance, the owners of properties, mines and factories should share their incomes with their employees and give a fairly certain percentage of their products to their workingmen in order that the employees may receive, beside their wages, some of the general income of the factory so that the employee may strive with his soul in the work.

'No more trusts will remain in the future. The question of the trusts will be wiped away entirely. Also, every factory that has ten thousand shares will give two thousand shares of these ten thousand to its employees and will write the shares in their names, so that they may have them, and the rest will belong to the capitalists. Then at the end of the month or year whatever they may earn after the expenses and wages are paid, according to the number of shares, should be divided among both' ('Abdu'l-Bahá, *Foundations of World Unity*, p. 43).

enumerates the specific ways in which humanity will benefit from this redistribution of energies.*

Charitable Giving as the Heart of any Solution

In addition to the immense and almost incalculable benefits that will be derived from the transference of energy and monies from armaments to public welfare and the general economy, another prominent source of revenue for the common good will derive, in addition to whatever legislated means are devised for redistribution of resources, from a reorientation of the human society (and eventually the human heart). That is, when energies are focused away from an adversarial relationship and towards mutual benefit of the common household, the voluntary or charitable redistribution will also become a major factor, perhaps the most important ingredient, in ameliorating the grievous injustices that currently tear at the vitals of society.†

Motivating such voluntary giving will be the emerging realization that everyone is equally an integral part of one social organism:

> And among the teachings of Bahá'u'lláh is voluntary sharing of one's property with others among mankind. This voluntary sharing is greater than equality, and consists in this, that man should not prefer himself to others, but rather should sacrifice his life and property for others.[18]

Related to this principle of giving are several requisites

---

* See p. 288.

† 'Abdu'l-Bahá states that 'The rich too must be merciful to the poor, contributing from willing hearts to their needs without being forced or compelled to do so' ('Abdu'l-Bahá, *Promulgation of Universal Peace*, p. 107).

that currently guide Bahá'ís in their own voluntary contributions within the Bahá'í Faith, principles which we can assume would most probably function equally effectively and importantly in the context of charitable contributions made within such a commonwealth. The first of these is the purely voluntary act of giving: funds should not be solicited. The motivation for giving thus becomes an internal spiritual process. Second is the principle of anonymity with regard to contributions. No matter how much or how little one gives, the community at large is not privy to information about what one chooses to give. A third principle is the idea of universal participation – that there is a special energy generated when everyone participates in this symbolic act, regardless of the extent to which they contribute. No doubt part of this energy derives from the spiritual force engendered by the unity of purpose as demonstrated in this metaphorical act. Finally, giving should involve some degree of sacrifice. Obviously this is a purely subjective determination, but for the process of giving to improve the spiritual condition of the giver, it must involve conscious effort.

Put simply, money is entirely symbolic in nature, and our relationships with it are inevitably loaded with symbolic meaning. Attachment to money obviously implies attachment to the things of this world that money represents. Likewise, the generous contribution of one's acquired wealth to the welfare of the public good is, symbolically, an expression of one's recognition of and love for the family of which he or she is a part, a giving of oneself. Therefore, this metaphorical exercise provides an exquisite means by which such understanding and perspective can be acquired on a systematic basis so that a budgetary analysis of one's expenditures would become tantamount to an assessment of one's values.

Huqúqu'lláh as the Solution

But if charitable giving will function as a helpful source of ameliorating economic disparity in that future common-wealth, Bahá'u'lláh has provided another method which will be the principal way in which the funding in all the needs of such a society can be met, as well as a crucial tool for the spiritual training of the citizenry: the law of Huqúqu'lláh ('the Right of God'). Both a law and a sacred institution, the Huqúqu'lláh represents 'one of the key instruments for constructing the foundation and sup-porting the structure of the World Order of Bahá'u'lláh'.[19] In general, the law states that one should give to this fund 19 per cent of all 'assessable possessions' in excess of the equivalent of 19 mithqáls of gold, excluding one's resi-dence and its 'needful' furnishings. This is paid only once on the excess that exists after one deducts living expenses, losses and taxes. Furthermore, this amount is not paid again until additional income in excess of the value of 19 mithqáls is acquired.

It is important to note, however, that even this fund, though commanded by law and 'crucial to the material well-being of the emerging Bahá'í commonwealth' is purely a matter between the individual and God:

> That the observance and enforcement of this law, so crucial to the material well-being of the emerging Bahá'í common-wealth, should thus have been left entirely to the faith and conscience of the individual, gives substance to and sheds light on what the beloved Master calls the spiritual solution to economic problems.[20]

Obviously the universal application of this law would have an amazing effect on the distribution of resources and the elimination of the extremes of poverty and wealth. Likewise, the examination of the law as a symbolic gesture reveals a dramatic method of expressing the recognition that one's well-being is entirely dependent on the grace of God. In addition, the law of Ḥuqúqu'lláh serves as a beneficial exercise in confirming the temporary nature of our relationship to the physical world in our eternal spiritual evolution.

Bibliography

'Abdu'l-Bahá. *Foundations of World Unity*. Wilmette, Ill.: Bahá'í Publishing Trust, 1945.
—— *The Promulgation of Universal Peace*. Compiled by Howard MacNutt. Wilmette, Ill.: Bahá'í Publishing Trust, 2nd edn. 1982.
—— *Selections from the Writings of 'Abdu'l-Bahá*. Translated by a Committee at the Bahá'í World Centre and by Marzieh Gail. Haifa: Bahá'í World Centre, 1978.
—— *Some Answered Questions*. Compiled and translated by Laura Clifford Barney. Wilmette, Ill.: Bahá'í Publishing Trust, 5th edn. 1981.
—— *Tablets of Abdul-Baha Abbas*. 3 vols. New York: Bahai Publishing Society, 1909–16.
—— *Will and Testament of 'Abdu'l-Bahá*. Wilmette, Ill.: Bahá'í Publishing Trust, 1944.
Abrams, M.H. *The Mirror and the Lamp: Romantic Theory and the Critical Tradition*. New York: Oxford University Press, 1953.
American Tradition in Literature. ed. Bradley, Beatty and Long. New York, W. Norton, 3rd edn. 1967.
Anderson, George K. *Literature of the Anglo-Saxons*. Princeton, N.J.: Princeton University Press, rev. edn. 1966.
Báb, The. *Selections from the Writings of the Báb*. Translated by Habib Taherzadeh and a Committee at the Bahá'í World Centre. Haifa: Bahá'í World Centre, 1976.
Bahá'í Prayers: A Selection of Prayers Revealed by Bahá'u'lláh, the Báb and 'Abdu'l-Bahá. Wilmette, Ill.: Bahá'í Publishing Trust, 1982.
Bahá'í World: An International Record. vol. 13. Haifa: Bahá'í World Centre, 1970.
Bahá'í World Faith: Selected Writings of Bahá'u'lláh and 'Abdu'l-

Bahá. Wilmette, Ill.: Bahá'í Publishing Trust, 2nd edn. 1976.

Bahá'u'lláh. *Epistle to the Son of the Wolf.* Wilmette, Ill.: Bahá'í Publishing Trust, 1988.

—— *Gleanings from the Writings of Bahá'u'lláh.* Wilmette, Ill.: Bahá'í Publishing Trust, 2nd edn. 1983.

—— *The Hidden Words.* Wilmette, Ill.: Bahá'í Publishing Trust, 1990.

—— *The Kitáb-i-Aqdas.* Haifa: Bahá'í World Centre, 1992.

—— *The Kitáb-i-Íqán.* Wilmette, Ill.: Bahá'í Publishing Trust, 2nd edn, 1989.

—— *Prayers and Meditations.* Wilmette, Ill.: Bahá'í Publishing Trust, 1987.

—— *The Proclamation of Bahá'u'lláh to the Kings and Leaders of the World.* Haifa: Bahá'í World Centre, 1967.

—— *The Seven Valleys and the Four Valleys.* Translated by Ali-Kuli Khan and Marzieh Gail. Wilmette, Ill.: Bahá'í Publishing Trust, 1991.

—— *Tablets of Bahá'u'lláh revealed after the Kitáb-i-Aqdas.* Translated by Habib Taherzadeh with the assistance of a Committee at the Bahá'í World Centre. Wilmette, Ill.: Bahá'í Publishing Trust, 1988.

Balyuzi, H. M. *Muḥammad and the Course of Islam.* Oxford: George Ronald, 1976.

—— *Bahá'u'lláh, the King of Glory.* Oxford: George Ronald, 1980.

The Bible. Revised Standard Edition.

Bell, Earl H. and Sirjamaki, John. *Social Foundations of Human Behavior: Introduction to the Study of Sociology.* New York: Harper & Row, 2nd edn. 1965.

Brooks, Cleanth and Warren, Robert Penn. *Understanding Poetry.* New York: Holt, Rinehart and Winston, 4th edn. 1976.

The Covenant: Its Meaning and Origin and Our Attitude Toward It. National Teaching Committee of the National Spiritual Assembly of the Bahá'ís of the United States. 1988.

Durkheim, Emile, *Elementary Forms of the Religious Life.* Translated by J. W. Swain. New York: Free Press, 1965.

English Romantic Poetry and Prose. ed. Russel Noyes. New York: Oxford University Press, 1956.

Esslemont, John E. *Bahá'u'lláh and the New Era*. Wilmette, Ill.: Bahá'í Publishing Trust, 1984.

Excerpts from the Writings of the Guardian on the Bahá'í Life. Compiled by the Universal House of Justice. Canada: National Spiritual Assembly of the Bahá'ís of Canada, 1974.

Ferguson, Marilyn. *The Aquarian Conspiracy: Personal and Social Transformation in the 1980s*. Los Angeles: J. P. Tarcher, Inc., 1980.

Finley, I. M. *The World of Odysseus*. New York: The World Publishing Company, 1963.

Fitzmyer, Joseph A. *Pauline Theology: A Brief Sketch*. Englewood Cliffs, N. J.: Prentice Hall, 1967.

Gail, Marzieh. *Bahá'í Glossary: A Glossary of Persian and Arabic Words Appearing in the Bahá'í Writings*. Wilmette, Ill.: Bahá'í Publishing Trust, 1965.

Hatcher, John S. *From the Auroral Darkness: The Life and Poetry of Robert Hayden*. Oxford.: George Ronald, 1984.

—— *The Purpose of Physical Reality: The Kingdom of Names*. Wilmette, Ill.: Bahá'í Publishing Trust, 1987.

—— *A Sense of History: A Collection of Poetry by John S. Hatcher*. Oxford: George Ronald, 1990.

Hayden, Robert E. *Collected Poems of Robert Hayden*. ed. Frederick Glaysher. New York: Liveright Publishing Corporation, 1985.

Hutcherson, Francis. *Inquiry Concerning Moral Good and Evil*. 1720.

The Koran. Translated by H. M. Rodwell. London: Dent (Everyman's Library), 1963.

Lights of Guidance: A Bahá'í Reference File. Compiled by Helen Hornby. New Delhi: Bahá'í Publishing Trust, 2nd edn. 1988.

Marx, Karl, *Critique of the Hegels 'Philosophy of Right'*. Translated by Annette Jolin and Joseph O'Mally. Cambridge: Cambridge University Press, 1977.

Masterworks of World Literature. eds. Edwin Everett, Calvin Brown and John Wade. New York: Holt, Rinehart and Winston, rev. edn. 1965.

Momen, Wendi. *A Basic Bahá'í Dictionary*. Oxford: George Ronald, 1989.

Murchie, Guy. *The Seven Mysteries of Life: An Exploration in*

Science and Philosophy. Boston: Houghton Mifflin Company, 1978.

Norton Anthology of English Literature. ed. M. H. Abrams. New York: W. W. Norton & Company, 5th edn. 1986.

Norton Anthology of Poetry. eds. Allison, Barrows, Blake, Carr, Eastman and English. New York: W. W. Norton & Company, 3rd edn. 1983.

Principles of Bahá'í Administration: A Compilation. London: Bahá'í Publishing Trust, 1976.

Rabbani, Rúḥíyyih. *The Guardian of the Bahá'í Faith.* New Delhi: Bahá'í Publishing Trust, 1988.

Schaefer, Udo. *The Light That Shineth in Darkness: Five Studies in Revelation after Christ.* Translated by Hélène Momtaz Neri and Oliver Coburn. Oxford: George Ronald, 1977.

Schmithals, Walter. *Paul and James.* Translated by Dorthea Barton. Naperville, Ill.: A. R. Allenson, 1965.

Shakespeare, William. *The Complete Works of Shakespeare.* Hardin Craig. Chicago: Scott, 1951.

Shoghi Effendi. *The Advent of Divine Justice.* Wilmette, Ill.: Bahá'í Publishing Trust, 1990.

—— *Citadel of Faith.* Wilmette, Ill.: Bahá'í Publishing Trust, 1970.

—— *God Passes By.* Wilmette, Ill.: Bahá'í Publishing Trust, 1974.

—— *High Endeavors: Messages to Alaska.* Alaska: National Spiritual Assembly of Alaska, 1976.

—— *Messages to America.* Wilmette, Ill.: Bahá'í Publishing Committee, 1947.

—— *Messages to the Bahá'í World: 1950–1957.* Wilmette, Ill.: Bahá'í Publishing Trust, 1958.

—— *The Promised Day is Come,* Wilmette, Ill.: Bahá'í Publishing Trust, 1980.

—— *Unfolding Destiny.* London: Bahá'í Publishing Trust, 1981.

Stumpf, Samuel Enoch. *Socrates to Sartre: A History of Philosophy.* New York: McGraw-Hill Book Company, 4th edn. 1988.

Taherzadeh, Adib. *The Revelation of Bahá'u'lláh.* vol. 4. Oxford: George Ronald, 1982.

Taylor, Paul W. *Normative Discourse.* Englewood Cliffs, N. J.: Prentice Hall, Inc., 1961.

The Universal House of Justice. *Constitution of the Universal House of Justice*. Haifa: Bahá'í World Centre, 1972.

—— *Messages from the Universal House of Justice 1968–1973*. Wilmette, Ill.: Bahá'í Publishing Trust, 1976.

—— *The Promise of World Peace*. Various editions, 1985.

—— *A Synopsis and Codification of the Kitáb-i-Aqdas*. Haifa: Bahá'í World Centre, 1973.

—— *Wellspring of Guidance*. Wilmette, Ill.: Bahá'í Publishing Trust, 1969.

—— *A Wider Horizon*. Riviera Beach, Fl.: Palabra Publications, 1992.

Tyson, J. *World Peace and World Government: From Vision to Reality*. Oxford: George Ronald, 1986.

Wellek, René. *Concepts of Criticism*. New Haven: Yale University Press, 1963.

References

References to the Kitáb-i-Aqdas are to paragraph numbers, not page numbers. References to the Bible are to the Revised Standard Edition. References to the Qur'án are to *The Koran*, translation by H.M. Rodwell, London: Dent (Everyman's Library), 1963.

Frontispiece

1. 'Abdu'l-Bahá, *Tablets*, p. 168.
2. 'Abdu'l-Bahá, *Questions*, p. 286.

Preface

1. 'Abdu'l-Bahá, *Selections*, p. 69.

1. The Subtle Art of Human Ascent

1. 'Abdu'l-Bahá, *Promulgation*, p. 10.
2. Bahá'u'lláh, *Bahá'í Prayers*, p. 4.
3. Bahá'u'lláh, *Gleanings*, p. 63.
4. ibid. p. 66.
5. ibid. pp. 47–8.
6. ibid. p. 184.
7. ibid. p. 143.
8. ibid. pp. 105–6.
9. Bahá'u'lláh, *Epistle*, p. 11.
10. Bahá'u'lláh, *Gleanings*, p. 260.
11. Bahá'u'lláh, *Íqán*, pp. 191–2.
12. 'Abdu'l-Bahá, *Selections*, p. 178.
13. Bahá'u'lláh, *Hidden Words*, Persian no. 81.
14. Bahá'u'lláh, *Tablets*, p. 24.

15. Bahá'u'lláh, *Hidden Words*, Persian no. 82.
16. 'Abdu'l-Bahá, quoted in *New Era*, p. 94.
17. The Báb, *Selections from the Writings*, p. 78.
18. Bahá'u'lláh, *Gleanings*, p. 332.
19. The Báb, *Selections from the Writings*, pp. 77–8.
20. Shoghi Effendi, cited in *Devotional Attitude*, p. 18.
21. Bahá'u'lláh, *Gleanings*, p. 65.
22. Hatcher, *Purpose*, p. 53.
23. Bahá'u'lláh, *Gleanings*, pp. 158–9.
24. 'Abdu'l-Bahá, *Questions*, p. 201.
25. Bahá'u'lláh, *Gleanings*, p. 215.
26. Bahá'u'lláh, *Aqdas*, no. 4.
27. Bahá'u'lláh, *Gleanings*, pp. 77–8.
28. Bahá'u'lláh, *Aqdas*, no. 1.
29. Bahá'u'lláh, *Íqán*, p. 176.
30. ibid. p. 178.
31. 'Abdu'l-Bahá, *Questions*, pp. 162–3.
32. Bahá'u'lláh, *Gleanings*, p. 5.
33. Shoghi Effendi, *America*, p. 24.
34. Bahá'u'lláh, *Aqdas*, no. 1.
35. 'Abdu'l-Bahá, *Promulgation*, p. 157.
36. 'Abdu'l-Bahá, *Questions*, p. 300.
37. ibid. p. 302.
38. Hatcher, *Purpose*, p. 83.
39. Bahá'u'lláh, *Hidden Words*, Persian no. 14.
40. 'Abdu'l-Bahá, *Promulgation*, p. 10.
41. Bahá'u'lláh, *Íqán*, pp. 254–5.
42. ibid. pp. 177–8.
43. ibid. p. 154.
44. ibid. p. 176.
45. Bahá'u'lláh, *Prayers and Meditations*, p. 321.
46. 'Abdu'l-Bahá, *Tablets*, p. 121.
47. Stevens, cited in *American Tradition*, vol. II, pp. 1529–30.
48. Keats, cited in *Norton Anthology*, vol. II, p. 823.
49. Coleridge, cited in ibid. p. 354.
50. ibid. p. 355.
51. ibid.
52. Coleridge, cited in *Romantic Poetry and Prose*, p. 427.
53. Bahá'u'lláh, *Tablets*, p. 51.
54. 'A Defense of Poetry', *Romantic Poetry and Prose*, p. 1101.
55. Hatcher, *Auroral Darkness*, p. 241.

56. Matt. 13:13–14.
57. Bahá'u'lláh, *Tablets*, p. 35.
58. Bahá'u'lláh, *Hidden Words*, Arabic no. 2.
59. Abrams, *Mirror*, p. 59.
60. Personal conversation with author, 4 May 1991.
61. Wellek, *Concepts*, p. 183.
62. Bahá'u'lláh, *Aqdas*, no. 124.
63. ibid. no. 125.
64. Gen. 2:18.
65. Gen. 1:26.
66. Gen. 1:20–2.
67. 'Abdu'l-Bahá, *Questions*, pp. 122–6.
68. Gen. 3:3.
69. Gen. 3:5.
70. Gen. 3:12.
71. Gen. 3:13.
72. Gen. 2:24.
73. Gen. 3:15.
74. Gen. 3:16.
75. Gen. 3:17–19.
76. 'Abdu'l-Bahá, *Selections*, p. 193.

2. The Social Imperative

1. 'Abdu'l-Bahá, *Selections*, p. 69.
2. Bahá'u'lláh, *Gleanings*, p. 215.
3. ibid. p. 143.
4. Hatcher, *Purpose*, pp. 115–17.
5. 'Abdu'l-Bahá, *Selections*, p. 69.
6. Bahá'u'lláh, *Hidden Words*, Arabic no. 68.
7. Bahá'u'lláh, *Gleanings*, p. 71.
8. Bell and Sirjamaki, *Social Foundations*, p. 21.
9. See Kingsley Davis, 'Extreme Social Isolation of a Child', *American Journal of Sociology*, January 1940, pp. 554–65 and J. A. L. Singh and Robert M. Zingg, *Wolf Children and Feral Man*. New York: Harper and Row, 1942, pp. 1–119.
10. Durkheim, *Elementary Forms*, pp. 16–17.
11. Bahá'u'lláh, *Gleanings*, p. 206.
12. Finley, *World of Odysseus*, p. 57.
13. Cited in Hatcher, *Sense of History*, p. 30. Often translated

under the title 'The Wanderer', this passage is my trans-
lation of lines 29 to 36 of folios 76b to 77b of the *Exeter
Book*, ed. G. P. Krapp and E. Dobbie. New York:
Columbia University Press, 1936, pp. 134–5.

14. 'Abdu'l-Bahá, *Foundations*, p. 38.
15. ibid.
16. Hatcher, *Purpose*, p. 115.
17. Schwartz, 'The Heavy Bear', quoted in *Understanding
Poetry*, p. 380.
18. Yeats, 'Sailing to Byzantium', quoted in *Norton Anthology*,
vol. II, p. 1951.
19. Gail, *Bahá'í Glossary*, p. 15.
20. Shoghi Effendi, quoted in *Compilations*, p. 238.
21. Abu'l-Faḍl, *Bahá'í Proofs*, pp. 93–4.
22. Bahá'u'lláh, *Seven Valleys*, p. 5.
23. Petrarch, quoted in *Masterworks*, vol. II, p. 218.
24. Bahá'u'lláh, *Seven Valleys*, p. 8.
25. ibid. p. 14.
26. ibid. p. 12.
27. ibid. p. 17.
28. ibid. p. 30.
29. ibid.
30. ibid. p. 28.
31. ibid. p. 26.
32. ibid. pp. 24–5.
33. ibid. p. 32.
34. ibid.
35. ibid. pp. 31–2.
36. ibid. p. 32.
37. ibid.
38. ibid. p. 33.
39. ibid. p. 34.
40. ibid. p. 39.
41. ibid. pp. 39–40.
42. ibid. pp. 37–8.
43. ibid. p. 38.
44. ibid. pp. 40–1.
45. Hayden, 'Words in the Mourning Time', *Collected Poems*,
p. 90.
46. Hayden, 'Richard Hunt's "Arachne"', ibid. p. 113.
47. Arnold, 'Dover Beach', quoted in *Norton Anthology*, p. 794.

48. Whitman, 'Song of Myself', quoted in ibid. p. 760.
49. Yeats, quoted in ibid. p. 883.
50. Shoghi Effendi, *God Passes By*, p. 100.
51. Shoghi Effendi, *Promised Day*, p. 1.
52. 'Abdu'l-Bahá, quoted in *World Order*, pp. 164–5.
53. Shoghi Effendi, *World Order*, pp. 42–3.
54. ibid. p. 43.
55. ibid.
56. Bahá'u'lláh, *Íqán*, p. 4.
57. Qur'án (The Cow) 2:82, p. 346.
58. Matt. 23:37.
59. 'Abdu'l-Bahá, quoted in *World Order*, p. 111.

3. A Wheel within a Wheel

1. 'Abdu'l-Bahá, *Questions*, p. 182.
2. See Hatcher, *Purpose*, pp. 46 ff.
3. 'Abdu'l-Bahá, *Selections*, p. 193.
4. 'Abdu'l-Bahá, *Questions*, p. 180.
5. Bahá'u'lláh, *Gleanings*, p. 184.
6. Bahá'u'lláh, *Hidden Words*, Persian, no. 29.
7. 'Abdu'l-Bahá, *Questions*, p. 201.
8. Bahá'u'lláh, *Gleanings*, pp. 158–9.
9. See Hatcher, *Purpose*, pp. 52 ff.
10. 'Abdu'l-Bahá, *Questions*, p. 151.
11. ibid. p. 225.
12. 'Abdu'l-Bahá, 'Tablet to Dr Forel', *Bahá'í World Faith*, pp. 346–7.
13. 'Abdu'l-Bahá, *Questions*, p. 180.
14. ibid. pp. 193–4.
15. ibid. p. 192.
16. ibid. p. 198.
17. Hatcher, *Purpose*, p. 60.
18. Shoghi Effendi, quoted in *High Endeavors*, p. 71.
19. John 12:49.
20. Bahá'u'lláh, quoted in *God Passes By*, p. 101.
21. John 6:15.
22. 'Abdu'l-Bahá, *Selections*, p. 52.
23. Bahá'u'lláh, *Íqán*, p. 152.
24. ibid.

25. 'Abdu'l-Bahá, *Promulgation*, p. 222.
26. The Universal House of Justice, quoted in *Compilations*, vol. 1, p. 111.
27. 'Abdu'l-Bahá, *Promulgation*, p. 222.
28. 'Abdu'l-Bahá, *Bahá'í World Faith*, p. 358.
29. 'Abdu'l-Bahá, *Questions*, p. 164.
30. ibid.
31. ibid.
32. Jonah 47.
33. Shoghi Effendi, *World Order*, p. 202.
34. Bahá'u'lláh, *Íqán*, pp. 199–200.
35. 'Abdu'l-Bahá, *Promulgation*, pp. 141–2.
36. 'Abdu'l-Bahá, *Questions*, pp. 160–1.
37. 'Abdu'l-Bahá, *Promulgation*, p. 220.
38. ibid.
39. Shoghi Effendi, letter to an individual believer, 14 July 1943, quoted in a letter to the author from the Research Department of the Universal House of Justice, 12 August 1991.
40. Qur'án (The Confederates) 33: 40, p. 438.
41. Shoghi Effendi, *God Passes By*, p. 57.
42. Bahá'u'lláh, *Gleanings*, p. 11.
43. ibid. p. 39.
44. Shoghi Effendi, *Messages to the Bahá'í World*, p. 155.
45. Rev. 3:12.
46. 'Abdu'l-Bahá, *Questions*, p. 161.
47. 'Abdu'l-Bahá, quoted in *World Order*, p. 167.
48. Shoghi Effendi, *God Passes By*, pp. 54–5.
49. 'Abdu'l-Bahá, *Questions*, p. 161.
50. Quoted in *Compilations*, vol. 2, p. 4.
51. 'Abdu'l-Bahá, quoted in *World Order*, p. 38.
52. Bahá'u'lláh, *Tablets*, p. 88.
53. Letter written on behalf of Shoghi Effendi, quoted in *Lights*, no. 1955, p. 472.
54. Letter written on behalf of Shoghi Effendi, quoted in a letter to the author from the Research Department of the Universal House of Justice, 12 August 1991.
55. 'Abdu'l-Bahá, quoted in *Compilations*, vol. 2, pp. 346–7.
56. Shoghi Effendi, *Citadel*, p. 80.
57. Shoghi Effendi, *World Order*, p. 163.
58. ibid. p. 114.

4. New Wine and Old Skins

1. Matt. 9:14–17.
2. Luke 22:19–20.
3. Matt. 5:17.
4. See Balyuzi, *Muḥammad*, p. 150.
5. ibid. p. 153.
6. ibid. p. 188.
7. Letter written on behalf of Shoghi Effendi, quoted in *Compilations*, vol. 2, p. 4.
8. Hayden, *Collected Poems*, p. 41.
9. 'Abdu'l-Bahá, *Tablets*, p. 266.
10. Bahá'u'lláh, *Seven Valleys*, p. 15.
11. Bahá'u'lláh, quoted in *God Passes By*, p. 99.
12. Bahá'u'lláh, *Íqán*, p. 4.
13. Qur'án (The Believers) 23:23–5, p. 146.
14. Bahá'u'lláh, *Íqán*, pp. 3–4.
15. Matt. 7:15–20.
16. Matt. 12:38–40.
17. Qur'án (The Poets) 26:178, p. 109.
18. ibid. 187–8.
19. Bahá'u'lláh, quoted in *God Passes By*, p. 144.
20. Bahá'u'lláh, *Íqán*, p. 208.
21. ibid. p. 209.
22. Exodus 4:12.
23. John 14:9–10.
24. Qur'án (The Confederates) 33:40, p. 438.
25. ibid. (The Family of Imran) 38.
26. The Báb, quoted in *God Passes By*, p. 21.
27. The Báb, *Selections*, p. 11.
28. ibid. p. 167.
29. Bahá'u'lláh, *Proclamation*, p. 7.
30. Bahá'u'lláh, *Aqdas*, no. 82.
31. Bahá'u'lláh, quoted in *God Passes By*, p. 102.
32. The Báb, *Selections*, p. 16.
33. Bahá'u'lláh, *Íqán*, p. 57.
34. ibid.
35. ibid. p. 55.
36. ibid. p. 57.
37. ibid. p. 15.
38. ibid. pp. 44–5.

39. Matt. 24:29.
40. Qur'án (The Earthquake) 99:1–8, p. 44.
41. Bahá'u'lláh. *Hidden Words*, Persian no. 13.
42. 'Abdu'l-Bahá, *Questions*, p. 163.
43. Balyuzi, *Muḥammad*, p. 189.
44. Bahá'u'lláh, *Hidden Words*, Persian no. 79.
45. Matt. 23:16.
46. Bahá'u'lláh, *Hidden Words*, Persian no. 24.

5. Adam and Eve Get Divorced

1. Shoghi Effendi, *World Order*, p. 5.
2. Schaefer, *Light*, p. 85.
3. ibid.
4. ibid. p. 87.
5. Bahá'u'lláh, *Tablets*, p. 156.
6. Matt. 5:17–20.
7. Matt. 5:32.
8. Matt. 7:21.
9. Matt. 7:26–7.
10. James 1:22–5.
11. James 2:8–17.
12. James 3:13.
13. 2 Peter 3:15–16.
14. 2 Peter 3:17.
15. Acts 15:5.
16. Acts 11:7–10.
17. Acts 15:10–11.
18. Acts 15:19–20.
19. Acts 11:9.
20. Romans 3:28.
21. Gal. 3:11.
22. Gal. 3:13.
23. Bahá'u'lláh, *Aqdas*, no. 1.
24. Fitzmyer, *Pauline Theology*, p. 65.
25. Romans 3:27.
26. Romans 3:31.
27. Bahá'u'lláh, *Aqdas*, no. 4
28. Gal. 3:19.
29. Gal. 3:24.

30. Schmithals, *Paul and James*, p. 63.
31. Gal. 2:11–16.
32. Gal. 1:18ff.
33. Schmithals, *Paul and James*, pp. 42–3.
34. 'Abdu'l-Bahá, *Questions*, p. 93.
35. ibid.
36. ibid. p. 94.
37. Shoghi Effendi, *God Passes By*, p. 31.
38. ibid. p. 32.
39. ibid. p. 33.
40. ibid, pp. 32–3.
41. Bahá'u'lláh, *Íqán*, p. 51.
42. John 1:1.
43. Gal. 3:28.
44. Stumpf, *Socrates to Sartre*, p. 169.
45. Martin Luther, quoted in ibid. p. 209.
46. ibid. p. 210.
47. ibid.
48. ibid.
49. Marx, *Critique*, introduction.
50. Zukov, *Dancing Wu Li Masters*, p. 330.
51. Ferguson, *Aquarian*, p. 402.
52. ibid. p. 407.
53. Murchie, *Seven Mysteries*, p. 643.
54. See Hatcher, *Purpose*, p. 69.
55. 'Abdu'l-Bahá, *Paris Talks*, p. 143.
56. Bahá'u'lláh, *Gleanings*, p. 242.
57. ibid. pp. 249–50.

6. The Choice Wine at the Family Reunion

1. Bahá'u'lláh, *Gleanings*, p. 28.
2. See Qur'án (The Resurrection) 75, p. 55.
3. Qur'án (The Pilgrimage) 22:5, p. 44.
4. Baha'u'lláh, *Íqán*, p. 120.
5. ibid. p. 117.
6. ibid.
7. ibid. p. 144.
8. Bahá'u'lláh, *Gleanings*, p. 28.
9. ibid. pp. 319–20.

10. Bahá'u'lláh, *Prayers and Meditations*, p. 279.
11. Bahá'u'lláh, *Hidden Words*, Arabic no. 68.
12. Shoghi Effendi, *World Order*, p. 65.
13. ibid. p. 43.
14. ibid. pp. 163–4.
15. ibid. pp. 162–3.
16. Matt. 20:1–16.
17. John 15:1–2.
18. John 15:4.
19. Bahá'u'lláh, *Epistle*, p. 145.
20. 'Abdu'l-Bahá, *Selections*, p. 86.
21. 'Abdu'l-Bahá, *Tablets*, p. 30.
22. ibid. p. 537.
23. ibid. p. 121.
24. Bahá'u'lláh, quoted in *Compilations*, vol. 2, p. 245.
25. ibid. pp. 245–6.
26. Bahá'u'lláh, *Íqán*, pp. 254–5.
27. Bahá'u'lláh, *Epistle*, p. 15.
28. Shoghi Effendi, *God Passes By*, p. 172.
29. ibid. p. 138.
30. Balyuzi, *King of Glory*, p. 164.
31. ibid. pp. 164–5.
32. Bahá'u'lláh, *Íqán*, p. 152.
33. ibid. p. 142.
34. Shoghi Effendi, *God Passes By*, p. 139.
35. ibid.
36. Qur'án (Those Who Stint) 83:4–5, 15, 17, 24–6, pp. 57–8.
37. Shoghi Effendi, *God Passes By*, p. 140.
38. ibid. p. 139.
39. Bahá'u'lláh, *Aqdas*, no. 5.
40. Bahá'u'lláh, *Tablets*, p. 105.
41. Bahá'u'lláh, *Epistle*, pp. 113–14. See also pp. 44, 83, 88 and 105.
42. Bahá'u'lláh, *Gleanings*, p. 213.
43. Shoghi Effendi, *God Passes By*, p. 99.
44. Shoghi Effendi, *World Order*, p. 59.
45. Shoghi Effendi, *God Passes By*, pp. 411–12.
46. Shoghi Effendi, *Messages to America*, p. 33.
47. Hutcherson, *Inquiry*, sec. 3.
48. Ibsen, quoted in *Masterworks*, vol. II, p. 815.

49. ibid. p. 817.
50. Bahá'u'lláh, *Gleanings*, p. 250.

7. From the Lesser Peace to a Golden Age

1. Shoghi Effendi, *World Order*, p. 202.
2. Shoghi Effendi, *Citadel*, p. 126.
3. Shoghi Effendi, *Promised Day*, p. 122.
4. The Universal House of Justice, *Promise*, para. 39.
5. Shoghi Effendi, *World Order*, pp. 41–2.
6. ibid. p. 202.
7. Bahá'u'lláh, quoted in ibid. p. 169.
8. Bahá'u'lláh, quoted in *Promised Day*, p. 3.
9. Shoghi Effendi, *God Passes By*, p. 305.
10. Shoghi Effendi, *World Order*, p. 46.
11. Shoghi Effendi, *Promised Day*, p. 3.
12. Letter written on behalf of Shoghi Effendi, quoted in *Lights*, no. 431, p. 129.
13. Shoghi Effendi, *Citadel*, p. 125.
14. ibid. p. 126.
15. ibid. pp. 126–7.
16. ibid. pp. 122–3.
17. Letter written on behalf of Shoghi Effendi, quoted in *Lights*, no. 447, pp. 133–4.
18. ibid. p. 134.
19. ibid. no. 439, p. 131.
20. Rev. 16:16.
21. Rabbani, *Guardian*, p. 77.
22. ibid.
23. Tyson, *World Peace*, p. 85.
24. Letter written on behalf of the Universal House of Justice, quoted in *Lights*, no. 426, p. 127.
25. ibid. no. 428, p. 128.
26. ibid.
27. ibid. no. 433, p. 129.
28. ibid. no. 431.
29. ibid.
30. ibid. no. 425, p. 127.
31. Shoghi Effendi, quoted in *Unfolding Destiny*, p. 225.

32. Letter written on behalf of Shoghi Effendi, quoted in *Lights*, no. 434, p. 130.
33. Bahá'u'lláh, *Tablets*, p. 165.
34. Sub-title in Shoghi Effendi, *World Order*, p. 191.
35. Shoghi Effendi, *World Order*, p. 40.
36. 'Abdu'l-Bahá, *Secret*, pp. 64–5.
37. ibid. p. 65.
38. 'Abdu'l-Bahá, *Promulgation*, p. 317.
39. ibid.
40. Shoghi Effendi, *World Order*, p. 191.
41. ibid. pp. 191–2.
42. ibid. p. 192.
43. The Universal House of Justice, Riḍván letter, 1991, para. 3.
44. ibid. para. 4
45. Letter written on behalf of the Universal House of Justice, quoted in *Lights*, no. 1428, p. 436.
46. Shoghi Effendi, *World Order*, p. 41.
47. ibid. p. 45.
48. Shoghi Effendi, *Citadel*, p. 39.
49. Shoghi Effendi, *World Order*, p. 40.
50. ibid. p. 203.
51. ibid. pp. 40–1.
52. ibid. p. 203.
53. 'Abdu'l-Bahá, *Promulgation*, p. 440.
54. Shoghi Effendi, *Administration*, p. 47.
55. Shoghi Effendi, *World Order*, pp. 40–1.
56. Tyson, *World Peace*, p. 46.
57. 'Abdu'l-Bahá, *Selections*. p. 306.
58. ibid.
59. Shoghi Effendi, *World Order*, p. 41.
60. ibid. p. 203.
61. Letter written on behalf of Shoghi Effendi, quoted in *Lights*, no. 1077, p. 320.
62. Tyson, *World Peace*, p. 63.
63. 'Abdu'l-Bahá, *Selections*, p. 306.
64. Shoghi Effendi, *World Order*, p. 203.
65. 'Abdu'l-Bahá, *Selections*, p. 306.
66. Shoghi Effendi, *World Order*, p. 41.
67. 'Abdu'l-Bahá, *Selections*, pp. 306–7.
68. Letter written on behalf of Shoghi Effendi, quoted in *Lights*, no. 1412, p. 431.

69. Shoghi Effendi, *Messages to the Bahá'í World*, p. 155.
70. Letter of the Universal House of Justice, 23 March 1975.
71. Shoghi Effendi, *God Passes By*, p. 239.
72. 'Abdu'l-Bahá, *Questions*, p. 171.
73. *Bahá'í World,* vol. XIII, pp. 341–6.
74. Shoghi Effendi, *Citadel*, p. 6.
75. The Universal House of Justice, quoted in *Lights*, no. 427, p. 128.
76. Shoghi Effendi, *Messages to the Bahá'í World,* p. 155.
77. The Universal House of Justice, quoted in *Lights*, no. 1430, pp. 436–7.
78. ibid. no. 1428, p. 436.

8. The Kingdom Come

1. Shoghi Effendi, *World Order*, p. 203.
2. Rev. 21:2–3.
3. 'Abdu'l-Bahá, *Promulgation*, p. 102.
4. ibid.
5. ibid.
6. 'Abdu'l-Bahá, *Questions*, pp. 67–8.
7. 'Abdu'l-Bahá, *Selections*, p. 12.
8. ibid. p. 59.
9. Shoghi Effendi, *God Passes By*, p. 213.
10. Shoghi Effendi, *World Order*, p. 157.
11. ibid. p. 163.
12. Bahá'u'lláh, *Íqán*, pp. 243–4.
13. Letter written on behalf of the Universal House of Justice, quoted in *Lights*, no. 1376, p. 415.
14. Letter written on behalf of Shoghi Effendi, quoted in *Lights*, no. 1607, p. 483.
15. ibid. no. 1713, pp. 507–8.
16. Shoghi Effendi, *World Order*, p. 203.
17. ibid. pp. 203–4.
18. ibid. p. 204.
19. ibid.
20. 'Abdu'l-Bahá, quoted in ibid. p. 205.
21. Shoghi Effendi, *World Order*, p. 204.
22. ibid.
23. ibid.

24. ibid. p. 203.
25. Rev. 21:3–4 quoted in ibid. pp. 205–6.
26. Shoghi Effendi, *World Order*, p. 204.
27. ibid. p. 19.
28. ibid. p. 152.
29. ibid.
30. The Universal House of Justice, *Messages*, p. 38.
31. Shoghi Effendi, quoted in ibid.
32. ibid. p. 39.
33. ibid. p. 40.
34. The Universal House of Justice, *Wellspring*, pp. 86–7.
35. Bahá'u'lláh, *Tablets*, p. 221.
36. The Universal House of Justice, *Constitution*, Preamble to By-Laws.
37. The Universal House of Justice, *Messages*, p. 92.
38. Shoghi Effendi, *World Order*, p. 203.
39. Shoghi Effendi, *Messages to the Bahá'í World*, p. 79.
40. Gen. 9:13.
41. Taherzadeh, *Revelation*, vol. 4, p. 361.
42. Bahá'u'lláh, *Tablets*, p. 5.
43. Taherzadeh, *Revelation*, vol. 4, p. 361.
44. The Báb, *Selections*, p. 12.
45. Momen, *Dictionary*, p. 185.
46. Shoghi Effendi, *Citadel*, p. 95.
47. ibid. p. 96.
48. Shoghi Effendi, *World Order*, p. 163.
49. The Universal House of Justice, *Constitution*, Preamble to By-Laws.
50. Shoghi Effendi, letter of 17 June 1933, quoted in a letter from the Research Department of the Universal House of Justice to the author, 18 November 1990.
51. Shoghi Effendi, *World Order*, p. 7.
52. 'Abdu'l-Bahá, quoted in *Lights*, no. 1061, p. 314.
53. The Universal House of Justice, quoted in ibid. no. 1072, p. 318.
54. Shoghi Effendi, *World Order*, pp. 6–7.
55. Shoghi Effendi, *Bahá'í Administration*, p. 63.
56. Shoghi Effendi, *World Order*, pp. 152–3.
57. ibid. p. 153.
58. ibid.
59. ibid.

60. ibid. p. 154.
61. ibid.

9. The Heart of the Commonwealth

1. Letter written on behalf of Shoghi Effendi, 2 November 1933, quoted in a letter from the Research Department of the Universal House of Justice to the author, 12 August 1991.
2. Shoghi Effendi, *World Order*, p. 163.
3. Letter written on behalf of Shoghi Effendi, quoted in *Lights*, no. 128, p. 36.
4. Letter written on behalf of the Universal House of Justice, quoted in ibid. no. 730, p. 218.
5. The Universal House of Justice, quoted in *Compilations*, vol. 2, p. 29.
6. The Universal House of Justice, *Messages*, p. 48.
7. ibid.
8. Finley, *World Of Odysseus*, pp. 79–80.
9. Anderson, *Anglo-Saxons*, p. 14.
10. Bahá'u'lláh, *Aqdas*, no. 30.
11. Shoghi Effendi, *Bahá'í Administration*, p. 38.
12. ibid. p. 63.
13. ibid. p. 65.
14. ibid. p. 64.
15. Momen, *Dictionary*, p. 151.
16. Bahá'u'lláh, *Aqdas*, no. 115.
17. ibid. note 168, p. 237.
18. Momen, *Dictionary*, p. 151.
19. Letter written on behalf of the Universal House of Justice, quoted in *Lights*, no. 1836, p. 541.
20. Shoghi Effendi, *God Passes By*, p. 340.
21. Letter written on behalf of the Universal House of Justice, quoted in *Lights*, no. 1884, p. 555.
22. The Universal House of Justice, quoted in ibid. no. 1848, p. 545.
23. ibid. pp. 544–5.
24. Letter written on behalf of the Universal House of Justice, quoted in ibid. no. 1884, p. 555.
25. ibid.

26. Shoghi Effendi, *Advent*, p. 7.
27. Letter written on behalf of Shoghi Effendi, quoted in *Lights*, no. 329, p. 96.
28. Bahá'u'lláh, *Aqdas*, p. 105, question 3.
29. 'Abdu'l-Bahá, *Selections*, pp. 132–3.
30. Shakespeare, *Othello*, II:iii.
31. ibid.
32. Letter of the Universal House of Justice, 23 February 1976, quoted in a letter to the author 26 September 1989. See also Bahá'u'lláh, *Aqdas*, para. 45.
33. Bahá'u'lláh, *Tablets*, p. 27.
34. 'Abdu'l-Bahá, *Questions*, p. 269.
35. ibid.
36. ibid. p. 270.
37. ibid.
38. Letter of the Universal House of Justice, 23 February 1976, quoted in a letter to the author, 26 September 1989.
39. Hayden, *Collected Poems*, pp. 90–8.
40. ibid. p. 62.
41. Letter written on behalf of Shoghi Effendi, quoted in *Lights*, no. 1843, p. 542.
42. Shoghi Effendi, *Bahá'í Administration*, p. 66.
43. Gail, introduction to Bahá'u'lláh, *Epistle*, p. vi.
44. ibid. p. vii.
45. Bahá'u'lláh, *Prayers and Meditations*, p. 111.

Appendix A: Some Distinctive Features of Operation

1. Shoghi Effendi, *Bahá'í Administration*, p. 88.
2. ibid. p. 63.
3. 'Abdu'l-Bahá, *Selections*, p. 88.
4. ibid. p. 87.
5. 'Abdu'l-Bahá, *Bahá'í World Faith*, p. 411.
6. 'Abdu'l-Bahá, *Promulgation*, pp. 72–3.
7. 'Abdu'l-Bahá, *Tablets*, p. 554.

Appendix B: A Divine Economy

1. Taylor, *Normative Discourse*, p. 129.
2. Shoghi Effendi, *World Order*, p. 19.

3. 'Abdu'l-Bahá, *Promulgation*, p. 102.
4. ibid. p. 107.
5. ibid. pp. 181–2.
6. Letter written on behalf of Shoghi Effendi, quoted in *Lights*, no. 1868, p. 550.
7. The Universal House of Justice, *Promise*, para. 30.
8. See Shoghi Effendi, *World Order*, p. 203.
9. See Shoghi Effendi, *God Passes By*, p. 281.
10. 'Abdu'l-Bahá, *Foundations*, p. 39.
11. ibid. p. 37.
12. Letter written on behalf of Shoghi Effendi, quoted in *Lights*, no. 1867, p. 550.
13. 'Abdu'l-Bahá, *Foundations*, p. 40.
14. ibid. p. 39.
15. ibid. p. 40.
16. ibid. p. 39.
17. Letter written on behalf of Shoghi Effendi, quoted in *Lights*, no. 1869, p. 550.
18. 'Abdu'l-Bahá, *Selections*, p. 302.
19. The Universal House of Justice, *Horizon*, p. 172.
20. ibid. p. 173.